Beethoven's Only Beloved:

Josephine!

John E Klapproth

Beethoven's Only Beloved: *Josephine!*

Copyright © John E Klapproth 2011.

All Rights Reserved.

ISBN-13: 978-1461186380

ISBN-10: 1461186382

Cover Design by Andrea M Jaretzki.

Front cover photograph: Martonvásár Garden, Copyright © Zsuzsanna Bernáth 2011.

Back cover photographs: Martonvásár Lake and (insert) Martonvásár Castle, Copyright © Zsuzsanna Bernáth 2011.

Published by CreateSpace, North Charleston, SC, U.S.A.

First Edition, released on 14 August 2011.

Contents

Introduction 6
Praeludium 9
Overture 15
   1799: First Meeting 16
   1800: Joseph and Josephine 23
   1801: Temptation 27
   1802: Depression 30
   1803: To Prague 33
Largo sostenuto 35
   1804: Widow 36
   1805: Hope 42
   1806: Jealousy 47
   1807: Forced Withdrawal 51
Inter Lacrimas et Luctum 61
   1808: A Journey 62
   1809: Home again – with Baggage 66
   1810: State of Ferment 72
   1811: Family Life 81
1812: Intermezzo 85
   January to June: Dissolution 86
   The Month of July: Encounter 93
   August to December: Aftermath 97

Adagio molto e cantabile 101
  1813: Minona 102
  1814: A Kidnapping 107
  1815: Tohuwabohu 117
  1816: The Last Yearning 123
  1817: Resignation 135

Finale 139
  1818: The Last Letter 140
  1819: Final Visit 143
  1820: Final Illness 147
  1821: Death and Oblivion 150

Reflections 155
  The Letter 156
  The Wisdom of Solomon 170
  Beethoven's Diary 202
  Christoph von Stackelberg 207

Conclusion 219

Appendix 223
  Chronology 224
  Comparison of a Surviving Fragment of Beethoven's
    Diary with Gräffer's Copy 227
  Websites 233
  Movies 235
  List of Songs 239
  List of Works 241

Literature 247

Index 261

Be to yourself, be to your world, as much as you can, an angel, thus it will be to you, as much as it can, a heaven.[1]

---

[1] "Sey dir, Sey deiner Welt so viel du kan[n]st ein Engel, so wird sie dir so viel sie kann ein Himmel seyn." (Josephine's Diary, ca. 4 July 1812, in Steblin 2007, p. 159.) Two days later, Beethoven began to write a Letter to his "Immortal Beloved", addressing her as "My **angel**", and went on to refer to their love as "a true edifice in **Heaven**".

Introduction

When Ludwig van Beethoven died on 26 March 1827, he had already become a legend in his own lifetime. For his funeral at the Währing cemetery in Vienna more than 20,000 people turned up. Dignitaries and luminaries, the rich and the famous jostled to be his pallbearers. Obituaries and eulogies were full of superlatives.

> But there was someone else waiting for Ludwig: A woman, who due to the snobbery of her family had been repeatedly separated from him and driven to death. Almost exactly six years before Beethoven, Josephine von Brunsvik had been quietly interred at the Währing cemetery.
>
> Two, who could not come together during their lifetimes. In death, they could be together, at last.[1]

* * *

Josephine Countess von Brunsvik, who was buried without ceremony, without obituary, even without any mourners. No tombstone on her grave. She, who was to be condemned to total oblivion, is the subject of this book. I want to trace her short life of 42 years, more than half of which she spent "so near, so far" to Beethoven.

Separated together, but always united in spirit.

They were in love, quite simply. Within the constraints (massive and daunting as they were) of the early nineteenth-century Austro-Hungarian society, dominated by a rotten and rotting aristocracy, doomed to be blown away by the winds of economic change (though still delayed by the brutal regime of Metternich's secret police), who kept musicians and composers like pets. And where women were still second-class citizens (within their respective class, naturally).

It was **music** that enabled, triggered, sustained, and ultimately transcended their love, in this world. And in the next. It was in music that Beethoven spoke to her, often only and exclusively to her. And it was Josephine – maybe only she – who understood it. Understood him. Because she could hear it.

This is the story of Josephine Countess von Brunsvik, about whom very little is known, and much less was ever published (at least in English). It is the story of a modest and humble woman, whom Beethoven called an "Angel" – "**My Angel**".

Hers is the story of a life begun in wealth and luxury, in joy and happiness, of being caught up in the conflict between love and duty, between class constraints and freedom, and ending in many agonizing years of illness, poverty, and suffering.

The story of her life (of which Beethoven was an integral part) is told here in six parts, with one chapter per year – from their first meeting in 1799 to her death in 1821. The footnotes contain mainly the original German (sometimes French) texts of the many quotations (all translated by me), and auxiliary remarks.

The full story is told here – for the first time in English – in the words of the main protagonists, collecting the most important passages published so far, by and about Josephine, her sisters Therese and Charlotte, Beethoven and other contemporaries.

* * *

Acknowledgments are due to those, who provided help, encouragement and information (though any remaining errors and misrepresentations in this book are entirely my own responsibility): Bernhard Appel of the Beethoven-Haus in Bonn, Heidrun Beißwenger of http://www.adelinde.net/, Zsuzsanna ("Bizsu") Bernáth in Martonvásár, Michael Hedley Burton[2] in Sydney, William Connor in my hometown Greytown (NZ), Leo Ensel in Oldenburg, James F Green of http://www.unheardbeethoven.org/, Wolfram Heinrich of http://www.theodor-rieh.de/, Mária Hornyák of http://brunszvikterez.hu/, Steffen Kreft of http://www.national-park.co.nz/, Joyce Maier of http://www.beethovensite.eu/, Dominique Prévot of http://www.lvbeethoven.com/, Edith Seegel of the Estonian Historical Archives in Tallinn, Wolfhart von Stackelberg in Bonn, Rita Steblin in Vienna, Victoria St John in Auckland, Jan Swafford in Boston, and Edward Walden in Canada.

And last but not least my wife Andrea M Jaretzki, my only beloved.

Papawai, Greytown, New Zealand, 30 July 2011

J.E.K.

---

[1] "Aber noch jemand erwartet hier Ludwig. Eine Frau, die durch den Standesdünkel ihrer Familie immer wieder von ihm getrennt und in den Tod getrieben wurde. Fünf [!] Jahre vor Beethoven wurde Josephine auf dem Währinger Friedhof in aller Stille verscharrt. Zwei, die zu Lebzeiten nicht zusammen kommen konnten, im Tode dürfen sie endlich beieinander liegen." (Pichler 1994, p. 10.)

[2] Michael Burton wrote and performed a remarkable one-man play for the theater, called "Being Beethoven", which was performed to much acclaim in New Zealand (see http://www.lvbeethoven.com/Spectacles/Events.html, 17 Jul 2011).

Poetry, aesthetics and fine arts – that was our life.[1]

Praeludium

On 8 April 1818, Josephine Baroness von Stackelberg, née Countess von Brunsvik, widowed Countess Deym, wrote a letter to an unnamed person. She had just turned 39, and she was already terminally ill – a kind of nervous consumption, with bouts of mental confusion. Josephine was suffering from frequent fever attacks.

The day was Minona's fifth birthday, her fifth daughter, her seventh child, who was in far away Estonia, with Christoph Baron von Stackelberg, Josephine's estranged husband (her second), who took the three children of their marriage with him. Never to be seen again. This had happened four years before. She did not even know what Minona looked like.

Stackelberg had not only stolen her children, he had also ruined her completely. Left her without a single penny. She had hardly enough to pay for daily expenses, a servant and a cook, doctor's visits and the annual summer vacation in a spa.

A rather frugal lifestyle, compared to earlier, happier days when she, as Countess Deym, was the star at the many balls and parties in Vienna and Budapest. And with all the gallants at her feet!

Even this modest lifestyle she could now only sustain with a little income from letting some of the 80 rooms in her villa, and the occasional donations from her brother Franz or her mother. And maybe even (though secretly, no one ever knew about it) Beethoven.

For – as we shall see presently – Ludwig van Beethoven was (most likely) the addressee of this letter, because he was (most likely) Minona's father.

* * *

In 1846, Therese Countess von Brunsvik, now in her seventies, began to write her memoirs, titled "My Half-Century".[2] It would take her until 1855 to finish them – still well before her death in 1861. Forty years after her sister Josephine's death.

Therese's Memoirs are the main source for biographical data about Josephine, but – apart from the occasional lack of accuracy, after so many decades – they contain, strangely, absolutely nothing about the love relationship between Josephine and Beethoven.

Much more revealing are some entries in Therese's Diary[3] – like this one:

> Beethoven! It is like a dream, that he was the friend, the confidant of our house – a beautiful mind! Why did not my sister Josephine, as widow Deym, take him as her husband? Josephine's soul mate! They were born for each other. She would have been happier with him than with Stackelberg. Maternal affection made her forgo her own happiness.[4]

* * *

Ludwig van Beethoven was born in December 1770 in Bonn as the second son of a court musician. He was named after his grandfather, who had been an excellent singer and keyboard player.

The first child, born nearly two years before, had also been named Ludwig (Ludwig Maria), but died after a few days. Strangely, Ludwig "the second" never knew his own date of birth![5]

This was not helped by his father, who took him on tours around the country, to exhibit him as a child prodigy, advertising him as "the new Mozart". And he cheated on the boy's age, claiming he was two years younger.

Young Ludwig displayed his musical talents early on. He soon learned to play the piano, the viola and the organ; he was also a choirboy. His first major composition, at 11 years, was a set of Piano Variations.[6]

In his teens, Ludwig became acquainted with members of the Bonn nobility, who appreciated his talents, and he was soon a favorite at the Court. In 1787, he was urged to travel to Vienna, in order to meet – and learn from – W A Mozart.

There is an anecdote that Mozart saw him playing and remarked: "Watch out for this one, he will become great one day!" True or not, and maybe even without having met Mozart, Ludwig returned as his mother fell ill.[7]

Soon after, his mother died, and he had to look after his two younger brothers, Carl and Johann, as well as his father, who developed into a derelict alcoholic. Ludwig took over his father's position and salary as a court musician.

Beethoven composed the "Ritterballett" music WoO 1 (1790–1791) – as a "ghostwriter" – for his patron Ferdinand Count Waldstein, who had it performed as his own work. As a reward, Ludwig obtained useful letters of introduction by Waldstein and others to leading aristocrats in Vienna, where he traveled again in late 1792 – after a brief meeting with Joseph Haydn in Bonn (and French troops on their way to occupy his home town). This time he stayed for good.

Haydn was very impressed by the young man – now 21 – and promised to take him on as a pupil. Little did he know that Beethoven proved to be a difficult character, with no respect for received traditions! His first compositions published with Opus numbers – Three Piano Trios, Three Piano Sonatas and a String Trio[8] – were already showing signs of genius that were beyond the old master.

Haydn soon lost interest in teaching a pupil who was too restless to follow his more balanced approach. Beethoven continued his studies of counterpoint and composition with Johann Georg Albrechtsberger and Court Musician Antonio Salieri – who both in due course suffered the same bewilderment.

Albrechtsberger for a while even thought that Beethoven was a good-for-nothing – how wrong he was! Not only did the young man learn the ropes quickly and continued to churn out new and original compositions – his fame became firmly established due to his skills as a pianist, which he displayed during his frequent invitations to the salons of the nobility.

Beethoven was an outstanding virtuoso at the keyboard, enrapturing the noble ladies with sentimental adagios. He was able to improvise the most astounding melodies. What a pity that no one recorded or memorized them...

He won so many piano playing and improvising contests with the top pianists at the time that their noble mentors ordered their protégés not to compete any more, to spare them the humiliation.

At the end of the century, Beethoven's fame was worldwide – at least in Vienna, which was the capital of what was then the "World" (in continental Europe): the Austro-Hungarian Empire, with Hungary in particular being just a rural backwater.[9]

* * *

In 18th century Hungary, the Brunsviks[10] were a noble family with a keen interest in music. They traced their ancestry back to the crusader Heinrich Duke von Braunschweig ("Henry the Lion", 1139–1195). In Martonvásár near Budapest, on what was previously a desert-like puszta, they had built themselves a magnificent castle, with gardens and lakes – a little paradise out in the country.

Anna Countess von Brunsvik, née Baroness von Seeberg, had been a widow since 1792.[11] She had four children, who were now (in 1799) approaching marriageable age: The only son and designated sole heir Franz, born in 1777, was an accomplished cello player. And there were three daughters: Therese, born in 1775, Josephine, born in 1779, both talented piano players and keen admirers of Beethoven and his music, and Charlotte, born in 1782.

Therese had suffered from the "Rickets"[12] as a child, and she was not as beautiful as her younger sisters. She was to remain single.[13] Anna's intention was to get her younger daughters married off to rich noblemen, especially the beautiful Josephine.

Therese and Josephine were and would remain always very close to each other, and together with their younger sister Charlotte they had been living a carefree life in a fantasy world of their own making. They read the Greek classics, romantic poets and famous writers of the time (like Goethe), and they learned to play musical instruments.

In the luxury of their castle, they were protected from the vicissitudes of life in the outside world, and they knew little about the attractions (and distractions) of city life – as represented by the big capital of Vienna.

> [We] were always dreamers ... visionaries – living in an elevated realm of the psychic, outside of this world – how could we be happy in this world, on this planet, which we did not recognize? ... The Ideal attracted us, we followed happily.[14]

As a young girl, Therese had spent some time in Vienna where she had heard about Beethoven – perhaps she even saw him perform. In any case, the announcement by her mother to take her and Josephine to Vienna in order to see the great Beethoven must have been exciting news!

---

[1] "Poesie, Aesthetik und schöne Künste war unser Leben." (Therese's Memoirs, in La Mara 1909, p. 63.)

[2] First published (in German) by La Mara (1909), pp. 58–135.

[3] The term "Diary" is not very precise: The documents quoted here – as far as they have been published, in the case of Therese mainly by Czeke (1938) – are often just notes, letters or fragments, undated and out of order, in the handwriting of the time ("Kurrentschrift", not to be confused with "Sütterlin"). They were kept (and found, many only recently) in the estates of the Brunsviks and the Deyms in the Czech Republic, Slovakia and Hungary, and literally thousands of documents are still hidden somewhere, untranscribed...

[4] "Beethoven! ist es doch wie ein Traum, [daß] er der Freund, der Vertraute unseres Hauses war – ein herrlicher Geist – warum nahm ihn meine Schwester J. nicht zu ihrem Gemahl als Witwe Deym? Josephines Herzensfreund! Sie waren für einander geboren. Sie wäre glücklicher gewesen als mit St[ackelberg]. Mutterliebe bestimmte sie – – auf eigenes Glück zu verzichten." (Therese's Diary, 4 February 1846, in Schmidt-Görg 1957, p. 23.)

[5] In 1818, Beethoven was talking "about the first and the second Ludwig" [vom ersten und zweiten Ludwig]. (Beethoven's Diary, in Solomon 2005, p. 99.) He was then again doubting his own certificate of baptism (dated 17 December 1770), thinking it was that of his older brother, born 18 months earlier (and dead soon after).

[6] 9 Variations for Piano in C minor on a March by Ernst Christoph Dreßler WoO 63, 1782. Even though Mozart's legendary genius had emerged already at a much earlier age, Beethoven's achievements as a composer in his teens (before he went to Vienna, and before being fully educated in the art of counterpoint) are truly outstanding.

[7] According to Haberl (2006), Beethoven arrived in Vienna on ca. 14 January 1787 and had plenty of time to meet with Mozart, until he left Vienna on ca. 28 March 1787 (before knowing of his mother's illness). Beethoven learned that his mother was ill only after arriving in Augsburg on 26 April 1787.

[8]   3 Piano Trios Op. 1, 1792–1794; 3 Piano Sonatas Op. 2, 1793–1795; String Trio in *E flat major* Op. 3, 1794. For more details about Beethoven's works, see Cooper (1991), and for discussions of his major compositions, Lockwood (2003).

[9]   Strictly speaking, Vienna at the time was still the capital of the Holy Roman German Empire, which included Austria (but not Hungary), and Franz II was German Emperor. Due to the obliteration of the rest of Germany caused by the Napoleonic wars, it became obvious that there was no such thing as a "German Nation" any more, and he decided to abdicate a meaningless title and called himself henceforth (the first) Emperor of Austria and King of Hungary, as Franz I. Not that Napoleon cared – he occupied Vienna twice soon after (1805 and 1809). And the (no longer existing) German crown was later (in 1871) picked up by Bismarck and handed to the King of Prussia.

[10]   The name "Brunsvik", derived from the German "Braunschweig", is also spelled "Brunßwick" or "Brunswick" in German, "Brunšvik" in Czech/Slovakian, and "Brunszvik" in Hungarian.

[11]   It is intriguing that the main protagonists in this story lost their father relatively early, and in the same year of 1792: Beethoven (just after his departure to Vienna), the Brunsvik kids (some sources say 1793), and also Josephine's second husband Christoph von Stackelberg.

[12]   "Rickets" is a softening of bones in children, potentially leading to fractures and deformity. It is nowadays among the most frequent childhood diseases in many developing countries. The predominant cause is a vitamin D deficiency. The majority of cases occur in children suffering from severe malnutrition.

[13]   "When I was 16 years old, I consecrated myself ... as a **Priestess of Truth**, and I decided never to marry." [Als ich 16 Jahre alt war, weihte ich mich ... zur **Priesterin der Wahrheit** und beschloß, mich nie zu vermählen.] (Therese's Memoirs, in La Mara 1909, p. 62.) Therese makes this appear like a solemn act of early wisdom that befell her.

[14]   "[Wir] waren immer Träumerinnen ... Visionärinnen, – im psychischen[,] im ausserweltlich Höheren lebend – wie kön[n]t' es uns auf dieser Welt, in dieser Welt, die wir nicht geachtet, gut gehn? ... Das Ideale riß uns hin, wir folgten gerne." (Therese's Diary, 1841, in Tellenbach 1983, p. 94.)

We were young, cheery, beautiful, childish, naïve.[1]

Overture

---

[1] "Wir waren jung, frisch, schön, kindlich, naiv." (Therese's Memoirs, in La Mara 1909, p. 65.)

At that time, the intimate, deep friendship with Beethoven was formed that lasted until his death.[1]

1799: First Meeting

Let's hear from Therese's Memoirs, how it all began:
> When, in May 1799, we stayed for those remarkable 18 days in Vienna, my mother wished to provide her two daughters, Therese and Josephine, with Beethoven's inestimable music lessons. Beethoven, we were told, would not be persuaded to follow an invitation, but "if Your Excellency is comfortable to climb three flights of a narrow spiral staircase at St Peter's Square to pay him a visit", we might have a chance.
>
> This we did. We entered. I was carrying my Beethoven sonata with violin and violoncello accompaniment[2] under my arm. The immortal, dear Louis van Beethoven was very friendly and as polite as he could be. [He] placed me at his out-of-tune piano, and I played pretty well.
>
> This delighted him so much that he promised to come every day to our hotel. He was very diligent, and from 12 o'clock he used to stay, instead of one hour, often until 4 or 5, and he never tired to hold down and bend my little fingers. The noble man must have been very happy with us, because during 16 days, he did not miss a single lesson.[3]

On that fateful day in early May 1799, the 28-year-old Beethoven fell in love at first sight with the beautiful 20-year-old Josephine. The "noble" and "immortal" composer went to the trouble of spending half a day every day, for more than a fortnight, with three rather obscure Countesses from far away Hungary, for no payment and no obvious prospects of winning yet another lucrative patronage.

Therese expressed the infatuation she suffered clearly enough:
> At that time, the intimate, deep friendship with Beethoven was formed that lasted until his death.[4]

This must have included Josephine, who would later admit as much:
> My soul was already **enthusiastic** for you even before I knew you personally – this was increased through your affection. A feeling deep in my soul, incapable of expression, made me love you. Even before I knew you, your Music made me **enthusiastic** for you. The goodness of your character, your affection increased it.[5]

Therese mused, towards the end of her memoirs:
> A beautiful word from the Persian, full of meaning: **En-thousias**: To Be In God.[6]

However, being in a hotel room, with her sister and her mother around all the time, there was little chance for Ludwig and Josephine to exchange more than glances. Beethoven came as close as he possibly could to a declaration of love, using his mastery of music by composing a song after a poem by Goethe, "Ich denke dein" [I Am With You], originally called "Nähe des Geliebten" [The Beloved Nearby].

He wrote an excerpt into the sisters' diary, on 23 May 1799:

> *I am with you,*
> *However far away you might be,*
> *You are near me!*

adding:
> My greatest wish is that you, at least sometimes, when playing and singing this little musical offering, remember your Ludwig v. Beethoven, who adores you truly.[8]

Beethoven composed several versions with piano variations of this song[9], and later dedicated the music to both Therese and Josephine.[10]

But first there was to be a wedding.

* * *

Apart from the apparently quite happy encounter with Beethoven and the musical education of her daughters, Mother Anna von Brunsvik had another important topic on her agenda, and that was to find a wealthy husband for at least one of them. And the "ugly duckling" Therese was not a likely candidate.

One day, as part of their daily sightseeing outings,

> Mother took us to the then very popular Müller's Art Gallery near the Red Tower. We entered, not knowing what was going to happen. An elderly gentleman met us. He was very knowledgeable and entertained us in a very friendly manner – it was Mr Müller (alias Count Deym), the owner. My future brother-in-law!
>
> Josephine had made the deepest impression upon him. He said to himself: "She is the one, who must become my wife."[12]
>
> Deym saw the incomparable beauty which was, as it were, still hidden in Josephine as in a bud, and at first sight he was aflame with violent passion.[13]

Joseph Count Deym von Střítež was 47 years old in 1799, and he already had a colorful past behind him. He had met Mozart just before his death (in 1791), and even took a death mask of him. Deym also knew Haydn, and he had managed to persuade both of them to contribute compositions for Musical Clocks in what was to become the major tourist attraction of the Austrian capital – his Art Gallery cum Wax Museum and Curiosities Cabinet (see Hatwagner 2008).

Deym had been forced to leave the country after a duel in his youth, and he later returned from exile under the pseudonym of "Müller". It was also rumored that the three "adopted" daughters, who lived with him in his 84-room villa, were actually his illegitimate children (Steblin 2007, p. 155, n. 44). He was a personal friend of the Emperor, to whom he immediately went after falling in love with Josephine. The Emperor in due course pardoned him and returned to him the title of "Count". Now he could be certain to be an acceptable son-in-law for the status-conscious Countess Anna.

The inevitable happened:

> Müller was our daily companion. At the end of our holidays, he came to us as usual early at 9 o'clock in the morning and asked my mother for a talk. After a few

minutes, Josephine was called into her room, and my mother introduced her to – Count Deym. "Dear Josephine", she said, "you can make me and your sisters very happy!" After a brief inner struggle, a scarcely audible "Yes" floated from her trembling lips – and for this "Yes" she sacrificed the happiness of her whole life, she, the noble minded! She did not know what she was doing, what she was to expect! Soon after, she threw her arms around my neck and wept a flood of tears.[14]

And with fiery zeal, Deym demanded the execution of the marriage with incredible haste.[15]

On 29 July 1799, Josephine von Brunsvik and Joseph Count Deym were married by the Bishop of Weißenburg in the chapel of Martonvásár. Then they drove westwards, with huge dark storm clouds overhead. Therese, the Cassandra of the family, the Priestess of Truth, had a premonition, and she said: "She is facing a difficult fate! As black as the sky!"[16]

Thus, the outcome of this brief "holiday" stay in the big capital was that

our mother took us, as it were, out of the nursery straight to Vienna. For 18 days and 3 hours, we stayed there – and everything was decided: Josephine was to be married. From then on, the most bitter days and tragic events were our lot.[17]

Well – not yet. And not straight away. Therese was exaggerating, with the benefit of hindsight, to add dramatic effect. However, Josephine's happy childhood was definitely over – gone were the days of innocent bliss:

We were young, cheery, beautiful, childish, naïve. Whoever saw us, loved us.[18]

---

[1] "Damals ward mit Beethoven die innige, herzliche Freundschaft geschlossen, die bis an sein Lebensende dauerte." (Therese's Memoirs, in La Mara 1909, p. 64.)

[2] Probably the Trio for Piano, Violin & Cello in *B flat major* Op. 11, 1797–1798.

[3] "Als wir jene merkwürdigen 18 Tage in Wien waren, wünschte meine Mutter ihren zwei Töchtern Therese und Josephine den unschätzbaren Musikunterricht Beethovens zu verschaffen. Beethoven ... würde nicht zu bewegen sein, der bloßen Einladung zu folgen; wenn aber Ihre Excellenz sich bequemen, die

drei Treppen der engen Wendeltreppe am St. Petersplatz zu erklimmen, und ihm die Visite zu machen, so möchte er für den Erfolg bürgen. – Dieß geschah. Meine Sonate Beethovens mit Violine und Violoncello=Begleitung ... unter dem Arm, traten wir ein. Der unsterbliche, liebe Louis von Beethoven war sehr freundlich und so höflich, als er es sein konnte. ... [Er] setzte ... mich an sein verstimmtes Piano und ich ... spielte dabei recht brav. Dieß entzückte ihn so sehr, daß er versprach, täglich zu kommen, in das Hotel ... Er kam fleißig, blieb aber statt einer Stunde von 12, bis oft 4 bis 5 Uhr, und wurde nicht müde, meine Finger ... nieder zu halten und zu biegen. Der Edle muß sehr zufrieden gewesen sein; denn durch 16 Tage blieb er nicht ein einzigsmal aus." (Therese's Memoirs, in La Mara 1909, p. 63 f.)

[4] "Damals ward mit Beethoven die innige, herzliche Freundschaft geschlossen, die bis an sein Lebensende dauerte." (Therese's Memoirs, in La Mara 1909, p. 64.)

[5] "Meine ohnedieß, für Sie **enthousiastische** Seele noch ehe ich Sie persönlich kannte – erhielt durch Ihre Zuneigung Nahrung. Ein Gefühl das tief in meiner Seele liegt und keines Ausdrucks fähig ist, machte mich Sie lieben; noch ehe ich Sie kan[n]te machte ihre Musick mich für Sie **enthousiastisch** – Die Güte ihres Characters, ihre Zuneigung vermehrte es." (Josephine to Beethoven, probably Winter 1806/7, draft, in Schmidt-Görg 1957, p. 20.)

[6] "Ein schönes bedeutungsvolles Wort aus dem Persischen: **En-thou-sias**: In Gott sein." (Therese's Memoirs, in La Mara 1909, p. 117.)

[7]
Ich bin bei dir
Du seist auch noch so ferne
Du bist mir nah!

This would become a prevailing theme in Beethoven's life long relationship to Josephine: Here he promised her already to be always "near" her (spiritually), no matter how "far" apart they might be (physically – or otherwise separated). Or, as we shall see, painfully near, but "far" in the sense of "unreachable"...

[8] "Ich wünsche nichts so sehr, als dass sie sich zuweilen beym durchspielen und singen dieses kleinen musikalischen Opfers, erinnern mögen an ihren sie wahrhaft verehrenden Ludwig v. Beethoven." (in La Mara 1920, p. 7.)

[9] Song "Ich denke dein" [I am with you] WoO 74#1, 1799–1803 (several versions); 6 Variations for Piano Duet in *D major* on "Ich denke dein" WoO 74#2, 1799–1803.

[10] This was to be the only composition he would ever dedicate officially to Josephine (though not alone to her). Please note that writing this kind of love poem into a good friend's album was a common practice of the time where romantic affection could take various forms. Surely it was **not** meant (and not understood) to be a declaration of true love, as Josephine was married at the time (or at least as good as engaged in May 1799), and Beethoven's moral stance was to always respect the institution of marriage. This is later to be born in mind in the context of

another love poem that Beethoven would write into a singer's album in 1811 (she was also married), a copy of which was then requested by his (married) friend Antonie Brentano. The American author Maynard Solomon – as we shall see – misleadingly interpreted this incident as "proof" of a true (yet adulterous!) love relationship.

[11] The "Red Tower" did not actually exist any more at the time, but was a common reference to the place, especially the building where Müller's Art Gallery was housed.

[12] "... führte uns die Mutter ... in die damals sehr gesuchte Müllerische Kunstgallerie am rothen Thurm. Ohne Ahnung traten wir ein; ... [da] kam uns ein ältlicher Herr entgegen, der über Alles Auskunft wußte und uns sehr freundlich unterhielt – es war H. Müller (Graf Deym), der Eigenthümer; mein künftiger Schwager! ... Josephinens Anblick hatte den tiefsten Eindruck auf ihn gemacht, und er hatte sich gesagt: 'Diese muß meine Frau werden'." (Therese's Memoirs, in La Mara 1909, p. 65.)

[13] "[Deym] sah die unvergleichliche Schönheit welche in Josephine gleichsam wie in der Knospe noch verborgen lag und entbrannte beim ersten Anblik von der heftigsten Leidenschaft." (Therese's Diary, in Tellenbach 1983, p. 58.)

[14] "Er wurde unser täglicher Begleiter. Am Ende des Séjours kam er wie gewöhnlich um 9 Uhr früh ... und bat die Mutter um eine Unterredung. Nach einigen Minuten wurde Josephine in's Nebenzimmer gerufen und meine Mutter stellte ihr den Grafen Deym ... vor. ... 'Du kannst', sprach sie, 'liebe Josephine, mich und deine Schwestern glücklich machen!' ... Nach kurzem innerlichen Kampf schwebte ein kaum vernehmbares 'Ja' über ihre zitternden Lippen – und diesem 'Ja' opferte sie ihr ganzes Lebensglück, die Edelmüthige! Sie wußte wohl nicht, was sie that, was sie einging! Bald darauf stürzte sie sich an meinen Hals und weinte einen Strom von Thränen." (Therese's Memoirs, in La Mara 1909, p. 66.) Therese's version of how Josephine was coerced (apparently by surprise, learning that Müller was indeed a Count, after all), and then regretted it straight away, is good movie material. In reality, it is much more likely, that Deym's proposal was – more or less – coolly received by the Brunsviks, and after some deliberation (involving all the senior family members) it was accepted, under the impression – as it turned out, wrongly – that Deym was very wealthy.

[15] "Mit Feuereifer drang Deym auf Vollziehung der Vermählung mit unglaublicher Hast." (Therese's Diary, in Tellenbach 1983, p. 58.)

[16] "6 Wochen darauf war Josephine durch den Bischof von Weißenburg in Martonvásár am Altare getraut. ... Josephine ... fuhr westwärts, wo ein ganz schwarzes Gewitter am Himmel stand. Therese, die Cassandra der Familie, die Priesterin der Wahrheit, ahnte und sprach es aus: 'Sie geht einem schweren Geschick entgegen! Schwarz wie das Firmament!'" (Therese's Memoirs, in La Mara 1909, p. 66 f.) Therese remembers the date of the wedding slightly incorrectly: It was not 6 weeks but two months later (Steblin 2007, p. 157). Perhaps because of that it was often reported later as 29 June 1799. And, of course, Therese's gloomy prediction was made with the benefit of hindsight (as so much in her – still valuable – memoirs).

[17] "Unsere Mutter führte uns so zu sagen aus der Kinderstube nach Wien. 18 Tage und 3 Stunden waren wir da und Alles war entschieden – nämlich Josephine wurde verheurathet. Von hier an waren die bittersten Tage und die tragischsten Ereignisse unser Loos." (Therese's Memoirs, in La Mara 1909, p. 63.) Therese exaggerates again, as the following years would be the happiest in Josephine's life. It must also be noted that the unmarried Therese (for good reason) developed the opinion that being married as such is already a tragedy for a woman... And, as so often, Therese refers to Josephine by using the plural "we" or "us", thus incorporating herself almost like a Siamese twin of her sister – whose life she shared so intensely.

[18] "Wir waren jung, frisch, schön, kindlich, naiv. Wer uns sah, liebte uns." (Therese's Memoirs, in La Mara 1909, p. 65; La Mara 1920, p. 7.) Again, she says "we" when in fact the beautiful and lovely one was her sister.

It is my divine wife, who keeps me going, she supplies my mind with new energy through her sincere sympathy... I shall be happy with her.[1]

1800: Joseph and Josephine

Josephine had a difficult time getting accustomed to the strange, old man. But soon she was a mother – on 5 May [1800], she gave birth to a little daughter, naming her Victoire [Viky], in honor of her aunt, Countess Golz, Deym's sister.[2]

Josephine was a complete mother, she nursed her child herself. Beautiful as an angel, only now had the bud come fully into blossom. She was delightful. "**Beautiful like an angel and fit to paint**", the fashionable ones called her [in French] when they saw her on the arm of her husband promenading through the streets.[3]

The storm clouds began to gather when it turned out that Deym's financial situation was not as rosy as he had made the Brunsviks believe, and he in turn was disappointed by Josephine's meager dowry. Anna von Brunsvik even made an attempt to have the marriage annulled.

Count Deym had reason to complain to his brother-in-law Franz:

I lived for nearly three months in such great agitation and had to suffer biting insults by your mother... It is my divine wife ... who keeps me going despite these sufferings, and she supplies my mind with new energy through her sincere sympathy. My honest manners towards her and my boundless unfeigned love have won me her whole heart, and I shall be ... happy with her.[4]

Something remarkable had happened: the little, fragile, shy, restrained and obedient daughter Josephine, who did not dare to give her mother anything other than "Yes" as an answer when "asked" to marry an old and strange man, now firmly stood with him, her husband and the father of her child. We discover here a strain of obstinacy in Josephine which, combined with the stubbornness of her rather simple-minded mother, did not bode well.

Very soon, Josephine and Joseph Count Deym, almost 30 years her senior, came to respect and really love each other, indeed much more than Therese's rather taciturn memoirs admit.[5]

* * *

And what about Beethoven? Josephine's marriage must have upset him. Yet he remained on friendly terms with her as well as with Deym and the Brunsviks.

> Beethoven was the steadfast visitor of the young Countess – he continued to give her free lessons. There were musical soirées. Brother Franz came to visit, and he became acquainted with Beethoven. The two musical geniuses were to become intimately linked, and my brother never left his friend alone when he was suffering financial troubles, until his, alas! **all too premature end!**[6]

Franz Count von Brunsvik was the only son of Anna. After the early death of his father in 1792, as the only male, Franz became the de-facto head of the family. He was a gifted violoncello player, and became a lifelong friend of Beethoven – one of the few whom the composer would address in his letters with the intimate "Du".[7]

Franz was designated to manage and eventually inherit the Brunsvik estates, and his mother was anxious not to reduce his expected inheritance by giving away expensive dowries to her daughters. (Like Josephine, Charlotte, the youngest, was also soon married to a Count – namely Emerich Teleki, a fellow Hungarian.)

Beethoven became like a member of the Brunsvik family, whose castle in Martonvásár he also visited. He continued to see Josephine in Deym's villa (at least weekly). Count Deym did not show any signs of jealousy; on the contrary, he behaved like Beethoven's paternal friend. The composer returned the favour by presenting Deym with several compositions for Musical Clock,[8] to add to his growing collection of curiosities (Goldschmidt 1977, p. 252).

During the entire duration of her marriage to Deym, Josephine continued her piano lessons with Beethoven and made considerable progress. In December 1800, she appeared as a pianist in a performance of – among others – Beethoven's new Violin Sonatas[9] in a concert for Franziska von Hohenheim, Princess of Württemberg,[10] who soon after became the godmother of Josephine's second child, her first son, Friedrich (Fritz), born on 3 May 1801.

Josephine played so brilliantly, that they spoke of her as
> this divine Countess Deym, the master of the piano and the ruler of all hearts.[11]

---

[1] "Mein göttliches Weib ... ist es, die mich ... aufrecht haltet und durch aufrichtige Theilnahme meinem Geist neuen Schwung giebt ... ich werde mit ihr ... glücklich sein." (Deym to Franz von Brunsvik, 1 August 1800, in La Mara 1920, p. 9.)

[2] "Schwer gewöhnte sich Josephine an den fremden, alten Mann. ... Aber sie war bald Mutter – am 5. May [1800] gebar sie ein Töchterchen, welches der Tante, Gräfin Golz, zu Ehren Victoire genannt wurde." (Therese's Memoirs, in La Mara 1909, p. 67.)

[3] "Josephine war ganz Mutter; sie nährte ihr Kind selbst. Schön wie ein Engel; erst da war die Kospe völlig zur Blüte gekommen ... war sie zum Entzücken. ...'*Belle comme un ange et mise a peindre*', sagten die Fashionablen von ihr, wenn sie ... an dem Arm des Gemahls durch die Straßen wandelte." (Therese's Memoirs, in La Mara 1909, p. 68.)

[4] "... in welcher Agitation ich nun beynahe drey Monathe lebe und welche beißende Kränkungen deiner Mutter leyden mußte. ... Mein göttliches Weib ... ist es, die mich in diesen Leyden aufrecht haltet und durch aufrichtige Theilnahme meinem Geist neuen Schwung giebt. Mein aufrichtiges Benehmen gegen sie und meine gränzenlose ungeheuchelte Liebe hat mir ihr ganzes Herz gewonnen und ich werde mit ihr ... glücklich sein." (Deym to Franz von Brunsvik, 1 August 1800, in La Mara 1920, p. 9.)

[5] There were, recently discovered (as mentioned in Goldschmidt 1977, p. 484), over 100 love letters between the newly weds, indicating that a healthy erotic relationship was growing between the spouses. Steblin (2007, p. 155, n. 41) announced a forthcoming publication of these letters.

[6] "Beethoven war der standhafte Besucher der jungen Gräfin – unentgeltlich gab er ihr Unterricht. ... Man gab musikalische Soirées. Der Bruder kam ... und machte Bekanntschaft mit Beethoven. Die beiden Musikgenies verbanden sich innig und nie verließ mein Bruder den in seinen Finanzen oft zerrütteten Freund, bis an sein, hélas! **zu frühes Ende!**" (Therese's Memoirs, in La Mara 1909, p. 69.) Implying that Franz von Brunsvik supported Beethoven later in

life financially is ironic and sounds like dissembling. The sad truth is that the Brunsviks – Franz as their de-facto *pater familias* in particular – eventually discontinued their financial aid to Josephine, who was to die alone and in poverty, whereas Beethoven probably gave her money – secretly (though this is not confirmed). Possibly, maybe even money he had received from Franz! (As we shall see later, Beethoven also received considerable sums from the other Franz, Brentano, which he may have passed on to his only beloved...)

[7]   Only five letters of Beethoven to Franz von Brunsvik survived, and all about rather trivial matters (they are all printed in La Mara 1909, pp. 23–28). Why were all the others lost? What is remarkable in these few letters is not only that Beethoven addresses Franz using the intimate "Du", but even more that he calls him "brother" (brother-in-law?). With the additional mystery that not a single entry by Franz is to be found in Beethoven's – surviving – conversation books (of which several were destroyed by Schindler, who in turn was in contact with Franz von Brunsvik), it must be assumed that there were a few secrets shared between them...

[8]   5 Pieces for Musical Clock WoO 33, 1799; Grenadier March for Mechanical Clock in *F major* Hess 107, 1798.

[9]   3 Sonatas for Piano & Violin Op. 12, 1797–1798.

[10]   Usually – but incorrectly – Julia von Giovane is named as the hostess of this concert (see more in Steblin 2009, p. 124).

[11]   "... dieser göttlichen Gräfin Deym, der Meisterin des Klaviers und Herrin aller Herzen." (Therese's Diary, 1800, in Tellenbach 1983, p. 62.)

> *After two years, I am again enjoying some moments of bliss, and it is the first time that – I feel that marriage could make me happy, but unfortunately she is not of my station.*[1]

1801: Temptation

Julie Countess Guicciardi, a cousin of the Brunsvik children, was born in 1782[2] (like Charlotte). In January 1801, she appeared in Vienna, and Josephine noted how
> she is making quite a stir: She is only ever called "the beautiful Guicciardi". And she is on intimate terms with the Gallenbergs.[3]

In early November 1801, Julie joined her cousins in taking piano lessons with Beethoven, who instantly fell in love (or became infatuated) with her. He wrote to his friend Wegeler in Bonn about
> a sweet, enchanting girl, who loves me and whom I love. After two years, I am again enjoying some moments of bliss, and it is the first time that – I feel that marriage could make me happy, but unfortunately she is not of my station – and now – I certainly could not marry now.[4]

Even though he had fallen under the spell of this young, exuberant, enchanting girl, he was fully aware that for him marriage into a noble family was out of the question. Beethoven also made it clear that he had to wait for "two years" to feel such "bliss" again – two years since Josephine got married:
> You can hardly believe how desolate, how sad my life has been since these last two years.[5]

In March 1802, Beethoven dedicated his Piano Sonata #14 Op. 27#2[6] to Julie, as a kind of "retaliatory" measure, because he – again – did not accept any payment from a pupil whom he liked. He was angry about a gift from Julie's mother. Beethoven certainly had his pride – he could not be bought!

However, as it soon turned out, the young Countess was only flirting with him, practicing her skills.[7] On 14 November 1803 (Steblin 2009, p. 145), she married the handsome (but not very wealthy) Count Gallenberg, a rather mediocre ballet composer, who considered himself a rival of (and even better than) Beethoven, who had already composed a ballet of his own, titled "The Creatures of Prometheus"[8] – a theme that was to become prominent in future characterizations of Beethoven's life as a "Promethean" struggle to wring fire from the gods and bring it to humankind (see Rolland 1928)...

* * *

However, this ballet was to be his only one – maybe he was just too annoyed to compete with the likes of Gallenberg. Nevertheless, he recycled several times one of the most beautiful melodies of this ballet – its finale, which is also to be found in one of his Contre-Dances, as the theme of the so-called "Eroica" Variations, and in the final movement of his groundbreaking "Eroica" Symphony.[9]

---

[1] "Es sind seit 2 Jahren wieder einige seelige Augenblicke, und es ist das erstemal, daß ich fühle, daß – heirathen glücklich machen könnte, leider ist sie nicht von meinem stande." (Beethoven to Wegeler, 16 November 1801, in La Mara 1909, p. 9.)

[2] Usually Julie is reported as being born in 1784, making her two years younger. But two years can be quite a difference for a girl under 20! (For the full story, see Steblin 2009.)

[3] "Julie Guicciardi macht hier geradezu Aufsehen. Man nennt sie nur die schöne Guicciardi ... Sie ist mit den Gallenbergs intim." (Josephine to her sisters, January 1801, in La Mara 1920, p. 14.)

[4] "... ein liebes zauberisches Mädchen ..., das mich liebt und das ich liebe; ... Es sind seit 2 Jahren wieder einige seelige Augenblicke, und es ist das erstemal, daß ich fühle, daß – heirathen glücklich machen könnte, leider ist sie nicht von meinem stande – und jetzt – könnte ich nun freilich nicht heirathen..." (Beethoven to Wegeler, 16 November 1801, in La Mara 1909, p. 9; La Mara 1920, p. 22.)

[5] "Du kannst es kaum glauben, wie öde, wie traurig ich mein Leben seit 2 Jahren zugebracht." (Beethoven to Wegeler, 16 November 1801, in La Mara 1909, p. 9; La Mara 1920, p. 22.)

[6] Piano Sonata #14 "quasi una Fantasia" in *C sharp minor* Op. 27#2 (later nicknamed *Moonlight* – but not by Beethoven), 1800–1801. On the dedication page, being all in Italian, she is called "Giulietta" – a name that has stuck ever since. However, she was always called "Julie" (Steblin 2009, p. 90).

[7] This was later dramatized as a heart-wrenching love affair in the French film "**Un amour de Beethoven**" (1936) by Abel Gance. Needless to say, Julie became a prime suspect in the "hunt" for the unknown addressee of the "Letter to the Immortal Beloved". However, she moved immediately with her husband to Italy, and during the next 20 years she returned only a few times to Vienna. In fact, on one such occasion, Beethoven snubbed her (Steblin 2009, p. 151).

[8] Ballet Music "Die Geschöpfe des Prometheus" [The Creatures of Prometheus] Op. 43, 1800–1801; Ballet Music "Die Geschöpfe des Prometheus" for Piano (arr. Op. 43) Hess 90, 1801.

[9] Contredance for Orchestra #7 in *E flat major* WoO 14, 1800–1802; 15 Variations with Fugue for Piano in *E flat major* ("Eroica Variations" – should really be called "Prometheus Variations") Op. 35, 1802; Symphony #3 in *E flat major* "Eroica" Op. 55, 1803.

> *Today I am holding a great party.*[1]
> *I must live like an exile.*[2]

1802: *Depression*

On 27 July 1802, Josephine & Joseph Deym's third child Carl was born. Apart from finding happiness as a mother, the experience of life during most of the four and a half years of Josephine's marriage to Count Deym was like a dream: Her life was like a never ending ball; she almost tumbled from one party to the next. Life in the noble circles of Viennese (and Budapest) High Society was full of refined entertainment – and Beethoven was one of the stars providing it.

They enjoyed life to the fullest, as Josephine reported to her sisters:

> Quartets by Beethoven were played; ... and I played, accompanied by Zmeskall, the Horn Sonata.[3] The day after, we had a small ball at Aunt Finta's, the following day a delightful one at Aunt Guicciardi's, then again a picnic.[4]
>
> Today I am holding a great party. I have invited the [Princess] Esterházy and her entourage to tea and dinner. Yesterday the [Countess] Guicciardi had a great breakfast. Today we had a musical matinée at Zmeskall's... We heard quartets by Beethoven, Julie played, and the divine Beethoven presented us with divine variations.[5]
>
> You have no idea how busy I am. I am embroidering a silken dress with chenille,[6] and I have many things to prepare for the ball. Beethoven is so assiduous; he demands that I be it, too.[7]

* * *

During 1801, Beethoven had noticed increasingly unsettling problems with his hearing, which he confessed in emotional letters to his old friend Wegeler (who was a doctor) and his friend Amenda, in June and July 1801, respectively. He had noticed hearing problems for the first time around 1797 (after a typhus infection).

Beethoven's following summer stay at Heiligenstadt was dominated by a very severe depression. On 6 and 10 October 1802 he drafted a letter to his two brothers, later known as the "Heiligenstadt Testament", found after his death in his desk (i.e., never sent). In this document, he was pouring out his grief over his hardness of hearing, which – as he was forced to expect – could result in complete deafness.

His pupil and friend Ferdinand Ries was visiting him in Heiligenstadt. During a walk, Ries pointed out the beautiful sound of a shepherd's flute – but Beethoven could not hear anything!

> And yet it was not possible for me to say to the people around me: speak louder, shout, for I am deaf; oh how could it be possible then that I should have to indicate the weakness of a sense, that in me should be developed in a more than perfect degree, compared to others, a sense which I once possessed in the greatest perfection... But what humiliation when someone stood beside me and heard a flute from a distance, and I heard nothing, or someone heard a shepherd singing, and I again eard nothing.[8]

---

[1] "Heute habe ich große Gesellschaft." (Josephine to her sisters, ca. 1801, in La Mara 1920, p. 39.)

[2] "... wie ein Verbannter muß ich leben." ("Heiligenstadt Testament", in Pichler 1994, p. 367.)

[3] Sonata for Piano & Horn in F major Op. 17, 1800.

[4] "Quartette von Beethoven wurden gespielt; ... und ich spielte, von Zmeskall begleitet, die Sonate mit Horn. Am Tag darauf hatten wir einen kleinen Ball bei Tante Finta, am folgenden einen sehr reizenden bei Tante Guicciardi, darauf wieder ein Pique=nique." (Josephine to her sisters, ca. 1801, in La Mara 1920, p. 38 f.)

[5] "Heute habe ich große Gesellschaft. Ich gebe der Esterhazy und den Ihrigen einen Theeabend. Gestern veranstaltete die Guicciardi ein großes Frühstück. Heute hatten wir bei Zmeskall eine musikalische Matinee... Wir hörten Beethovensche Quartette, Julie spielte und der göttliche Beethoven beschenkte uns mit göttlichen Variationen." (Josephine to her sisters, ca. 1801, in La Mara 1920, p. 39.)

[6] "Chenille" is French for "caterpillar"; it is the name of a fabric.

[7] "Ihr habt keine Idee, wie beschäftigt ich bin. Ich sticke mir ein seidenes Kleid mit Chenille und habe für den Ball noch vieles andere vorzubereiten. Beethoven ist so eifrig, er verlangt daß ich es auch sei." (Josephine to her sisters, October 1803, in La Mara 1920, p. 42.)

[8] "Und doch war's mir noch nicht möglich den Menschen zu sagen: sprecht lauter, schrejt, denn ich bin taub, ach wie wär es möglich dass ich dann die Schwäche eines Sinnes angeben sollte; der bej mir in einem vollkommenern Grade als bej andern sein sollte, einen Sinn den ich einst in der grössten Vollkommenheit besass ... aber welche Demüthigung wenn jemand neben mir stund und von weitem eine flöte hörte und ich nichts hörte; oder jemand den Hirten Singen hörte, und ich auch nichts hörte". ("Heiligenstadt Testament", in Pichler 1994, p. 368.)

1803: To Prague

Despite his hearing problems, Beethoven experienced an extremely productive phase of his career, with two big concert performances of his latest works on 5 April[1] and 24 May 1803.[2] Among his major compositions during this year were the Variations on "God Save the King" WoO 78 and "Rule Britannia" WoO 79, and then – as an early culmination of his achievements – the sensationally innovative Symphony #3 in *E flat major* "Eroica" Op. 55.

* * *

In June 1803, the Deyms, with their oldest child, moved to Prague, into a house that was only a few blocks away from the inn "Zum schwarzen Roß" – where Beethoven would stay later in 1812 (and where he probably met his "Immortal Beloved"). The two boys stayed with Grandmother Anna and Aunt Therese in Budapest.

Count Deym, who had many relatives in Bohemia and originated from Moravia (as indicated by his full name Deym von Střítež), wanted to return to his home country, which had the added advantage of a more affordable lifestyle (compared to the expensive world city Vienna). And then, his oldest children were soon approaching school age. (Naturally, as aristocrats they would not be obliged to attend public schools – they would have personal tutors and private teachers to educate them according to their station.)

Little did he know that this, his last, move was to be a fatal one.

* * *

Interestingly, towards the end of 1803 – just when the Deyms moved to Prague – Beethoven was also making plans to go there (Goldschmidt 1977, p. 254).

[1] He premiered the Symphony #2 in *D major* Op. 36 and the Piano Concerto #3 in *C minor* Op. 37, playing the solo part himself. The Symphony #1 in *C major* Op. 21 was also performed.

[2] First performance of the Violin Sonata #9 in *A major* Op. 47, with the English virtuoso George Bridgetower as soloist to whom Beethoven had originally dedicated the sonata, but after Bridgetower made an insulting remark about a lady, Beethoven withdrew the sonata from him and dedicated it instead to the violinist Rodolphe Kreutzer, who in turn never performed it – finding it "unplayable".

I love you, and I appreciate your moral character – You have shown so much love and kindness to me and my children, I will never forget it, as long as I live.[1]

Largo sostenuto

---

[1] "Ich liebe Sie, und schätze ihren moralischen Charackter – Sie haben viel Liebe, und Gutes mir und meine Kindern erwiesen, daß werde ich nie vergessen … so lange ich lebe." (Josephine to Beethoven, 1805, draft, in Schmidt-Görg 1957, p. 25.)

> *Dying I beg You, Your Highness,*
> *do not abandon my good wife*
> *and my under-aged children.*[1]

1804: Widow

On 27 January 1804, Count Deym died of pneumonia in his new home in Prague – disaster had struck, as prophesied by "Cassandra" Therese.

> Josephine lost this good-natured husband, who was oppressed by worry and grief, and whom she had hardly got used to, after she had borne him two boys and was pregnant with their fourth child, after a short illness.[2]

On 4 December 1803, already exhausted from the stress and the anxieties surrounding the move of part of his family to a new home in Prague (and his wife pregnant again),

> Deym had traveled to Budapest to pick up his two boys. He arrived with a terrible cough. During the worst time of the year, he traveled to Prague. The doctors diagnosed the galloping consumption, and after seven days of terrible agony, he, the admirable, was a corpse! Josephine stood by his bedside day and night with unparalleled patience and perseverance. He made his will. ... He transferred to his young wife the guardianship of their children and his assets.[3]

This was rather unusual at the time, as widows (let alone divorced women) were normally not assigned the custodianship of their own children – and, as we shall see, the threat of having this guardianship removed was hanging over Josephine for the rest of her life (when she died in 1821, even her oldest child was still a minor).[4]

Deym wrote the last letter of his life on his deathbed to his friend Emperor Franz:

> Most Gracious Monarch! Close to death, I use my last remaining strength to thank Your Majesty for all the benefits I received from You, and dying I beg You, Your Highness, do not abandon my good wife and my under-aged children.

Your Majesty's most grateful and faithful subject, Joseph Count Deym. Prague, 22 January 1804.[5]

* * *

Josephine went to see the Emperor, who had always been a protector of Deym. The Emperor was moved and very kind to her.[6]

Only, he promised but did not give her any money.

On 24 February 1804, shortly after Deym's funeral, Josephine's fourth child, the second girl, was born. She named her Josepha – in memory of her beloved husband.

There was, however, not much time for bereavement. Because now the young mother of four – as part of the inheritance – was

> overwhelmed with business matters that she had to learn from scratch: an art gallery with daily admission fees to be administered, and 80 rental rooms in a magnificent building to be managed.[7]

Josephine had now also the company and assistance of her younger sister Charlotte, who observed, later that year, how Josephine was having a nervous breakdown,[8] after all the stress, as she reported to Therese:

> You can imagine how her fever attacks upset me, what I am suffering here. The nights were particularly awful, she had terrible nervous attacks, sometimes she laughed, sometimes she wept, after which extreme fatigue set in. ... How sad![9]

* * *

During the summer of 1804, Beethoven's love of Josephine was rekindled and intensified, as documented by at least 15 love letters that he wrote to her over the following ca. five (maybe six) years – i.e., letters that survived (because Josephine kept them).

What is more, the young widow soon reciprocated in kind, revealing her love to Beethoven in many letters (often exchanged – concealed – in books they borrowed each other), none of which however survived – only a few drafts.

The initially very rapid development of Beethoven's devotion to Josephine can be traced by the words he used in his greetings – a fascinating correspondence.

Summer 1804:
> Farewell, dear good Countess – your most devoted Beethowen.[10]

November 1804:
> Until we meet again ... your Beethowen, who worships you.[11]

December 1804:
> My dear, my good J. ... Your – your – your Beethowen.[12]

January/February 1805:
> **You**, you, my everything, my happiness ... Beat only silently, my poor heart – you cannot otherwise. For **you** – always for **you** – only **you** – forever you – to my grave only you – my solace – my everything.[13]

March/April 1805:
> Oh beloved J., it is not the drive to the opposite sex that attracts me to you, no, **only you, your whole self** with all its characteristics – has my respect – all my feelings – my whole sensibility enthralled by you ... Long – long – may our love last – it is so noble – so much founded on mutual respect and friendship – even great similarity in so many things, in thoughts and feelings.
>
> Oh you, let me hope that **your heart** will continue to beat for me for a long time – **mine** can only – stop – to beat for you – if – it **beats no more – beloved J.**[14]

April 1805:
> Farewell, Angel – of my heart – of my life.[15]

April/May 1805:
> Here **your – your** – *Andante* – and the *Sonata* ... Farewell Angel of my heart.[16]

May 1805:
> Farewell, my beloved, my only J.[17]

From mid 1804 until the end of May 1805 (at least), there was a continuous crescendo in Beethoven's affection for Josephine, as expressed in these letters: She was his "dearest", his "only", his "beloved", his "everything" – his "**angel**".

He continued to visit her frequently, under the pretext of giving her piano lessons – but after six years of continuous study, several public performances, and already having been quite versed and very talented in any case, who would now be fooled in believing that she still needed a teacher?[18]

Beethoven had dedicated his Piano Sonata #21 in *C major* Op. 53 to his former patron in Bonn, Ferdinand Count von Waldstein, but he replaced the original slow movement by another one. This separate little piece that he took out was to be known as the *Andante favori* WoO 57.[19]

It was "Josephine's Theme".

---

[1] "... Euer Majestät ... als Sterbender anzuflehen ... mein guttes Weib mit meinen unmündigen Kindern nicht verlassen [zu] wollen." (Deym to Emperor Franz, 22 January 1804, in Hatwagner 2008, p. 29.)

[2] "Und diesen, von Sorgen und Kummer gedrückten, aber gutmüthigen Gemahl, an den sie sich kaum gewöhnt hatte, verlor sie, nachdem sie ihm noch zwei Knaben geboren und mit dem vierten Kinde guter Hoffnung war, auch an einer kurzen Krankheit." (Therese's Memoirs, in La Mara 1909, p. 67.)

[3] "Deym war ... den 4. Dezember nach Ofen gereist, um seine beiden Knaben abzuholen. Er kam mit einem gräulichen Husten an. ... Er reiste ... in der schlimmsten Jahreszeit bis Prag. ... Die Aerzte erklärten die galoppirende Lungensucht, und nach siebentägiger, schrecklicher Agonie war er, der Treffliche, eine Leiche! Josephine ... stand an seinem Bette Tag und Nacht ... mit beispielloser Geduld und Ausharrung. Er machte sein Testament. ... Er übertrug der jungen Frau die Vormundschaft über Kinder und Vermögen." (Therese's Memoirs, in La Mara 1909, p. 69 f.)

[4] Beethoven was later to take advantage of this discrimination against women in the law, when he battled with his widowed sister-in-law over the guardianship of his nephew.

[5] "Gnädigster Monarch! Nahe dem Tode wende ich meine letzte Kraft an, Euer Majestät für die mir erwiesenen Wohltaten zu danken, und als Sterbender anzuflehen, daß allerhöchst dieselben, mein guttes Weib mit meinen unmündigen Kindern nicht verlassen wollen. Eurer Majestät danckbahrst getreuster Unterthan Jos. Gr. Deym[.] Prag, 22. Jener 1804." (Deym to Emperor Franz, 22 January 1804, in Hatwagner 2008, p. 29.)

[6] "Josephine ... ging zum Kaiser, der immer ein Protector Deyms war. ... Der Kaiser war gerührt und gütig." (Therese's Memoirs, in La Mara 1909, p. 70 f.)

[7] "Nun war aber die junge Mutter mit vier Kindern von Geschäften überhäuft, die sie erst zu führen lernen mußte: einer Kunstgallerie mit täglich zu verrechnenden Eintrittspreisen, 80 zu vermiethenden Zimmern eines Prachtgebäudes." (Therese's Memoirs, in La Mara 1909, p. 71.)

[8] It appears that after almost every childbirth (she bore in total eight children), Josephine suffered a more or less severe illness, what we now call "postnatal syndrome" and/or "postnatal depression". Even today little is known about this condition. It is related to deficiencies of vitamins and/or hormones that can upset a woman's system, and in the case of Josephine we must assume an existing propensity of becoming ill due to her general frailty (which can also be gleaned from her portraits). On this occasion, the additional stress due to the inherited duties was probably the main cause. – Rolland (1928) suspects, not unreasonably, the feverish conditions of the swampy surroundings in Martonvásár (it seems many of the Brunsviks suffered from fever).

[9] "Du kannst dir vorstellen, wie die Fieberanfälle mich beunruhigen, was ich dabei leide. Die Nächte besonders waren furchtbar, sie hatte schreckliche Nervenzufälle, bald lachte, bald weinte sie, darnach trat äußerste Mattigkeit ein. ... Wie traurig!" (Charlotte to Therese, 16 September 1804, in La Mara 1920, p. 45.)

[10] "... leben sie wohl liebe gute Gräfin – ihr ergebenster Beethowen." (Beethoven to Josephine, Summer 1804, in Schmidt-Görg 1957, p. 8.) Apparently, he wrote his name with a "w" because in German, "v" is usually pronounced like an "f" (see also Steblin 2009b).

[11] "... auf glükliches Widersehen ... ihr Sie anbetender Beethowen." (Beethoven to Josephine, end of November 1804, in Schmidt-Görg 1957, p. 9.)

[12] "... liebe Gute J. ... – ihr – ihr – ihr Beethowen." (Beethoven to Josephine, beginning of December 1804, in Schmidt-Görg 1957, p. 11.)

[13] "**Sie** Sie mein Alles meine Glückseeligkeit ... Stille schlage nur armes Herz – weiter kannst du nichts – . Für **Sie** – immer für **Sie** – nur **Sie** – ewig Sie – bis ins Grab nur Sie – Meine Erquickung – mein Alles". (Beethoven to Josephine, first quarter of 1805, in Schmidt-Görg 1957, p. 15.)

[14] "O geliebte J., nicht der Hang zum andern Geschlechte zieht mich zu ihnen, nein **nur sie ihr ganzes Ich** mit allen ihren Eigenheiten – haben meine Achtung – alle meine gefühle – mein ganzes Empfindungsvermögen an sie gefesselt... Lange – Lange – Dauer – möge unsrer Liebe werden – sie ist so edel – so sehr auf wechselseitige Achtung und Freundschaft gegründet – selbst die große Ähnlichkeit in so manchen sachen, im Denken und empfinden – o sie laßen mich hoffen, daß **ihr Herz** lange – für mich schlagen werde – **das meinige** kann nur – au[f]hören – für sie zu schlagen – wenn – es **gar nicht mehr schlägt – geliebte J.**" (Beethoven to Josephine, March/April 1805, in Schmidt-Görg 1957, p. 14.)

[15] "... leb [!] wohl Engel – meines Herzens – meines Lebens." (Beethoven to Josephine, end of April 1805, in Schmidt-Görg 1957, p. 19.) Here the term "**leb wohl**" is clearly using the intimate "**Du**" form of addressing, as opposed to the usual "Sie" as in "Leben **Sie** wohl". 200 years ago, the observation of formalities was much

stricter in the use of the German language, at least in its written form. This particular "slip" seems to reveal that **Ludwig and Josephine were already on intimate speaking terms**, even though they adhered to tradition in their written communication. It was common in those days that couples would not change from "Sie" to "Du" before marriage; likewise children had to address their parents via "Sie". This is an interesting point to remember when we come to discover the famous Letter to his "Immortal Beloved" where Beethoven used the intimate "Du" throughout. It is also very interesting in this context that Antonie Brentano admitted in a letter to her husband Franz (Goldschmidt 1977, p. 123) not only how much she loved him (her husband – **not** Beethoven!), but also that it took her several years into their marriage until she could bring herself to address him via "Du".

[16]   "... hier **ihr** – **ihr** – *Andante* – und die *Sonate* ... leben sie Wohl Engel meines Herzens." (Beethoven to Josephine, April/May 1805, in Schmidt-Görg 1957, p. 17.) The "*Andante*" was of course the *Andante favori*.

[17]   "... leben sie Wohl geliebte einzige J." (Beethoven to Josephine, end of May 1805, in Schmidt-Görg 1957, p. 18.)

[18]   Astonishingly, the love between Josephine and Beethoven was a **secret** until 1957 (when the first 13 of his so far unknown love letters were published) – almost: There were some who speculated and concluded from the few available hints that Josephine was the one and only, e.g., La Mara (1920) and Kaznelson (1954). Rolland (1928) also came close.

[19]   Andante grazioso con moto for Piano in *F major* ("Andante favori") WoO 57, 1803–1804.

> *My heart you have won long ago, dear Beethoven... My love of you is unspeakable - like a pious mind loves another one.*[1]

1805: Hope

Beethoven had composed the Song "An die Hoffnung" [To Hope][2] at the end of 1804. This heart-wrenching melody, more than matching the text, was dedicated to none other than Josephine – the only piece of music that he ever dedicated to her alone.

However, only in private! There was to be no official dedication on the published version. Therefore, when one day Prince Lichnowsky spotted the song with the dedication on Beethoven's desk, this was a great embarrassment for the composer. Moreover, as Lichnowsky obviously knew (or sensed) what was going on, Beethoven had some explaining to do.

In a lengthy letter to Josephine – the longest of them all – he tried to dissuade her from any reason to be worried:

> As I said the matter with L[ichnowsky] is not that bad, my beloved J., as you were made to believe – L. saw, by chance, **the song "An die Hoffnung" [To Hope] at my place** without me noticing it...
>
> L. said that he himself was all too familiar with delicacy, **to tell but a single word to anyone, even if he were to assume a closer relationship** – on the contrary, he wished nothing so much as that such a relationship between you and me might arise, if it were possible,[3] because, due to what he had been told about **your character**, it could only be advantageous for me. ...
>
> An event occurred that for a long time made me despair of all happiness of **life here on earth** – now it is not half that bad, I have won **your heart**, oh I am certain of this, how I must **appreciate** this, my activity will increase again, and – herewith I promise you highly and dearly, in a short time I will be standing more worthy of **me and you**. ...
>
> Oh beloved J., it is not the drive towards the opposite sex which attracts me to you, no, **only you, your whole self**

with all its characteristics – have my respect – all my feelings – my whole sensibility enthralled by you. When I met you for the first time – I was determined not to let a spark of love germinate in me, but you have conquered me – I wonder if **you wanted this?** – or did you **not want it?** – perhaps J. could answer this question for me...

Oh heaven, what more I would like to tell you – how I think of you – what I feel for you – but how weak, how paltry is this language – mine at least – Long – Long – may our love last – it is so noble – so much founded on mutual respect and friendship – even great similarity in so many things, in thoughts and feelings – oh let me hope that **your heart** – will continue to beat for me for a long time – **mine** can only – stop – to beat for you – if – it **does not beat any more – beloved J.**[4]

Beethoven then gave the *Andante favori* as a special gift to Josephine, and he published the Song "Ich denke dein" (plus 6 Variations for Piano Duet in *D major*) WoO 74 with a dedication to Josephine and Therese.

Another letter draft to Josephine around this time speaks

of you – the only beloved – why is there no language expressing what is more than respect – far more than everything – which we can name – oh, who can call **you**, and not feel no matter how much he talks about you – that all this can hardly – reach **you** – – only in **music** –

Oh, I am not too proud when I believe that notes are more willing to me than words – **you**, you, my everything, my happiness – Oh no – not even in **my musical notes** can I express it, even though nature gifted me with some talents in this respect, it is still too little for **you**. Silently may my poor heart beat – that is all I can do. –

For **you** – always for **you** – only **you** – forever you – to my grave only you –

My solace – my everything, oh Lord watch over you – Bless your days – send all hardship to me not to **you** – might He strengthen you, bless you, console you – in this wretched yet blissful existence of mortal men – – would you not exist, who chained me to life again, even without this you would be my everything.[5]

Sure enough, there was a reply by Josephine – though much more measured:

> My heart you have won long ago, dear Beethoven ... The greatest proof of my love – my respect you receive, by this confession, by this my trust! – It is what ennobles you the most. – The fact that you appreciate it – that you know the value of the possession, the most precious possession of my **self**, which I hereby assure you – you will show to me – if you are satisfied with this –
>
> Do not tear my heart apart – – Do not further insist – My love of you is unspeakable – like a pious mind loves another one – Are you not capable of such an alliance? – I am not now susceptible to any other kind of love.[6]

Soon after, Josephine contacted Beethoven (probably via one of those book exchanges):

> Dear, good **Beethoven**! How are you? What are you doing? – Quite often – very often I am occupied with these questions.[7]

This was probably a coded invitation that she wanted to see him during their summer holidays, after which Charlotte the chaperone married Count Teleki (in September 1805), and they left for their honeymoon.

There was also a draft letter that broke off (and therefore was probably not sent), but indicates Josephine's state of mind (her children were most important to her):

> I love you, and I appreciate your moral character – You have shown so much love and kindness to me and my children, I will never forget it, and as long as I live, I will always be partaking in your fate, and contribute what I can to make you happy.[8]

* * *

In November 1805, the French army was in Vienna and the great little Corporal was in Schönbrunn as [French] Emperor. Josephine bought two horses and drove alone in her brother's carriage to Martonvásár.[9]

Like the Brunsviks, most of the Viennese aristocracy preferred to be elsewhere during the French occupation:

> We had lived very brilliantly during the Winter of 1805/6. The [Austrian] Emperor had fled to Hungary.[10]

And Beethoven did not regret his decision to withdraw from his *Eroica* Symphony the original dedication to the French general.

---

[1] "Mein Herz haben Sie schon längst, lieber Beethoven ... Ich liebe Sie unaussprechlich – wie ein frommer Geist den andern." (Josephine to Beethoven, first quarter of 1805, draft, in Tellenbach 1983, pp. 67, 74.)

[2] Song "An die Hoffnung" [To Hope], 1st setting, Op. 32, 1804–1805. A 2nd setting, Op. 94, occupied him from 1813 to 1815 – during the aftermath of 1812 (as was the opera *Leonore/Fidelio* and its central theme, the aria by Leonore "Komm Hoffnung!" [Come, Hope!] in 1814). The theme of "Hope" would again be reflected in an Arietta in the set of Italian Love Songs Op. 82, 1809–1810, and finally in the Piece for Piano in *G major* "O Hoffnung!" [Oh Hope!] WoO 200, 1818.

[3] "... if it were possible..." has been interpreted as a qualification indicating that the relationship between Beethoven and Josephine was in fact an impossible one – there was no chance he could ever marry a Countess (as he had observed already with regard to Julie Guicciardi). And this was – as this letter in particular makes clear – the main reason why their love had to be kept secret.

[4] "Wie ich sagte die Sache mit L[ichnowsky] ist nicht so arg meine Geliebte J. als man sie ihnen machte – L. hatte durch Zufall **das Lied an die Hoffnung bej mir liegen** sehen, **ohne daß ich es bemerkte** ... L. sagte selbst, daß er selbst zu sehr mit Delikatesse Bekannt sej, als daß er auch nur ein Wort **gesagt hätte, wenn er für gewiß ein engeres Verhältniß vorausgesezt hätte** – im Gegentheil wünsche er nichts so sehr als daß ein solches Verhältniß zwischen ihnen und mir entstehen möge, wenn es möglich wäre, indem, so viel man ihm **von ihrem Kharakter** berichtet habe, dieses nicht anders als Vortheilhaft für mich sejn könne. ... Ein Ereigniß machte mich lange Zeit an aller Glückseeligkeit des **Lebens hienieden** zweiflen – nun ist es nicht halb mehr so arg, ich habe **ihr Herz** gewonnen, o ich weiß es gewiß, **welchen Werth** ich drauf zu legen habe, meine Thätigkeit wird sich wieder Vermehren, und – hier verspreche ich es ihnen hoch und theuer, in kurzer Zeit werde ich **meiner und ihrer** Würdiger da stehn. ... o geliebte J., nicht der Hang zum andern Geschlechte zieht mich zu ihnen, nein **nur sie ihr ganzes Ich** mit allen ihren Eigenheiten – haben meine Achtung – alle meine gefühle – mein ganzes Empfindungsvermögen an sie gefesselt – als ich zu ihnen kam – war ich in der festen Entschlossenheit, auch nicht einen Funken Liebe in mir keimen zu laßen, sie haben mich aber überwunden – ob sie **das wollten?** – oder **nicht wollten?** – diese Frage könnte mir J. wohl einmal auflösen – Ach himmel, was mögt ich ihnen noch alles sagen – wie ich an sie denke – was ich für sie fühle – aber wie schwach wie armseelig diese sprache – wenigstens die meinige – Lange – Lange – Dauer – möge unsrer Liebe werden – sie ist so edel – so sehr auf wechselseitige Achtung und Freundschaft gegründet – selbst die große Ähnlichkeit in so manchen sachen, im

Denken und empfinden − o sie laßen mich hoffen, daß **ihr Herz** lange − für mich schlagen werde − **das meinige** kann nur − au[f]hören − für sie zu schlagen − wenn − es **gar nicht mehr schlägt − geliebte J.**" (Beethoven to Josephine, March/April 1805, in Schmidt-Görg 1957, pp. 12–14.)

5 "Von ihr − der einzig Geliebten − warum giebt es keine Sprache die das Ausdrücken kann was noch weit über Achtung − weit über alles ist − was wir noch nennen können − o wer kann **Sie** aussprechen, und nicht fühlen daß so viel er auch über Sie sprechen möchte − das alles nicht **Sie** − erreicht − − nur in **Tönen** − Ach bin ich nicht zu stolz, wenn ich glaube, die Töne wären mir williger als die Worte − **Sie** Sie mein Alles meine Glückseeligkeit − Ach nein − auch nicht in meinen Tönen kann ich es, obschon du Natur mich hierin nicht karg beschenktest, so ist [es] doch zu wenig für **Sie**. Stille schlage nur armes Herz − weiter kannst du nichts − . Für **Sie** − immer für **Sie** − nur **Sie** − ewig Sie − bis ins Grab nur Sie − Meine Erquickung − mein Alles[,] o Schöpfer wache über Sie − Seegne ihre Tage − eher über mich alles ungemach nur **Sie** − Stärke seegne tröste Sie − in dem armseeligen und doch so glükseeligen Daseyn, der Sterblichen Menschen − − wäre auch Sie nicht die mich wieder an das Leben angekettet auch ohne dieses wäre sie mir alles −." (Beethoven to Josephine, first quarter of 1805, in Schmidt-Görg 1957, p. 15.)

6 "Mein Herz haben Sie schon längst, lieber Beethoven ... den größten Beweis meiner Liebe − meiner Achtung empfangen Sie, durch dieß Geständniß, durch daß Vertrauen! − Es ist das, was Sie am meisten adelt, daß Sie es zu schätzen wissen − daß Sie den Werth kennen, dessen Besitz ich Ihnen hie[r]mit − den Besitz des edelsten meines **Ich's**, daß ich Ihnen hiemit versichre − werden Sie mir beweisen. − wenn Sie damit zufrieden − Nicht mein Herz zerreißen − − Nicht weiter in mich dringen − Ich liebe Sie unaussprechlich − wie ein frommer Geist den andern − Sind Sie dieses Bündnißes nicht fähig? − Andrer Liebe bin ich nicht für jetzo nicht empfänglich." (Josephine to Beethoven, first quarter of 1805, draft, in Tellenbach 1983, pp. 49, 74.)

7 "Lieber guter **Beethoven**! Wie geht es Ihnen? was machen Sie? − Recht oft − sehr oft beschäftigen mich diese Fragen." (Josephine to Beethoven, 3 June 1805, draft, in Schmidt-Görg 1957, p. 20.)

8 "Ich liebe Sie, und schätze ihren moralischen Charackter − Sie haben viel Liebe, und Gutes mir und meine Kindern erwiesen, daß werde ich nie vergessen, und so lange ich lebe, werde ich stets Antheil an ihrem Schicksale nehmen, und was ich kann zu ihrem Glücke beitragen −." (Josephine to Beethoven, 1805, draft, in Schmidt-Görg 1957, p. 25.)

9 "[November] 1805 war die französische Armee in Wien und der große kleine Corporal in Schönbrunn als Kaiser. ... Josephine ... kaufte 2 Pferde und fuhr in des Bruders Wagen ... allein bis Martonvásár." (Therese's Memoirs, in La Mara 1909, p. 75.)

10 "Den Winter ... 1805 auf 6 hatten wir sehr brillant gelebt. Der Kaiser war geflüchtet ... nach ... Ungarn." (Therese's Memoirs, in La Mara 1909, p. 77.)

Coquetry and childish vanity are far from me – as my soul is far superior... Only my faith in your inner value made me love you.[1]
Believe me, my dear good Beethoven, that I am much more, much more suffering than you ... much more![2]

1806: Jealousy

When dancing through the winter in Budapest, Josephine met Count Wolkenstein, who developed a crush on her.

> Obersthofmeister Count Wolkenstein formally courted my Josephine, who radiated at the time in all the splendor of youth and beauty, with spirit, wit and intellect.[3]

Not surprisingly, to the dismay of Beethoven. However, the much infatuated Count did not stay around for long.

Beethoven felt he had reason to be jealous due to Josephine's "affair" with Wolkenstein – and he let her know it. He composed a song "Empfindungen bei Lydiens Untreue" [Feelings about Lydia's Infidelity] WoO 132, later renamed "Als die Geliebte sich trennen wollte" [When the Beloved Wanted to Separate]:

> *Hope's last glimmer sinks from sight!*
> *With barely a moment's thought she broke all her vows;*
> *May the knowledge that I was once too happy*
> *Vanish forever by way of consolation!*
> *...*
> *Ha, fair Hope, come back to me;*
> *Stir all my passion with a single glance!*
> *However great love's anguish may be,*
> *He who loves never feels his lot to be wholly unhappy!*[4]

Josephine did not hesitate to reassure him of her unwavering love:

> Believe me, my dear good Beethoven that I am much more, much more suffering than you ... much more! – If you value my life, then do act with greater protection – And above all – do not have any doubts about me ...
>
> This suspicion that you so often, so insultingly expressed towards me, that is what hurts me beyond all expression – It is far from me. I hate these low, very low advantages of my sex! – – They are far below me – And I certainly do not need them!
>
> Coquetry and childish vanity are far from me – as my soul is far superior ... Only faith in your inner value made me love you ... Always bear in mind that you gave your goodwill, your friendship to a creature – that certainly is quite worthy of you.[5]
>
> Assuming that I am good to you, that I value your friendship, how can you hurt me, me, who I had, trustfully, let you look deep into my soul, more than our brief acquaintance should permit, because of that you ought to know how little cause for gladness I have – and you may grieve me, through lack of confidence in the strength of my character![6]

* * *

With his beloved away,[7] Beethoven experienced a rather momentous collision with his friend and patron Prince Lichnowsky, leading to a significant cooling of their relationship (and an end of the sponsorship), when he was staying at Lichnowsky's country estate near Troppau in Silesia.

There were also some French officers visiting, and they asked him to play. Beethoven, once a sincere admirer of the French, refused (he was rarely inclined to play on request, anyway). Lichnowsky tried to force him, but Beethoven impulsively left on foot, in pouring rain, and spent the night at an unknown place.

He traveled back home to Vienna where he threw Lichnowsky's bust to the ground. And in his fury, Beethoven wrote him this letter:

> Prince! What you are, you are through the accident of your birth. What I am, I became through myself. There have

been, and there will be thousands of Princes. However, there is only one Beethoven.[8]

* * *

On 25 May 1806, Carl van Beethoven married Johanna Reiss, who was already more than five months pregnant, much to the displeasure of his elder brother. Ludwig's nephew Karl was born on 4 September 1806.

---

[1] "Coquetterie, und kindische Eitelkeit seyen gleich weit von mir entfernt – So wie meine Seele weit erhaben ist ... Nur der Glaube an Ihren innern Werth machte mich Sie lieben." (Josephine to Beethoven, probably 24 April 1806, draft, in Goldschmidt 1977, p. 196.)

[2] "Glauben Sie l[ieber] g[uter] B[eethoven], dass ich viel mehr, viel mehr leide als Sie... viel mehr!" (Josephine to Beethoven, probably 24 April 1806, draft, in Goldschmidt 1977, p. 196.)

[3] "Obersthofmeister Graf Wolkenstein machte förmlich die Cour meiner Josephine, welche damals in allem Glanz der Jugend und Schönheit strahlte, mit Geist, Witz und Verstand." (Therese's Memoirs, in La Mara 1909, p. 77; see also La Mara 1920, p. 69.) Interestingly, this Count was actually a widower, who had remarried but did not tell the Brunsviks anything about this. His passionate love letters to Josephine (and to Therese about Josephine, see La Mara 1920, pp. 70–72) have to be taken with a grain of salt (see Goldschmidt 1977, p. 227). That the sisters should have met him again two years later according to Therese's Memoirs (La Mara 1909, p. 78) must be a mistake – Wolkenstein was dead by then.

[4]
Der Hoffnung letzter Schimmer sinkt dahin!
Sie brach die Schwüre all mit flücht'gem Sinn;
So schwinde mir zum Trost auch immerdar
Bewußtsein, daß ich zu glücklich war!
...
Ha, holde Hoffnung, kehr zu mir zurücke;
Reg all mein Feuer auf mit einem Blicke!
Der Liebe Leiden seien noch so groß;
Wer liebt, fühlt ganz unglücklich nie sein Los!

[5] "Glauben Sie l[ieber] g[uter] B[eethoven], dass ich viel mehr, viel mehr leide als Sie ... viel mehr! Wenn Ihnen mein Leben lieb ist, so handeln Sie mit mehr Schonung – Und vor allem – zweifeln Sie nicht an mir... Dieser Verdacht den Sie so oft, so kränkend mir zu verstehen geben, ist das was mich über allen Ausdruck

schmerzt – Er seye fern von mir. Ich verabscheue diese niedrigen, äusserst niedrigen Vortheile unsers Geschlechts! – – Sie sind tief unter mir – Und ich glaube ihrer nicht zu bedürfen! – Coquetterie, und kindische Eitelkeit seyen gleich weit von mir entfernt – So wie meine Seele weit erhaben ist ... Nur der Glaube an Ihren innern Werth machte mich Sie lieben ... Denken Sie immer, Sie haben ihr Wohlwollen[,] Ihre Freundschaft einem Geschöpfe geschenkt – daß gewiß ganz Ihrer würdig ist." (Josephine to Beethoven, probably 24 April 1806, draft, in Schmidt-Görg 1957, p. 24.)

[6] "Vorausgesetzt daß ich Ihnen gut bin, daß ich Werth in ihre Freundschaft setze, wie können Sie mich kränken, mich die [ich] Sie vertrauungsvoll tiefer in meiner Seele lesen ließ, als unsre kurze Bekan[n]tschaft es eigentlich erlaubte, die Sie eben dadurch wissen, wie wenig Ursache zum Frohseyn [ich] habe – und sie können mich betrüben, durch Mangel an Vertrauen an Festigkeit in meinem Charackter!" (Josephine to Beethoven, Spring 1806, draft, in Schmidt-Görg 1957, p. 24.)

[7] "In 1806, Josephine returned to Hungary, and at the end of May we traveled together to Transsylvania." [1806 kam Josephine wieder nach Ungarn und wir reisten zusammen Ende May nach Siebenbürgen.] (Therese's Memoirs, in La Mara 1909, p. 75.)

[8] "Fürst! Was Sie sind, sind Sie durch Zufall und Geburt. Was ich bin, bin ich durch mich. Fürsten hat es und wird es noch Tausende geben. Beethoven gibt's nur einen." (Beethoven to Prince Lichnowsky, 1806, in Pichler 1994, p. 246.)

Beethoven and Pepi, what is this going to be? She must be on her guard! Her heart must have the strength to say no, a sad duty.[1]

1807: *Forced Withdrawal*

Charlotte had reported to Therese (already in December 1804) dutifully and in much detail the development of Beethoven's interest in Josephine:

> Beethoven was twice with us. Pepi invited him the other day for dinner, after which we had music – quartets – and he was so kind to play immediately on request a sonata and variations, the same I sent you. He played divinely.[2]
>
> Beethoven is very kind, he comes almost every second day, and he gives Pepi lessons. ... Now he is composing an opera, and he has played to us already several wonderful pieces from it.[3]

The Opera *Leonore* (later renamed *Fidelio*) was to be Beethoven's only one. Its celebration of Conjugal Love, of Hope, and its plot – the heroic liberation of a doomed man by his courageous wife – were obviously topics high on the composer's mind in 1804/5.

The song "An die Hoffnung" [To Hope], dedicated secretly to Josephine, was shared by the whole Brunsvik family:

> Beethoven was just here ... He comes almost every day, and he is infinitely charming. He has composed a song for Pepi which she is sending you; however she asks you not to show it to anyone ... I am sure you will love it, **particularly the beginning**.[4]
>
> You are an angel, my dear, good mother and never can I thank you as much as I should and express my feelings. Hopefully we are now for the last time forced to ask you for your help and can pay you back your charitable advances. You took a load off my mind by this. ...
>
> I am tormented by a horrible headache. ... Good Beethoven wrote a beautiful song for me, "An die Hoffnung" [To

Hope], as a present ... During Holy Week, Beethoven's new symphony will be performed.[5]

While her mother must have been alarmed (a marriage to a poor musician was out of the question), her sister was impressed:

Beethoven's song is heavenly beautiful.[6]

Therese felt compelled to compose a poem as a "reply" to Beethoven's meanwhile published song "Ich denke dein" [I am with you], which she sent to her sisters with the remark: "After Geniuses, there are first and foremost those, who are able to appreciate them."

I am with you when I awake serenely
And thinking of you I fall asleep;
And when asleep, dreams make me happy -
Then I am with you.

I am with you at any hint of joy,
At every quietly subdued pain,
And when in tears I abandon hope -
So I am with you.

I am with you as long as I can breathe,
And when I am no more one day,
Even beyond this world of grief
I am only with you![7]

After the bereavement year was over, the Brunsvik sisters were again enjoying Life as a Ball (partying in Budapest):

Now we are going to revel in party after party ... We are going to have a carousel with masks, also a masked ball on 23 February [1805]... Everybody is occupied with preparations – it will be delightful.[8]

We danced until early in the morning and returned home only at 9 o'clock. Pepi too stayed that long, and now she is asleep. I have entertained myself excellently ... I have danced so much that I can no longer move my feet or hands.[9]

* * *

When at the end of the year 1804, Charlotte got wind of Beethoven's erotic interest in Josephine, she started to worry. The alarm bells began to ring, and she informed not only Therese but also brother Franz, the head of the family:

> Beethoven is very often here, he gives Pepi lessons – this is a bit **dangerous**, I must confess.[10]
> Beethoven is almost daily with us, teaching Pipschen – **you hear my heart!**[11]

At the beginning of 1805, Therese had already reacted to Charlotte's reports, and she reminded her youngest sister of her duties as a chaperone:

> Your song, my dearest, is my delight, since I got it. After two days I knew it by heart. ... But tell me, Beethoven and Pepi, what is this going to be? She must be on her guard! ... **Her heart must have the strength to say no**, a sad duty.[12]

The line was then drawn by Charlotte in October 1805:

> The only advice I have for you is to be on your guard with Beethoven: the law is that you never see him alone; the best is: never see him in your house; may God give you the strength to carry out what I advise you! That He returns you to your family, to your children; He will bring back peace and happiness to your heart.[13]

Charlotte kept reminding her sister Josephine with regard to Beethoven:

> Never be alone with him![14]

The Brunsvik family, conscious of the difference in social position, was anything but enthusiastic about Beethoven's overtures. After the last two years' developments, there was a real danger that Beethoven, being so frequently together with the young widow, could make a move and propose to her.

* * *

The year 1807 began with a letter by Josephine to inform Ludwig of her predicament:

> My soul was already **enthusiastic** for you even before I knew you personally – this was increased through your affection. A feeling deep in my soul, incapable of

> expression, made me love you. Even before I knew you, your Music made me **enthusiastic** for you.
>
> The goodness of your character, your affection increased it – this preference you granted me, the pleasure of your company, could have been the greatest adornment of my life if you loved me less sensually – that I cannot satisfy this sensual love – don't be angry with me –
>
> I would have to violate sacred bonds if I gave in to your request – Believe me – that I, by doing what is my duty, suffer the most – and that surely noble motives were guiding my actions.[15]

It is conceivable that Beethoven's "request" was to marry Josephine, and she was forced to say "no" because of the "sacred bonds" she could not "violate" – her duty as a mother to look after and, most importantly, to keep her four children. This was a much more serious obstacle than the fact that a marriage with a commoner was undesirable from the noble Brunsviks' point of view. It was simply a fact that Josephine in case of a marriage to Beethoven would have lost the custodianship of her children (Tellenbach 1988) – to whom she was tied by "sacred bonds".

And Beethoven was fully aware of this, as well as the Brunsvik family's efforts to keep him away from Josephine:

> My dear, good, beloved, – – – J. ... I will try this evening to find you, my beloved, dear, dear J., if not, well, then I will curse your relatives to catch all the evils there are – farewell beloved [J], I love you so much as you do not love me. Your faithful L v Beethowen.[16]

What was new, however: Ludwig now (in 1807) repeatedly emphasized his never-ending **faithfulness** – just when she (reluctantly) began to withdraw from him:

> Beloved, only J. ... farewell, beloved, dear J. – I am not well – and I feel even worse, because I could not see you yesterday and today, your faithful Beethowen.[17]

After recovering from his illness, he was still full of hope to see her again:

> Beloved J. ... I hope to feel better in a few days, and then I will see you again my beloved, only J.[18]

He found it impossible to respect her wish to stay away from her:

> My dear, beloved, only J.! – even a few lines again from you – would cause me great delight – How often did I,

> beloved J., struggle with myself, not to violate the ban which I imposed upon myself – but it is in vain, a thousand voices are always whispering to me, that you are my only girlfriend, my only beloved – I can no longer comply with what I imposed upon me, oh beloved J., let us walk again on that path without worries where we were often so happy.
>
> Tomorrow or the day after I shall see you, may the heavens bestow onto me an undisturbed hour, when I can be with you, to have the long awaited talk, when my heart and my soul can again meet you – my condition was so far still suffering, yet slowly I am getting better...
>
> Hardly was I for one day in Vienna again, when I went to see you **twice** – but I had no luck – to see you[.] It hurt me – and I surmised that your **attitude might perhaps** have changed – but I am still hopeful ... do not forget – do not condemn – your eternally faithful devoted Beethowen.
>
> [PS] I happen to be going to the city today – and I could almost deliver my letter in person – but I have doubts – that I might for the third time fail to see you.[19]

And not being able to talk to her may also have caused some misunderstandings:

> My dear, beloved J. ... my head is beginning to get better, and so – I am becoming more lonely – all the more, because here I can find hardly any company – You are not well – how it hurts me that I cannot see you – yet it is better for your and my serenity not to see you –
>
> You did not offend me – I was touchy for some other reason than you think the matter to be – yet today I cannot write about this in more detail, whatever might become of this, rest assured, ... our opinion of each other is so favorably founded, that trifles can never come between us – yet trifles can create **reflections** ... nothing against you my dear J., everything – everything for you – and yet it must be – farewell beloved J. – in a few days more.[20]

Josephine responded, reassuring him:

> I did not want to offend you! My dear **B**...[21]

* * *

Alas, it was not to be, and his last letter before her departure indicated his resignation – and his bewilderment:

> Dear J. since I must almost fear that you can no longer **be found** by me – and I no longer want to be subjected to the rejections by your servant – thus I can no longer come to see you – unless you care to reveal to me your opinion about this –
>
> Is it really the case – that you do not want to see me any more – so – please do be **frank** – I surely deserve it from you – when I walked away from you, I thought I had to, because it seemed to me that this was your wish – although I suffered much through this – however, I controlled myself...
>
> Tell me dear J. – your opinion, nothing shall bind you – I cannot and must not say anything to you any more, given the circumstances – farewell my dear beloved J.[22]

* * *

Among the documents found after Beethoven's death (apart from the "Heiligenstadt Testament" and "The Letter to the Immortal Beloved") there was also a brief note:

> Only love – yes, only love can give you a happier life! Oh God – let me find her – finally find her – who will strengthen my virtue – who is **allowed** to be mine –
>
> Baden, 27 July [1807.] When the M. drove by and it appeared as if she looked at me.[23]

"The M" was of course Mother Anna von Brunsvik, and we can imagine how her disapproving look pierced the heart of poor Ludwig, who realized that her daughter would never be allowed to be his.

---

[1] "Beethoven und Pepi, was soll daraus werden? Sie soll auf ihrer Hut sein! ... **Ihr Herz muss die Kraft haben nein zu sagen**, eine traurige Pflicht." (Therese to Charlotte, 20 January 1805, in La Mara 1920, p. 54.)

[2] "Beethoven était deux fois chez nous. Pepi l'a invité l'autre jour a dîné; après, on a fait musique, des quattors, et lui étais si aimable qu'il a tout de suite joué comme on l'a prié une sonate et des variations, les mêmes que je t'envoie,

divinement." (Charlotte to Therese, 10 November 1804, German transl. in La Mara 1920, p. 48.) Josephine was nicknamed "Pepi" or "Pipschen".

[3] "Beethoven ist äußerst liebenswürdig, er kommt fast jeden zweiten Tag und gibt Pepi Stunden. ... Jetzt komponiert er eine Oper und hat uns schon mehrere herrliche Stücke daraus vorgespielt." (Charlotte to Therese, 20 November 1804, in La Mara 1920, p. 48.)

[4] "Beethoven war gerade da ... Fast jeden Tag kommt er und ist unendlich liebenswürdig. Er hat ein Lied für Pepi komponiert, das sie dir schickt; doch bittet sie dich, es niemandem zu zeigen ... Es wird dir, dessen bin ich gewiß, gefallen, **namentlich im Eingang.**" (Charlotte to Therese, January 1805, in La Mara 1920, p. 52.)

[5] "Sie sind ein Engel, liebe gute Mutter, und nie kann ich Ihnen, so wie ich möchte, danken und meine Gefühle ausdrücken. Hoffentlich sind wir jetzt zum letztenmal gezwungen Ihre Hilfe zu erbitten und können Ihnen bald Ihre uns so wohlthätigen Vorschüsse zurückerstatten. Sie nahmen mir damit einen Stein vom Herzen. ... Mich plagen fürchterliche Kopfschmerzen. ... Der gute Beethoven hat mir ein hübsches Lied 'an die Hoffnung' für mich geschrieben, zum Geschenk gemacht ... In der Charwoche wird die neue Symphonie von Beethoven ... aufgeführt." (Josephine to her mother, 24 March 1805, in La Mara 1920, p. 59.)

[6] "Beethovens Lied ist himmlisch schön." (Therese to Charlotte, 24 January 1805, in La Mara 1920, p. 55.)

[7] "Nach Genies kommen zunächst diejenigen, die sie zu schätzen verstehen:"

Ich denke dein beim heitern Früherwachen
Und dein gedenkend schlaf ich ein;
Und wenn im Schlaf mich Träume glücklich machen –
Dann denk' ich dein.

Ich denke dein bei jedem Wink der Freude,
Bei jeder still verhaltnen Pein,
Und wenn ich weinend von der Hoffnung scheide –
So denk' ich dein.

Ich denke dein, so lang ich athmen werde,
Und werd' ich einstens nicht mehr sein,
Auch jenseits dieser kummervollen Erde
Denk' ich nur dein!

(Therese to her sisters, 2 February 1805, in La Mara 1920, p. 56.)

[8] "Jetzt werden wir Feste über Feste feiern ... Wir werden ein Karussell in Masken haben, auch einen Maskenball ... am 23. Februar... Alle Welt ist mit

Vorbereitungen beschäftigt – es wird köstlich werden." (Therese to her sisters, February 1805, in La Mara 1920, p. 56.)

9 "Bis in den hellen Tag hinein haben wir getanzt und kamen erst um 9 Uhr nach Hause. Pepi blieb ebenso lange und schläft jetzt. Ich habe mich ausgezeichnet unterhalten ... Ich habe so viel getanzt daß ich weder Fuß noch Hand mehr rühren kann." (Charlotte to Therese, 18 February 1805, in La Mara 1920, p. 58.)

10 "Beethoven vient très souvent, il dône des leçons à Pepi – c'est un peu **dangereux**, je t'avoue." (Charlotte to Therese, 19 December 1804, German transl. in La Mara 1920, p. 51.)

11 "Beethoven ist fast täglich bei uns, gibt Pipschen Unterricht – **vous m'entendez mon cœur**!" (Charlotte to Franz Brunsvik, 21 December 1804, in La Mara 1920, p. 51.)

12 "Dein Lied, Liebste, ist meine Wonne, seit ichs besitze. Nach zwei Tagen konnte ichs auswendig. ... Aber sage mir, Beethoven und Pepi, was soll daraus werden? Sie soll auf ihrer Hut sein! ... **Ihr Herz muss die Kraft haben nein zu sagen**, eine traurige Pflicht." (Therese to Charlotte, 20 January 1805, in La Mara 1920, p. 54.) The "Lied" referred to was of course "An die Hoffnung".

13 "... la seul chose pour la quelle je te conjure, c'ést d'être sur tes gardes avec B: fait toi la loi de ne jamais le voir seul; meilleur il servit encore de ne jamais le voir dans ta maison; que Dieu te donne la force d'exécuter ce que je te conseille! qu'il te redonne a ta Famille, a tes enfants: qu'il redonne a ton cœur la paix, et le bonheur." (Charlotte to Josephine, 20 October 1805, in Steblin 2002, p. 29; German transl. in Steblin 2007, p. 149.)

14 "Ne sois jamais seule avec lui!" (Charlotte to Josephine, ca. 1806, in Goldschmidt 1977, p. 328.)

15 "Meine ohnedieß, für Sie **enthousiastische** Seele noch ehe ich Sie persönlich kannte – erhielt durch Ihre Zuneigung Nahrung. Ein Gefühl das tief in meiner Seele liegt und keines Ausdrucks fähig ist, machte mich Sie lieben; noch ehe ich Sie kan[n]te machte ihre Musick mich für Sie **enthousiastisch** – Die Güte ihres Characters, ihre Zuneigung vermehrte es – dieser Vorzug den Sie mir gewährten, das Vergnügen Ihres Umgangs, hätte der schönste Schmuck meines Lebens seyn können[,] liebten Sie mich minder sinnlich – daß ich diese Sinnliche Liebe, nicht befriedigen kann – zürnen Sie [nicht?] auf mich – Ich müßte heilige Bande verletzen, gäbe ich Ihrem Verlangen Gehör – Glauben Sie – daß ich, durch Erfüllung meiner Pflichten, am meisten leide – und daß gewiß, edle Beweggründe meine Handlungen leiteten." (Josephine to Beethoven, probably Winter 1806/7, draft, in Schmidt-Görg 1957, p. 20 f.)

16 "Liebe gute liebe, – – – J. ... ich versuche es diesen Abend ob ich sie geliebte liebe, liebe, J. finde, ist es nicht, nun so fluche ich ihren Verwandten alle Übel an den Hals – leben sie wohl liebe [J,] ich habe sie so lieb, als sie mich nicht liebhaben. ihr tr[euer] L v Beethowen." (Beethoven to Josephine, probably 1807, in Schmidt-Görg 1957, p. 16.)

[17] "Geliebte einzige J. ... leben sie wohl, geliebte, liebe J. – ich bin nicht wohl – und befinde mich noch übler, weil ich sie gestern und heute nicht sehen konnte[,] ihr treuer Beethowen." (Beethoven to Josephine, May 1807, in Schmidt-Görg 1957, p. 25.)

[18] "Geliebte J. ... ich hoffe es wird mir in einigen Tägen besser gehn, und dann sehe ich sie meine geliebte einzige J. wieder." (Beethoven to Josephine, May 1807, in Brandenburg 1996, Letter #280.)

[19] "Liebe, geliebte, einzige J.! – auch wieder nur einige Zeilen von ihnen – machen mir große Freude – Wie oft habe ich geliebte J. mit mir selbst gekämpft, um das Verbot, welches ich mir auferlegte, nicht zu überschreiten – aber Es ist vergebens, Tausend Stimmen flüstern mir immer zu, daß sie meine einzige Freundin[,] meine einzige Geliebte sind – ich vermag es nicht mehr zu halten, was ich mir selbst auferlegt, o liebe J., lassen sie uß unbekümmert auf jenem Weege wandeln, worauf wir oft so glücklich waren – Morgen oder übermorgen sehe ich sie, möge der Himmel mir eine ungestörte Stunde bescheeren, wo ich mit ihnen bin, um einmal die lange Entbehrte unterredung zu haben, wo einmal wieder mein Herz und meine Seele ihnen wieder begegnen kann – mein Zustand war bisher noch immer leidend, doch geht es allgemach beßer ... kaum war ich einen Tag wieder in Vien angelangt, so war ich **2 mal** bej ihnen – konnte aber nicht so glücklich sejn – sie zu sehen[.] Es that mir wehe – und ich vermuthete, daß ihre **Gesinnung viel[l]eicht** sich geändert – doch hoffe ich noch ... vergeßen sie nicht – verdammen sie nicht – ihren ihnen ewig treu ergebnen Beethowen.

[PS] ich komme eben heute in die Stadt – und könnte bejnahe meinen Brief selbst übergeben – wenn ich nicht zweifelte – ob es mir nicht zum drittenmal fehlschlagen könnte sie zu sehn." (Beethoven to Josephine, 20 September [1807], in Goldschmidt 1977, p. 54 f.)

[20] "Liebe, liebe J. ... mein Kopf fängt an besser zu werden, und so – werde ich auch einsamer – um so mehr, da ich fast hier gar keine Gesellschaft für mich finde – sie sind nicht wohl – wie weh thut mir's, sie nicht sehen zu können – doch besser ist's für ihre[,] für meine Ruhe sie nicht zu sehen – sie haben mich nicht beleidigt – empfindlich war ich wohl aber aus einem ganz andern Grunde, als aus dem sie die Sache ansehen – heute kann ich ihnen nicht weitläufiger hierüber schreiben, was aber auch entstehen mag, unsere Meinung gegen einander ist wohl gewiß so vortheilhaft gegründet, daß Kleinigkeiten nie sie und mich entzweien können – doch können durch Kleinigkeiten wohl **Reflexionen** entstehn ... nichts wider sie liebe J. alles – alles für sie – aber doch muß es sejn – leben sie wohl geliebte J. – in einigen Tägen mehr." (Beethoven to Josephine, after 20 September 1807, in Schmidt-Görg 1957, p. 28.)

[21] "Ich wollte Sie nicht beleidigen! lieber **B**..." (Josephine to Beethoven, after 20 September 1807, draft, in Schmidt-Görg 1957, p. 28.)

[22] "Liebe J. da ich bejnahe fürchten muß, daß sie sich von mir gar nicht mehr **finden laßen** – und ich mich den Abweisungen ihres Bedienten nicht mehr unterziehen mag – so kann ich wohl nicht anders mehr zu ihnen kommen – als Wenn sie mir hierüber ihre Mejnung offenbaren – ist es wircklich an dem – daß sie mich nicht mehr sehen wollen – so – gebrauchen sie **Offenherzigkeit** – ich verdiene

sie gewiß um Sie – als ich mich von ihnen entfernte, glaubte ich dieses zu müßen, da es mir vorkam, als wünschten Sie dieses – obschon ich nicht wenig gelitten hierdurch –, so bemeisterte ich mich meiner doch ... sagen sie liebe J. – mir ihre Mejnung[,] nichts soll sie binden – ich kann und darf wohl in diesen Verhältnissen nichts mehr zu ihnen sagen – leben sie wohl liebe liebe J." (Beethoven to Josephine, after 20 September 1807, in Schmidt-Görg 1957, p. 28 f.)

[23] "Nur liebe – ja nur Sie vermag dir ein Glücklicheres Leben zu geben – o Gott – lass mich sie – jene endlich finden – die mich in Tugend bestärkt – die mir **erlaubt** mein ist – Baaden am 27. Juli [1807.] Als die M. vorbejfuhr und es schien als blickte sie auf mich –." (in Goldschmidt 1977, p. 57.)

What Josephine suffered and endured after her marriage to Stackelberg – entire books could be written about it.[1]

Inter Lacrimas et Luctum

---

[1] "Was Josephine litt und ausstand nach ihrer Vermählung mit Stackelberg, davon ließen sich ganze Bücher schreiben." (Therese's Memoirs, in La Mara 1909, p. 96; Goldschmidt 1977, p. 241.)

> *Stackelberg had become indispensable to her... Poor Josephine! in her lack of experience, she had no idea that she had to become the victim of his proposal.*[1]

1808: A Journey

Josephine, with Therese, embarked on a long journey, in order to find a teacher for her children. She had clearly made up her mind (or ... been brought to her senses by her relatives) that her school-age children and their education were now the main priority of her life. Therese recalls:

> In 1808, my mother was once again inclined to visit Carlsbad. We had a cousin, Elise Seeberg, with us, and we persuaded Josephine to join us... She came with the two boys, leaving her two daughters behind in Vienna, but well looked after, and I was allowed to accompany her to Gotha and Schnepfenthal. A new world was opened to us.[2]

However, they didn't like the rather rigorous methods they observed there, so they (minus Mother)

> moved on to Frankfurt am Main ... Here, Baron Schönberg and Countess Stolberg persuaded us to go to Pestalozzi in Yverdon – then at the height of his wisdom and fame as a teacher. The trip in a light carriage along the Rhine into Switzerland was unforgettably beautiful... Soon we arrived at Yverdon with the most intense expectations.[3]

They were not disappointed: Through Pestalozzi, Josephine and Therese became acquainted with and impressed by Christoph Baron von Stackelberg, a handsome, charming and learned young man. He became the children's teacher:

> Our boys attended classes regularly (October and November).[4]

Around that time, there were movements by French army units in the area, so a direct return to Austria was considered too risky. It was Stackelberg, who suggested a detour through northern Italy:

Josephine decided in Solothurn to make the return journey via Italy. Pestalozzi and Baron Stackelberg had accompanied us that far. In doing this, she followed the latter's wish – he had become very important to her and her children because of his refined educational views and his mature judgment.[5]

And again, our "Cassandra" sensed that disaster was looming:
> But the magic of destiny had spoken, and this decision was the second ring of fate, which decided the family's fortune and misfortune. Stackelberg had become indispensable to her. Such mature ideas, such willpower, such energy she had never met before. ... Poor Josephine! in her lack of experience, in her poetic sense, she had no idea that she had to become the victim of his proposal.[6]

However, at that time, Therese did not warn her.

The end of the year was not a happy one, as Josephine once again became ill, and this time very ill:
> In this mood, we flew through Savoy. On 4 December 1808, on one of those icy wet days we drove in the vicinity of Mont Blanc. ... Josephine's delicate constitution succumbed – a violent colic brought her to the brink of the grave. For four weeks, I stayed awake and looked after her. ... The trip over Mont Cenis was terrible under these circumstances.[7]

* * *

Beethoven meanwhile tried to placate his grief over Josephine's absence by composing four settings of Goethe's poem "Sehnsucht" [Yearning] WoO 134:

> *Only he who knows Yearning*
> *Knows what I am suffering!*
> *Alone and cut off*
> *From all joy,*
> *I'm gazing at the firmament*
> *On yonder side.*

Ah! she who loves and knows me
Is far away.
I am tottering, and burn
In my vitals.
Only he who knows Yearning
Knows what I am suffering![8]

And the Sonata for Piano and Violoncello #3 in *A major* Op. 69. It bears the heading "Inter Lacrimas et Luctum" [Amidst Tears and Sorrow].

---

[1] "Stackelberg war ihr unentbehrlich geworden. ... Arme Josephine! in ihrer Unerfahrenheit ... ahnte sie nicht, daß sie selbst das Opfer seines Antrages werden müßte." (Therese's Memoirs, in La Mara 1909, p. 87.)

[2] "1808 war meine Mutter nochmals geneigt Carlsbad zu besuchen. Wir hatten eine Cousine Elise Seeberg mit uns und beredeten Josephine uns zu folgen. ... Sie kam mit beiden Knaben, ihre zwei Töchter in Wien gut versorgt zurücklassend, und ... ich durfte sie begleiten ... nach Gotha und Schnepfenthal. Eine neue Welt war uns aufgethan." (Therese's Memoirs, in La Mara 1909, p. 83; La Mara 1920, p. 75 f.)

[3] "Wir ... zogen weiter nach Frankfurt a/M. ... Hier ... Baron Schönberg ... und ... Gräfin Stolberg ... beredeten uns ... Pestalozzi in Yverdon aufzusuchen, – damals auf dem Gipfel aller Pädagogen=Weisheit und seines Ruhmes. Unvergeßlich schön war die Reise im leichten Wagen, den Rhein entlang bis in die Schweiz. ... So zogen wir denn bald nach Yverdon mit den gespanntesten Erwartungen." (Therese's Memoirs, in La Mara 1909, p. 84.)

[4] "Unsere Knaben besuchten die Klassen regelmäßig ... (October und November)." (Therese's Memoirs, in La Mara 1909, p. 85.)

[5] "Josephine entschloß sich in Solothurn, lieber durch Italien die Rückreise zu machen. Pestalozzi und Baron Stackelberg hatten uns bis dahin begleitet, und dem Wunsch des Letzteren – der ihrer Kinder wegen durch seine geläuterten pädagogischen Ansichten und seines reifen Urteils wegen, ihr wichtig geworden war – zu willfahren." (Therese's Memoirs, in La Mara 1909, p. 86 f.; La Mara 1920, p. 76.)

[6] "Aber der Zauber des Schicksals hatte gesprochen, und dieser Entschluß war der zweite Schicksalsring, der über Glück und Unglück der Familie entschied. Stackelberg war ihr unentbehrlich geworden. So gereifte Ideen, solcher Willen, solche Thatkraft waren ihr noch nicht begegnet. ... Arme Josephine! in ihrer Unerfahrenheit, in ihrem poetischen Sinn ahnte sie nicht, daß sie selbst das Opfer seines Antrages werden müßte." (Therese's Memoirs, in La Mara 1909, p. 87.) The "ring of fate" Therese refers to is symbolized by the wedding ring, which once again

would bring much more unhappiness than happiness to her poor sister Josephine. Worse was to come. This time even much, much worse. And more quickly.

[7] "In dieser Stimmung durchflogen wir Savoyen. Den 4. Dezember 1808 fuhren wir an einem jener schneidend feuchten Tage in der Nähe des Montblanc spazieren. ... Josephinens zarte Constitution erlag – eine heftige Colik brachte sie an den Rand des Grabes. Durch vier Wochen wachte ich und pflegte sie. ... Die Reise über den Mont Cenis war furchtbar unter diesen Umständen." (Therese's Memoirs, in La Mara 1909, p. 87.)

[8]
Nur wer die Sehnsucht kennt,
Weiß, was ich leide!
Allein und abgetrennt
Von aller Freude,
Seh' ich ins Firmament
Nach jener Seite.

Ach! der mich liebt und kennt
Ist in der Weite.
Es schwindelt mir, es brennt
Mein Eingeweide.
Nur wer die Sehnsucht kennt,
Weiß, was ich leide!

> *Stackelberg's presence and his personality were displeasing ... the brother and the mother had furrowed brows.*[1]

1809: Home again – with Baggage

In March 1809, while Josephine was far away, Beethoven was suffering from his loneliness. His desire to find a female companion was expressed in a letter to his friend Ignaz Baron von Gleichenstein:

> Now, can you help me to look for a wife, if you can find a beautiful one over there in Freiburg, one who might, at times, sigh at my harmonies ... if so, make contact in advance – But she must be beautiful, I cannot love someone who is not beautiful – otherwise I would have to love myself.[2]

More seriously, he set to music another, more intense, version of the theme "Ich denke dein", the song "Andenken" [Memory] WoO 136, ending in:

> *I think of you*
> *With sweet agony*
> *And anxious yearning*
> *And burning tears.*
> *How do you think of me?*
>
> *Oh, think of me*
> *Until we are united*
> *On a happier star!*
> *No matter how far away,*
> *I am with you!*[3]

* * *

Meanwhile, the Brunsvik sisters and their companion were descending from the snow-capped mountains into northern Italy:
> Indescribable is the impression of permanent snow and ice ... to see us so suddenly transferred into the balmiest spring![4]

Therese enjoyed their time in Italy:
> I remember the days in Genoa and Florence with delight. ... April and May in the baths of Pisa![5]

However, not everything was bliss – there were shadows, not only sunshine. Therese was more and more under the impression that she was surplus to requirements:
> Stackelberg immediately took on the education and direction of the boys; he also instructed the mother. He was in love with her and I was no longer required. Things went so far that the boys were no longer entrusted to me, instead they took them away and left me alone at home. ... In Pisa and in Florence, where Josephine had to take the baths after her serious illness, I was left isolated.[6]

Therese experienced more reasons to feel dismayed:
> Stackelberg was always without money – he had already consumed his entire inheritance... We believed and trusted him. The de-facto split of the two loving sisters, the disregard of the faithful, loving aunt by the boys was his first accomplishment. He kept wisely silent about his lack of money, and he always expected shipments that never arrived.[7]

While the Estonian Baron was busy courting the young widow, her sister was left to herself:
> I walked alone, usually all the way to the castles high up in the forest, far away from the spa baths.[8]

Having sidelined the chaperone, Stackelberg was able to make his move.
> With his dangerous charm, and possessed by passion, he arrived at his goal in Geneva, when Josephine, barely recovered from her illness, was weakened in her resistance. She said later that "she had never loved him, never wanted to marry him, he went through all the tricks of seduction, he forced her to give herself ... against her will".[9]

> After continuing with the journey, she refused to give herself to him, and she told him bluntly that "she could not love him". ... How could this ever come to a happy end?[10]
>
> When he declared, after one year, that he could continue the education of her sons only as Josephine's husband, because he loved her, the coveted one agreed, albeit reluctantly, for the love of her children.[11]

But when Josephine returned home, the prospective husband she presented to her family was not welcomed:

> We had completed our whole trip in my sister's small carriage. ... Thus we arrived easily and lightheartedly in our mother's home. Stackelberg's presence and his personality were displeasing. Our extended stay was disliked ... even the trip to Pestalozzi; the brother and the mother had furrowed brows.[12]

Therese then used her ability of speaking in code, telling us that everyone could see (or knew) that Josephine was pregnant:

> But the return to our beloved home country was a sad one! Everywhere the spirit of pettiness; being misunderstood, we had to take refuge in silence! Mother and brother were completely inaccessible: they talked of excessive sentimentality and about being extravagant![13]

* * *

Josephine had not forgotten her faithful friend. Given that she was already six months pregnant and had, albeit reluctantly, promised to marry Stackelberg, her letter to Beethoven was as restrained as necessary:

> It is overdue that I received some news from you, how you are, and I would have asked you long ago, but modesty held me back. –
>
> Now tell me about you, what are you doing? How is your health, your mind, your way of life – the intimate sympathy that I have for everything that concerns you, and will have as long as I live [!], causes me to feel the need to know about it.
>
> Or does my **boyfriend** *Beethoven*, I think I am still allowed to call you that, suppose that I have changed? – What such a doubt would tell me is that you would not be the same any more.[14]

Thus, Josephine expressed in no uncertain terms her unchanged love of Beethoven, and clearly expected the same of him – she assured him of her "intimate sympathy" for "as long as I live"![15] Beethoven responded, renewing the relationship by once again stressing his **eternal** devotion, given the meanwhile changed circumstances:

> I thank you, for it appears that I am not completely banished from your memory, even if it happened, perhaps, more at the behest of others [!] – You want me to tell you how I am, a more difficult question cannot be put to me – and I prefer to leave it unanswered rather than – to answer it **too truly** – farewell beloved J. as always, eternally devoted to you, your Beethowen.[16]

As always!

---

[1] "Die Gegenwart Stackelbergs und seine Persönlichkeit mißfielen ... der Bruder, die Mutter hatten krause Stirnen." (Therese's Memoirs, in La Mara 1909, p. 95.)

[2] "Nun kannst du mir helfen eine Frau suchen, wenn du dort in F[reiburg] eine schöne findest, die viel[l]eicht meinen Harmonien zuweilen einen seufzer schenkt ... so knüpf im voraus an – Schön muss sie aber seyn, nichts nicht schönes kann ich nicht lieben – sonst müs[s]te ich mich selbst lieben." (Beethoven to Gleichenstein, ca. 14 March 1809, in Goldschmidt 1977, p. 332.)

[3]
Ich denke dein
Mit süßer Pein,
Mit bangem Sehnen
Und heißen Tränen.
Wie denkst du mein?

O denke mein
Bis zum Verein
Auf besserm Sterne!
In jeder Ferne
Denk' ich nur dein!

[4] "Unbeschreiblich ist der Eindruck, vom ewigen Schnee und Eis ... so plötzlich uns in den lautesten Frühling versetzt zu sehen!" (Therese's Memoirs, in La Mara 1909, p. 89.)

5 "Mit Wonne erinnere ich mich der Tage in Genua und in Florenz. ... April und May in den Bädern Pisa's!" (Therese's Memoirs, in La Mara 1909, p. 90.)

6 "Stackelberg nahm sich gleich der Erziehung und Leitung der Knaben an, er belehrte auch die Mutter; er liebte sie und ich wurde überflüssig. Die Sache ging so weit, daß man mir die Knaben nicht mehr anvertraute, sondern sie mit sich nahm und mich zu Hause ließ. ... In ... Pisa, wo Josephine nach der schweren Krankheit sowie in Florenz die Bäder brauchen mußte, daß ich so isoliert gelassen wurde." (Therese's Memoirs, in La Mara 1909, p. 92.)

7 "Stackelberg war immer ohne Geld – er hatte sein ganzes Erbtheil schon verzehrt. ... Wir glaubten und trauten ihm. Die quasi Entzweiung der beiden liebenden Schwestern, die Nichtachtung der treuen, liebevollen Tante bei den Knaben war sein erstes Werk. Wohlweise verschwieg er seine Geldlosigkeit und erwartete immer Sendungen, die nicht kamen." (Therese's Memoirs, in La Mara 1909, p. 93.) See also Tellenbach (1983, p. 90): "Stackelberg war gewohnt, sich um Geld nicht zu sorgen. Wenn er keines hatte, was öfter der Fall war, lieh er sich welches, sogar von Pestalozzi!" [Stackelberg was not used to worry about money. If he was short of cash, which was frequently the case, then he borrowed it, even from Pestalozzi!]

8 "Meine Spaziergänge machte ich größtenteils einsam auf die hohen Waldburgen, abseits von den Bädern." (Therese's Memoirs, in La Mara 1909, p. 93.)

9 "Mit seinem gefährlichen Charme, besessen von Leidenschaft, kam er in Genf bei der durch die gerade überstandene Krankheit in ihrer Widerstandskraft geschwächten Josephine zu seinem Ziel. Sie gab später an, 'sie habe ihn nie geliebt, ihn nie heiraten wollen, er habe durch alle Künste der Verführung sie gezwungen ihm sich hinzugeben ... wider ihren Willen'." (Tellenbach 1983, p. 90, quoting from Stackelberg's letter to Josephine, in Skwara/Steblin 2007.)

10 "Auf der Weiterfahrt hatte sie sich ihm verweigert und ihm klipp und klar erklärt, 'sie könne ihn nicht lieben'. ... Wie hätte das gut enden können?" (Tellenbach 1983, p. 91, quoting from Stackelberg's letter to Josephine, in Skwara/Steblin 2007.)

11 "Als er nach einem Jahr erklärte, die Erziehung ihrer Söhne nur als Gatte Josephinens fortsetzen zu können, da er sie liebe, willigte die Begehrte, wenn auch widerstrebend, aus Liebe zu ihren Kindern ein." (Therese's Memoirs, La Mara 1920, p. 77.)

12 "Wir hatten unsere ganze Reise im kleinen ... Wagen meiner Schwester zurückgelegt. ... So waren wir leicht und leichtsinnig im mütterlichen Hause angelangt. Die Gegenwart Stackelbergs und seine Persönlichkeit mißfielen. Unsere verlängerte Reise ... und schon die Reise zu Pestalozzi mißfielen; der Bruder, die Mutter hatten krause Stirnen." (Therese's Memoirs, in La Mara 1909, p. 95.)

13 "Unsere Rückkunft nach dem geliebten Vaterlande aber war traurig! Ueberall Kleinlichkeitsgeist, unverstanden mußten wir zum Schweigen unsere Zuflucht nehmen! Mutter und Bruder waren ganz unzugänglich: Schwärmerei hieß es, überspanntes Wesen!" (Therese's Memoirs, in La Mara 1909, p. 91.)

[14] "Schon längst hatte ich wohl gewünscht Nachricht von Ihrem Befinden zu haben, und lange schon würde ich mich darum erkundigt haben[,] hätte Bescheidenheit, mich nicht zurückgehalten. – Nun sagen Sie mir wie es Ihnen geht, was Sie machen? wie Ihre Gesundheit, Ihr Gemüth, Ihre Lebensart ist – der innige Antheil den ich an allem was Sie betrifft, nehme und so lange ich lebe nehmen werde macht es mir zum Bedürfnisse Nachricht darüber zu haben. Oder glaubt mein **Freund** *Beethoven*, darf ich sie wohl so nennen, ich habe mich geändert. – Was würde mir dieser Zweifel anders sagen als Sie selbst, wären nicht immer derselbe." (Josephine to Beethoven, ca. Autumn 1809, draft, in Schmidt-Görg 1957, p. 29.)

[15] This has to be seen against the background of her being now tied to Stackelberg.

[16] "Ich danke ihnen, daß sie noch scheinen wollen, als wäre ich nicht ganz aus ihrem Andenken verbannt, selbst, wenn es auch viel[l]eicht mehr auf Veranlassung andrer geschah – sie wollen, ich soll ihnen sagen, wie es mir geht, eine Schwerere Frage kann man mir nicht aufwerfen – und ich will sie lieber unbeantwortet laßen, als – sie **zu wahr** beantworten – leben sie wohl liebe J. wie immer ihr ihnen ewig ergebner Beethowen." (Beethoven to Josephine, ca. Autumn 1809, in Schmidt-Görg 1957, p. 30.)

> *Josephine, for the love of her children ... yielded to the sacrifice of her freedom in order to be forged once more under the yoke of marriage.*[1]

1810: State of Ferment

The year 1809 had ended with the birth of Stackelberg's first daughter Maria Laura – an event that was subsequently never mentioned by anyone. However, it was certainly the main reason why Josephine now had little choice but to marry him. Stackelberg had also threatened to leave immediately and to discontinue the education of the Deym children otherwise.

The wedding was only reluctantly accepted by the Brunsvik family, and took place – almost anonymously – on 13 February 1810. Therese reported it thus:

> Josephine decided to have a winter holiday in Gran [Esztergom]. ... Stackelberg accompanied her. ... There, he stated that he would not be able to stay and continue the education of the boys – because he loved her and found it impossible, unless the bond of marriage linked them together. ... Foreboding, Josephine agreed only reluctantly, for the love of her children. ... And at last she yielded to the sacrifice of her freedom in order to be forged once more under the yoke of marriage. With the consent of the Mother, they were married in Gran and there Maria Laura saw the light of day.[2]

Therese added that this birth happened exactly nine months later (after the wedding), however, in her efforts to dissemble she confused Maria Laura (who was already there) with Theophile, Stackelberg's second (and first legitimate) daughter, born in Vienna nine months after the wedding (Steblin, 2007, p. 157).[3]

The marriage was unhappy from the beginning – in fact, already well before that, as Therese noted in her Diary (later – too late) about Josephine's many sufferings which she so unwaveringly endured ... She reproached me that I should have acted in Geneva when she asked me for help – at that time, I could have saved her.[4]

In a diary note, Josephine tried to come to terms with her marriage to an unsociable husband:

> The purpose of my connection with Stackelberg is – to become better and more reasonable. – I have not yet reached the goal where I want to be. Therefore, I avoid parties, and through thinking it over and being alone, I will choose the most appropriate measures that lead to it. That is why I am calm externally, while much is happening inside me. It is a state of ferment.[5]

No more parties, no more balls – no more music!

Filled with ambivalent feelings, Josephine had felt obliged to marry Stackelberg, teacher of her children and father of her fifth child. Given the general disapproval by her family, the wedding had to take place away from home, in the absence of her mother and brother, though at least in the presence of her sister Therese (who was really struggling whether she should attend or not, as evidenced by her diary – she had arguments about this with her mother).

The newlyweds left immediately to Vienna. But here, Josephine was not happy with Stackelberg's idea to buy a small Austrian estate, and in May 1810, they purchased a large and expensive estate in Witschapp, Moravia, which involved a complex financial transaction. Stackelberg had to borrow significant amounts of money to finance it.

When Charlotte visited her two sisters, she was not particularly impressed by her new brother-in-law. And Therese had this to say about him:

> Stackelberg also believed, among other solid principles, that it was not appropriate for the delicate mind of a woman to deal with businessmen. ... He himself will do everything! But unfortunately he did not understand it! Everything was foreign to him, the learned book lover; together with his foreign dialect, he appeared almost ridiculous in his lack of knowledge of people and business matters.[6]

Stackelberg's wife, however, gave him not only the benefit of the doubt, but also her unconditional trust (and all her money) – at least initially:
> Josephine had ambition, [but she] overestimated the abilities of her husband.[7]

The costly purchase of the Witschapp estate would not be without consequences for the future, because
> it was significant that only Stackelberg had signed the contracts even though he did not contribute any money. Josephine's paternal inheritance of 150,000 Gulden was at stake: She had demanded that they both should sign, but he found a way to bypass her. This fact was later the main reason for their separation and the loss of the money![8]

Again, our Cassandra is foretelling the impending doom and gloom:
> And already we are approaching the catastrophe, which smashed everything to pieces and dispelled those involved into all directions. What Josephine suffered and endured after her marriage to Stackelberg – entire books could be written about it.[9]

After a brief summer trip to Karlsbad, where she met Goethe, Therese was back, walking with her sister in the countryside – and they were happy again.
> For several days, reunited with my beloved J in the most beautiful nature, on a notable summit.[10]

She also noticed that Josephine was no longer prepared to suffer under her husband without resistance:
> Today she said – it is not right to suffer, one has to change things, or one has to be content, or one must revolt against it.[11]

However, more telling insights were obtained about her sister's husband:
> Stackelberg: an egoist! This judgment, first by Josephine and now again by Charlotte, might contain some truth, after all. ... It is as if a heavy hand is pressing upon us, there is a lack of God's blessings felt throughout the whole house...
>
> Now I have to acknowledge that Stackelberg, who served me as my tenet and as a paragon, is a very weak and almost evil man; he has flattered and deceived us, and he does not make Josephine happy.[12]

Josephine confided to her diary:
> If I reveal myself to be a weak creature, then all my sacrifices will become worthless.[13]

* * *

During the first two months of 1810, Beethoven was suffering from a deep depression, and there was a marked decline in his compositional output. Although he said nothing about Josephine's second marriage, it must have hurt him deeply – any illusion of a possible union with his only beloved was now gone: She was "far" away and out of reach.

Among the few major works he wrote around this time were the Piano Sonata #26 in *E flat major* "Das Lebewohl" a.k.a. "Les Adieux" [The Farewell] Op. 81a (already in 1809),[14] and the Song "Wonne der Wehmut" [The Bliss of Melancholy] Op. 83#1:

> *Do not dry, do not dry,*
> *Tears of eternal love!*
> *Ah, to the only half-dry eye,*
> *How dreary, how dead the world appears!*
> *Do not dry, do not dry,*
> *Tears of unhappy love!*[15]

And a different song called "Sehnsucht" [Yearning] Op. 83#2:

> *What is tugging at my heart?*
> *What is driving me outside?*
> ...
> *She stays down there,*
> *I watch out for her.*
> *Here she comes, walking;*
> *I hurry to her,*
> ...
> *She lingers and listens*
> *And smiles inwardly:*
> *"He sings with such sweetness,*
> *He sings it for me."*
> ...

> *She walks by the stream*
> *Along the meadows,*
> *The light is now fading,*
> *Night covers her path.*
>
> *Suddenly, I appear*
> *As a twinkling star.*
> *"What shines above,*
> *So near yet so far?"*
>
> *And when with surprise*
> *You looked at that light,*
> *I lie at your feet,*
> *Filled with delight!*[16]

"So near yet so far" – a recurring theme in Beethoven's relationship to his Only, his Immortal, his Distant Beloved!

* * *

On 27 April 1810, Beethoven presented the Bagatelle for Piano in *A minor* WoO 59 to his pupil Teresa von Malfatti. It was to become famous under the title "Für Elise" (supposedly a misspelling of "Für Terese").[17]

Beethoven suddenly and painfully felt the need for a companion, or – as he used to call it – some "domesticity". Given that his beloved Josephine was lost to him, he did not consider himself bound not to marry, even though he did not feel the same affection towards the young Teresa, then 19 years old and a niece of his physician Dr Johann von Malfatti.

On 2 May, Beethoven wrote to his friend Wegeler in Koblenz, requesting urgently a copy of his baptismal certificate. Wegeler in due course traveled to Bonn, and sent him the document in early June. Apparently, Beethoven's marriage proposal was offered through an intermediary (Baron Gleichenstein), but Teresa von Malfatti rejected it.

The affair was concluded by a polite (and apologetic) letter:

> Farewell then, revered T., I wish you everything which is well and good in life, remember me, and gladly so – **forget**

my foolishness – be convinced that no one but me can wish your life to be gladder and happier, even if you do not take part in mine.[18]

"Forget my foolishness"!

* * *

While Teresa von Malfatti then disappeared more or less out of his life, Beethoven became acquainted with the Brentano family, first Bettina, then her brother Franz and his wife Antonie. He became a good friend of Franz (who would later support him financially), and he played for Antonie on the piano, when she was sick.

---

[1] "... aus Liebe zu ihren Kindern ... ergab sie sich dem Opfer ihrer Freiheit, um sich nochmals in das Joch der Ehe zu schmieden." (Therese's Memoirs, in La Mara 1909, p. 95.)

[2] "Josephine ... entschloß sich einen Winteraufenthalt in Gran zu machen. ... Stackelberg begleitete sie. ... Hier erklärte er, nicht bleiben zu können, die angefangene Erziehung der Söhne nicht fortzusetzen – denn er liebte [sie] und fand es unmöglich, außer das Band der Ehe verknüpfte Beide. ... Ahnungsvoll, nur mit Widerstreben willigte Josephine ein, aus Liebe zu ihren Kindern. ... Und endlich ergab sie sich dem Opfer ihrer Freiheit, um sich nochmals in das Joch der Ehe zu schmieden. Sie wurden mit Bewilligung der Mutter in Gran getraut und Maria Laura erblickte dort das Licht des Tages." (Therese's Memoirs, in La Mara 1909, p. 95.)

[3] There is still much confusion in the literature and on many (esp. genealogical) websites: Due to the secretiveness about the illegitimate birth of Maria Laura, Stackelberg's first two daughters (Maria Laura and Theophile) are often reported to have been born in 1810 and 1811 (i.e., in wedlock).

[4] "... vielen Leiden die sie so standhaft erträgt. ... Sie stellte mir vor wie ich in Genf hätte handeln sollen als sie mich um Hülfe ansprach – damals hätt' ich sie retten können." (Therese's Diary, 20 January 1810, in Tellenbach 1983, p. 91.)

[5] "Der Zweck meiner Verbindung mit Stackelberg ist – besser und vernünftiger zu werden. – Ich bin noch nicht an dem Ziel wo ich zu seyn will. Darum meide ich Gesellschaften und will mir durch nachdenken und allein seyn die zwekmäßigsten Maasregeln ergreifen[,] sie wählen welche dazu führen. Darum bin ich stille im äussern weil im[m]er in mir viel geschieht. Es ist ein Stand der Gährung." (Josephine's Diary, ca. 1810, in http://www.xs4all.nl/~ademu/Beethoven/.)

[6] "Stackelberg hatte unter anderen festen Grundsätzen auch den, daß es sich für die zarte Seele einer Frau nicht schicke mit Geschäftsleuten zu verkehren. ... Er wird alles thun! Aber leider er verstand es nicht! Alles war ihm fremd, dem

Gelehrten, dem Bücherfreund; seine ausländische Mundart, seine wenige Menschen= und Geschäftskenntniß machten ihn beinahe lächerlich." (Therese's Memoirs, in La Mara 1909, p. 96.)

[7] "Josephine hatte Ehrgeiz, [aber sie] überschätzte die Fähigkeiten ihres Gemahls." (Therese's Memoirs, in La Mara 1909, p. 97.) Sometimes this is interpreted as "she insisted on living beyond her means" or similar... It is difficult to assess these matters in a "neutral" way. Fact is that Stackelberg – as the man – made the decisions and that he did not (for various reasons) obtain any (or not sufficient) funds of his own, and why he decided to (try to) provide his wife with a lifestyle he could not afford, will forever remain a mystery. At the end of the day, the point is not to blame anyone, but to understand that, given the circumstances, these two people just managed to inflict more hardship upon themselves and each other than they could handle. It's the outcome which counts.

[8] "Für die Zukunft aber war es bedeutend, daß nur Stackelberg die Contracte unterzeichnet hatte ... obwohl er kein Schärflein Geld beigetragen. Josephinens ... väterliches Erbe 150000 Fl. waren im Spiele: Sie hatte beider Namen verlangt, er wußte es aber zu umgehen. Dieser Umstand war später der Hauptgrund ihrer Trennung und des Geldverlustes!" (Therese's Memoirs, in La Mara 1909, p. 99.)

[9] "Und schon nähern wir uns der Catastrophe, die Alles zertrümmerte und die Betheiligten in die vier Winde aus einander trieb. Was Josephine litt und ausstand nach ihrer Vermählung mit Stackelberg, davon ließen sich ganze Bücher schreiben." (Therese's Memoirs, in La Mara 1909, p. 96; Goldschmidt 1977, p. 241.)

[10] "Seit mehreren Tagen wieder vereinigt mit meiner geliebten J in der schönsten Natur auf einer beträchtlichen Höhe." (Therese's Diary, 11 August 1810, in http://www.xs4all.nl/~ademu/Beethoven/.)

[11] "Heute sagte sie – es sei nicht recht zu leiden, man müsse ändern, oder sich dahin stimmen zufrieden zu sein, oder sich erheben." (Therese's Diary, August 1810, in Tellenbach 1983, p. 93.)

[12] "St[ackelberg:] Ein Egoist! An diesem ersten Urtheil Jo[sephine]s und jetzt wieder Charlottens mag doch viel Wahres sein... es ist als ob eine schwere Hand auf uns liege; ein Mangel an Seegen Gottes ist durchs ganze Haus zu spüren... Ich muss zwar sehen, dass Stackelberg[,] der mir zum Canon diente und Muster, ein sehr schwacher und beinah schlimmer Mensch ist[;] er hat uns geschmeichelt und betrogen, er macht Jo[sephine] nicht glücklich." (Therese's Diary, September 1810, in Tellenbach 1983, p. 92 f.)

[13] "Wenn ich als schwaches Geschöpf mich zeige, verlieren alle meine Aufopferungen ihren Werth." (Josephine's Diary, 16 October 1810, in Tellenbach 1983, p. 93.)

[14] The "Farewell" Sonata, dedicated to Beethoven's pupil and patron Archduke Rudolph, has the following movement headings, as given by the composer: "Das Lebewohl" [Farewell], "Abwesenheit" [Absence], and "Das

Wiedersehen" [Reunion]. In May 1809, Vienna was bombarded and then occupied by Napoleon's army; as before in 1805, the aristocrats courageously left the city, whose inhabitants (including Beethoven) had to endure the warfare. It is often argued (e.g., Dahlhaus 1991, pp. 34-37; Lockwood 2003, pp. 299–303) that this Sonata is symbolizing Beethoven's emotional attachment to his beloved pupil Archduke Rudolph whose absence (and eventual return) he was – supposedly – "describing" in this piece of music. Dahlhaus (1991, p. 40) was so dazzled by this "'imagined' experience" that he was wondering "given the nature of the relationship between Beethoven and Archduke Rudolph, it is probably right to think of the expressive character of 'Les Adieux' as largely a matter of a fictive [fictitious] affect, although the work does not reveal the slightest trace of distancing [!] irony." Saying in so many words that the composer was actually quite happy to have his only (but demanding) pupil off his back... This common interpretation has also been questioned by L Poundie Burstein: "'Lebe wohl tönt überall' and 'Reunion after So Much Sorrow': Beethoven's Op. 81a and the Journeys of 1809." *Musical Quarterly* 93 (3-4), 2010, pp. 366-413, who conjectures that this Sonata might describe the "Farewell" to the departing soldiers, then (after the battle with the French was lost with huge casualties), the mourning over their absence, and the joy when peace and normality were restored... On the other hand, it makes perfect sense to interpret it as a reaction to Josephine's departure (the first movement was originally titled "**Abschied**" [The Parting]), his sadness during her absence, and his joyful feelings (though short-lived) about her coming home: There was **Hope** again!

15   *Trocknet nicht, trocknet nicht,*
Tränen der ewigen Liebe!
Ach, nur dem halbgetrockneten Auge,
Wie öde, wie tot die Welt ihm erscheint!
Trocknet nicht, trocknet nicht,
Tränen unglücklicher Liebe!

16   *Was zieht mir das Herz so?*
Was zieht mich hinaus?
...
Sie weilet da drunten,
Ich spähe nach ihr.
Da kommt sie und wandelt;
Ich eile sobald,
...
Sie weilet und horchet
Und lächelt mit sich:
"Er singet so lieblich
Und singt es an mich."
...

Sie wandelt am Bache
Die Wiesen entlang,
Und finster und finstrer
Umschlingt sich der Gang.

Auf einmal erschein' ich,
Ein blinkender Stern.
"Was glänzet da droben,
So nah und so fern?"

Und hast du mit Staunen
Das Leuchten erblickt;
Ich lieg' dir zu Füßen,
Da bin ich beglückt!

17   It is actually not known for sure if and when Beethoven gave this little work to Teresa Malfatti. Also the bearer of the name "Elise" (supposedly written on it) is still an unresolved mystery. Michael Lorenz: "Die 'Enttarnte Elise'. Elisabeth Röckels kurze Karriere als Beethovens 'Elise'." [The "Unmasked Elise". Elisabeth Röckel's Short Career as Beethoven's "Elise".] *Bonner Beethoven-Studien* 9, 2011, pp. 169-190 (http://homepage.univie.ac.at/michael.lorenz/beethovens_elise/, 24 Jul 2011), debunks a claim by Kopitz that "Elise" was instead one Elisabeth Röckel, as "based on flimsy evidence and cannot be upheld". – In this article, Lorenz has more to say about Kopitz: "I had noticed Kopitz up to now only by his strange views on the identity of the 'Immortal Beloved' [Kopitz 2001] and his faulty book *Beethoven from the Perspective of his Contemporaries in Diaries, Letters, Poems and Memories*. An awfully poor essay on Haydn's Vienna apartments could not increase my respect for him either. Kopitz is primarily blessed with a fertile imagination, as a renowned researcher on Burgmüller." [Mir war Kopitz bis dahin nur durch seltsame Ansichten zur Identität der "Unsterblichen Geliebten" [Kopitz 2001] und sein in biographischen Details fehlerhaftes Buch *Beethoven aus der Sicht seiner Zeitgenossen in Tagebüchern, Briefen, Gedichten und Erinnerungen* aufgefallen. Ein erschreckend schwacher Aufsatz über Haydns Wiener Wohnungen konnte meinen Respekt auch nicht fördern. Kopitz ist in erster Linie ein mit blühender Fantasie gesegneter, renommierter Burgmüller-Forscher.]

18   "Leben sie nun wohl verehrte T., ich wünsche ihnen alles, was im Leben gut und schön ist. Erinnern sie sich meiner, und gern – **vergessen sie das Tolle** – seyn sie überzeugt, Niemand kann ihr Leben froher [und] Glücklicher wissen wollen als ich, und selbst dann, wenn sie gar keinen Antheil nehmen." (Beethoven to Teresa von Malfatti, end of May 1810, in Tellenbach 1983, p. 275.)

> *The disagreement between
> Josephine and Stackelberg –
> it was like a dissolution![1]*

1811: Family Life

On 4 March 1811,
> after the birth of Theophile and an ensuing lengthy illness, Josephine wrote ... to Therese in Witschapp, giving detailed instructions for the set-up of her bedroom ... She made it quite clear that she would not be sleeping with Stackelberg, and even insisted that a maid sleep in the room between their separate bedrooms (Steblin 2007, p. 171).

Therese's Diary on 21 March 1811 once again illustrates that the marriage had been on the rocks for the whole preceding year:
> It is no wonder that their relationship last summer affected, confused and shocked me so much. The disagreement between Josephine and Stackelberg – it was like a dissolution! It was the non-existence of the most beautiful feelings, a betrayal of the most beautiful expectations![2]

In April, Stackelberg traveled to Prague to borrow a substantial sum of money from a banker, and signed a contract underwritten by Deym's cousin Franz, who eventually ended up with a huge loss (Steblin 2007, p. 169, n. 70; p. 170, n. 72). In May, Josephine was ill again. In August, she traveled, accompanied by Viky, her oldest daughter, to Karlsbad in Bohemia, for a cure, which she desperately needed.

Meanwhile, it became obvious that there was not enough money to pay for the Witschapp estate.[3] The previous owner, Countess Trautmannsdorf, demanded it back, which was followed by a lengthy lawsuit against Stackelberg. Eventually, the Moravian estate was lost, and Stackelberg ended up with huge debts (including lawyer's bills).

* * *

Stackelberg became known as a very unsympathetic, even slightly sadistic man, who seemed to have learned little from the great Pestalozzi. This is vividly illustrated by a comparison of the couple's diverging views on child education.

First, Josephine's "General thoughts on education":

> I think it is a good thing to tell a child something nice every morning – to put love into his heart through conversation or action. In order to encourage a child, one should not compare him to anyone else, because wanting passionately to be better than others produces only rivalry and consequently vices. A keen moral sense is required, such that from a **feeling** of superiority there should not arise the abuse of it. Nothing is more harmful than lecturing children. Always be good to them.[4]

Compare this to what can only be described as her husband's terror regime – Stackelberg's "Code of Law" with "Articles" like these:

> The children must not touch anything that is not theirs. If the children do not obey this Article, then their hands shall be tied together.
>
> Furthermore, they must not roll around on the floor. If this Article is not complied with, then the children are to be tied to their bed for a certain period.[5]

* * *

With Josephine unavailable, Beethoven continued to stay in contact with the other Brunsviks. He exchanged letters with Franz, and especially with Therese, who forwarded this letter by him verbatim to Josephine:

> Even without being sought out, the better people among us think of each other, as is the case with you and me, worthy admirable Therese: still I owe you sincere thanks for your beautiful picture, and ... I must appear as a beggar by entreating you ... to renew for me that little drawing, which I was unfortunate enough to lose. **An eagle looking towards the sun**, that was it, I cannot forget it.[6]

The "Eagle" drawing was probably a picture made by Josephine (see Tellenbach 1999) whom Beethoven obviously could not

contact directly. Therese was only too happy to oblige and soon after followed this up, reminding her sister:
> My request to you, dear Josephine, is now to bring that picture back to life, and only you can do it.[7]

It is not known whether Josephine reproduced this drawing again, nor whether Beethoven ever received it.

It was a difficult time for both of them.

---

[1] "Die Uneinigkeit Jo[sephine]s und St[ackelberg]s – es war eine Auflösung!" (Therese's Diary, 21 March 1811, in Tellenbach 1983, p. 93.)

[2] "Kein Wunder, wenn mich das Verhältniss des vorigen Sommers so ergriff, verwirrte und erschütterte. Die Uneinigkeit Jo[sephine]s und St[ackelberg]s – es war eine Auflösung! es war ein Nichtbestehen der schönsten Ahndung! ein Betrogensein in den schönsten Erwartungen." (Therese's Diary, 21 March 1811, in Tellenbach 1983, p. 93.)

[3] Not only that: "After most of the purchase price had already been paid, there was still outstanding the admission of Christoph v. Stackelberg into the Bohemian Knighthood, an indispensable condition for the transfer of ownership." [Als der Kaufpreis bereits größtenteils bezahlt war, stand noch immer die für eine Eigentumsübertragung unerläßliche Aufnahme von Christoph v. Stackelberg in die böhmische Ritterschaft aus.] (Wolfhart Stackelberg 2001, p. 5.) When the document (for a fee of 10,000 Gulden!) finally arrived, it was too late, thus giving the previous owner a(nother) pretext to revoke the deal…

[4] "Josephines … 'Allgemeine Gedanken zur Erziehung': … 'Ich finde es gut dem Kinde morgens etwas herzliches zu sagen – ihnen Liebe durch Gespräch oder Handlung in das Herz zu legen. … Man muß ein kind um es anzueifern mit niemand andrem vergleichen, weil das leidenschaftl[ich] besser sein wollen rivalität und folglich Laster erzeugt. … Ein geschärfter moralischer Sinn wird erfordert wenn aus dem **Gefühl** der Übermacht nicht der Mißbrauch derselben enstehen soll… Nichts ist schädlicher als hofmeistern bei Kindern. gegen selbe immer gut'." (Tellenbach 1983, p. 93 f.)

[5] "Stackelberg dagegen entwarf ein 'Gesetzbuch' mit 'Artikeln': 'Die Kinder sollen nichts anrühren, was ihnen nicht gehört … Wenn die Kinder diesen Artikel nicht halten, so werden ihnen die Hände zugebunden. … Auch sollen sie sich nicht auf den Dielen herumwälzen. Wird dieser Artikel nicht gehalten, so werden die Kinder für einige Zeit auf dem Bett festgebunden'." (Tellenbach 1983, p. 94.)

[6] "Auch ungesucht gedenken die besseren Menschen sich, so ist es auch der Fall bei Ihnen und mir, werthe verehrte Therese: noch bin ich Ihnen lieben Dank schuldig für Ihr schönes Bild, und … muß ich sogleich ein Bettler erscheinen, indem ich Sie ersuche …, mir doch jene kleine Handzeichnung zu erneuern, welche ich so unglücklich war zu verlieren. **Ein Adler sah in die Sonne**, so war's,

ich kann's nicht vergessen." (Beethoven to Therese, 2 February 1811, in La Mara 1920, p. 81.)

[7] "Meine Bitte an dich, liebe Josephine, ist nun jenes Bild, das nur du am besten wieder ins Leben zu rufen vermagst, wirklich herbei zu rufen." (Therese to Josephine, 23 February 1811, in La Mara 1920, p. 81.)

We are no longer married.[1]

1812: Intermezzo

---

[1] "Wir sind nicht mehr vermählt." (Josephine's Diary, February/March/April 1812, in Tellenbach 1983, p. 108.)

> *Stackelberg wants to leave me on my own. He is callous to supplicants in need... I want to see Liebert in Prague.*[1]

January to June: Dissolution

Beethoven must have heard about the problems Josephine had with Stackelberg. In January 1812, the composer wrote a letter to a publisher, referring to "Russians and Livlanders" disparagingly as "wind bags and braggarts".[2]

In February, the Brunsvik sisters discussed their holiday plans, taking no account of Stackelberg. Therese was all too aware that
> Josephine needs care and attention, amusement of the mind, clean air, scented herbs, baths, physical exercise.[3]

As before in 1811, they made plans to travel (in the summer)
> to Karlsbad and Eger; she with one child, the rest of us near Vienna in a country house on a mountain.[4]

In late December 1811, they had left Witschapp and returned to the Deym villa in Vienna (Steblin 2007, p. 173). Josephine accused her husband of having pasha airs when he preferred reading a book to talking with his wife:
> Take Stackelberg as he is ... clean up the mess he has created ... if he thinks to be that rich. How can you continue reading when you see a creature next to you in sorrow! Rather than helping me you are seeking distraction ... We are no longer married – because your companion's grief means nothing to you. ...
>
> He is not sincere – and not reliable. – In addition, he is tainted with an evil character. He tries to win the trust of others through hypocrisy, and to exploit them as he sees fit. ... This he did indeed very often with regard to me, in that he misused my most noble-minded trust – prattles about religion ... As long as Stackelberg does not use his own money for my house and does not maintain it – he is my guest. – Otherwise I would be his guest.[5]

Josephine was wondering if "my honor permits me to remain bound to him in the future".[6] In her desperation, she turned for advice to a priest:

> I am writing to you in the most wistful mood of my life, for I fear for the first time that Stackelberg can really do wrong! ... Stackelberg told me yesterday – that he is definitely [!] going away from here, and within a few days. I am well aware of the consequences, which such a step will have for my honor and for myself ...
>
> His pretext is that I do not want to hand over the administration of the property of my children – the real reason is more likely that he did not win any friends here. ... It is desirable that someone should hold him accountable, about how he acts against me, my fatherland, my friends and my family.[7]

On 3 April, a violent quarrel broke out between the spouses, witness the diary of the twelve-year-old daughter Viky:

> This morning, as misfortune would have it, I awoke to hear a scene that pierced my heart ... Mama's voice, and the angry voice of Papa ... I listened with pricked ears ...
>
> Dad told Mom that she was the martyrdom of his life ... In his terrible delusion, he told her a thousand insults ... I thought of the terrible consequences of her getting married with such haste for the love of us, which had caused my mother's misfortune, and by this important step it brought about her everlasting unhappiness. She did it for us.[8]

Probably, Stackelberg left in a huff after this incident, and returned for a short time a few weeks later – only to pack his suitcases and leave his wife, with six children (and mounting debts), once again.

Things seemed to have come to a head definitely soon after. On 8 June 1812, Josephine noted:

> Today has been a difficult day for me. – The hand of fate is resting ominously on me – I saw besides my own deep sorrows also the degeneration of my children, and – almost – all courage deserted me –!!![9]

And soon after:

> Stackelberg wants to leave me [!] on my own. He is callous to supplicants in need. ... I want to see Liebert in Prague [!]. I will never let the children be taken from me. ... On account of Stackelberg I have ruined myself physically, in

that I have incurred so much distress and illness through him.[10]

> **"I want to see Liebert in Prague"**: This piece of a Diary note by Josephine in June 1812 (after she learned that **Stackelberg was about to leave**), where she unambiguously expressed her **intention** to go to **Prague**, is the closest to a **proof** that she most likely actually went there!
> This (first published by Steblin 2007, p. 162) is absolutely **sensational**!
> A piece of solid evidence that was so long missing and has always been demanded by all those, who were determined to maintain – against all the other evidence – that Josephine could not even be considered a "candidate" for the enigmatic role of Beethoven's "Immortal Beloved" unless her presence in Prague in July 1812 can be "proved".[11]

The situation was by now such a difficult one for Josephine, that she not only required help to sort out the financial mess created by her incompetent husband, she was also so distraught that she desperately needed someone to talk to, to be comforted by a friend. There were certainly several acquaintances and relatives in Prague (or nearby) whom she could have decided to visit – incognito.

At the same time, Therese was horrified to read the diary left behind by Stackelberg:

> Josephine, remain steadfast! ... How weak, how powerless, how biased, how unfair is this highly touted Stackelberg! I am astonished. How callous, how unfair towards Josephine! How selfish, how conceited, how contrived... I would be ashamed to waste my time at this moment with such drivel of a diary.[12]

Therese vividly describes the break-up that occurred (most likely) in June 1812:
> Stackelberg was extremely irritated. The couple's peace was finally and irrevocably destroyed. As so often, when they had disputes, I threw myself on my knees before them and begged both of them to give in. Each of them appealed to reason – but each thought something different to be reasonable, in respect of education as well as regarding the administration of their estate.
>
> The pecuniary situation finally cut the Gordian knot. It was revealed that Stackelberg did not receive any funds from Russia.[13] ... His mind was paralyzed by too many disgusting thoughts. ... Josephine told him at last, she would give him no more money for his private expenses. She wanted to force him to act and locked away his clothes – he, angry, made a scene and left the house. We did not see him again for six months.[14]

* * *

> He said later that he had rented a small room, threw himself onto his bed, and in tears he was struggling for enlightenment and help, he prayed fervently to God, and behold, it was from above that help arrived – the Lord Himself with His grace entered into his heart, bare of all worldly hopes and wishes, and He filled it with solace, with love and faith.
>
> From that moment on, he belonged exclusively to the Lord. He left Vienna ... and prepared himself for that great mission which was to become his calling, to work on the improvement of Estonia, his home country.[15]

Therese's sarcastic comments about Stackelberg's hypocrisy must have been little consolation for Josephine, who was facing a severe financial crisis. Stackelberg wrote a letter dated 14 June 1812 to his mother in Reval, announcing to see her "this summer" with his family. There is no confirmation that this letter was ever sent; even so, it is just another example of his art of dissembling in the face of difficulties.

* * *

From mid June 1812 until several months later, the sisters' diaries have significant gaps – Josephine's diary even shows clearly that several pages had been carefully cut out!

This, together with the blank in Therese's (and everybody else's) memoirs, can only indicate that **something must have happened that had to be kept secret** (by those who knew), no matter what. Could it have had anything to do with Beethoven?

* * *

At the end of June 1812, Beethoven left Vienna, traveling to Teplitz via Prague for his summer holidays and to take the baths, as ordered by his physician Dr Jakob Staudenheim.

---

[1] "St. will daß ich mir selbst sitzen soll. er ist gefühllos für bittende in der Noth. ... Ich will Liebert in Prague [!] sprechen." (Josephine's Diary, June 1812, in Steblin 2007, pp. 159–162.)

[2] "... wie überhaupt die Russen und liefländer windbeutel und Grossprahler sind..." (Beethoven to Breitkopf & Härtel, 28 January 1812, in Tellenbach 1983, p. 97.) "Liefland" (or "Livland", also "Livonia") was another term for the Baltic state of Estonia (where Stackelberg was from).

[3] "Josephine braucht Pflege und Aufmerksamkeit, Erheiterung des Gemüths, reine Luft, Kräuterduft, Bäder, Übung des Körpers." (Therese's Diary, February 1812, in Goldschmidt 1977, p. 236.)

[4] "... nach Karlsbad und Eger; sie mit einem Kinde, wir übrigen in der Nähe von Wien in ein Landhaus auf einem Berg..." (Therese's Diary, 15 February 1812, in Goldschmidt 1977, p. 228.) When later (in July 1812) Beethoven was referring to "K" (= Karlsbad) this could mean that Josephine was still planning to go there (but – maybe – didn't).

[5] "St[ackelberg] nehmen wie er ist ... den Wirrwarr den er angerichtet hat wieder aufräumen ... wenn du so reich darinnen dich dünkst[.] Wie kan[n]st du lesen wenn du ein Geschöpf neben dir in Kummer siehst! Ehe du hilfst[,] magst du dich zerstreuen ... Wir sind nicht mehr vermählt – den[n] das Leiden der Gefährtin ist es nicht dem andren. ... Er ist nicht aufrichtig – und nicht zuverlässig. – Auch hat er eine tincture des bösartigen Charackters. Er sucht andren Vertrauen abzugewinnen durch heucheley, und sie nach seinem Belieben auszuholen. ... Dieß that er wirklich in hinsicht meiner sehr oft, daß er das edelste Vertrauen mißbrauchte – Schwatzt von Religion ... So lange St[ackelberg] nicht sein eigenes Vermögen für mein Haus verwendet u. es davon erhält – so ist er mein Gast – im vorhergehenden Fall würde ich der seinige seyn." (Josephine's Diary, February/March/April 1812, in Tellenbach 1983, p. 108 f.)

[6] 22 March 1812, in *The Beethoven Newsletter* vol 9 #2–3 (http://www.ringnebula.com/Beet/B_1812.htm, 27 Apr 2011).

[7] "Ich schreibe Ihnen in der wehmütigsten Stimmung meines Lebens, den[n] ich fürchte zum erstenmal das[s] St[ackelberg] wirklich unrecht handeln kan[n]! ... Stack[elberg] sagte mir gestern – daß er ganz bestimmt sey von hier weg zu gehen, und binnen einiger Tage. Ich sehe die Folgen ein, welche dieser Schritt für meine Ehre und für mich haben wird ... Zum Vorwand nimmt er[,] daß ich ihm die Verwaltung des Vermögens der Kinder nicht geben will – die wahre Ursache liegt wohl darin, daß er hier sich keine Freunde erwarb ... Es wäre doch zu wünschen[,] daß ihn jemand zu Rechenschaft zöge, wie er gegen mich, mein Vaterland, meine Freunde und Verwandte[n] handelt." (Josephine to a priest, Spring 1812, in Tellenbach 1983, p. 109.)

[8] "Ce matin a mon réveille le malheur voulut que j'entende une scène qui me perçat le cœur ... la voix de maman, et a son ton colère la voix de papa ... je prête l'oreille ... Papa ... ne voit en maman qu'une martyr de sa vie ... dans cette illusion affreuse mille injures ... je pensais aux suites affreuses de la übereilung [hâte] qui a fait le malheure de ma mère; qui par amour pour nous s'est marier et par ce pas important à fait pour toujours son malheur; elle l'a fait pour nous." (Viky Deym's Diary, 3 April 1812, in Goldschmidt 1977, p. 222; German transl., p. 529.)

[9] "Ich habe heute einen schweren Tag. – Die Hand des Schicksals ruht düster auf mir – Ich sah nebst meinem tiefen Kummer auch noch die Entartung meiner Kinder und – fast – aller Muth wich von mir –!!!" (Josephine's Diary, 8 June 1812, in Steblin 2007, p. 159.)

[10] "St. will daß ich mir selbst sitzen soll. er ist gefühllos für bittende in der Noth. ... Ich will Liebert in Prague [!] sprechen. ich will die Kinder nie von mir lassen. ... Ich habe Stackb zu liebe [mich] physisch zugrunde gerichtet indem ich ... noch so viele Kummer und Krankheit durch ihn zugezogen habe." (Josephine's Diary, June 1812, in Steblin 2007, p. 162.)

[11] Schmidt-Görg (1957, p. 34, n. 41) categorically demanded: "First of all ..., a document about Josephine's presence in Prague has to be provided before considering that this letter [to the 'Immortal Beloved'] was written to her." [Es ist ... zuerst ein Dokument für Josephines Prager Aufenthalt beizubringen, ehe man daran denken kann, daß dieser Brief [an die "Unsterbliche Geliebte"] damals an sie geschrieben wurde.] Well, here it is, and together with the near certainty that she traveled incognito, what more do we need? (She also mentions Stackelberg having left or about to leave her.)

[12] "Bleibe standhaft Joseph[ine]! ... Wie schwach, wie kraftlos, wie einseitig, wie ungerecht ist dieser hochgepriesene Stackelberg! Ich erstaune. Wie gefühllos, wie ungerecht gegen Josephine! Wie egoistisch, wie eingebildet, wie montirt. ... Ich würde mich schämen in diesen Moments meine Zeit mit einem solchen Gewäsch von Tagebuch hinzubringen." (Therese's Diary, 9 June 1812, in Goldschmidt 1977, p. 214; La Mara 1920, p. 86.)

[13] This was perhaps not Stackelberg's fault insofar as at the time Napoleon was marching towards Moscow. Also in the years before there were various wars

involving Austria as well as Russia which probably made the transfer of funds between these countries difficult or risky. According to Wolfhart von Stackelberg (2001, p. 5), Christoph had inherited considerable assets in Estonia (after his father's death in 1792). In any case, it seems that he had promised (or hoped) that these funds were guaranteed to arrive, and when they didn't, Josephine refused to provide any of her own (or her family's) money. The resulting frustration was too much for him. His reaction was to become a religious fanatic.

[14] "Stackelberg [war] aufs äußerste gereizt. Der Ehefriede war endlich unwiederbringlich zerstört. Wie oft, wenn sie disputirten ..., warf ich mich auf die Knie vor ihnen und beschwor den einen und den andern nachzugeben. Jeder berief sich auf die Vernunft – jeder aber hielt etwas anderes für vernünftig, sowohl in Rücksicht der Erziehung ... als in der Verwaltung des Vermögens. Die pecuniären Verhältnisse schnitten endlich den gordischen Knoten entzwei. Es zeigte sich: Stackelberg bekam aus Rußland keine Gelder. ... Sein Geist war gelähmt durch zu viele Widerwärtigkeiten. ... Josephine ... bedeutete ihm endlich, kein Geld für seine Privat=Auslagen ihm ferner geben zu können. Sie wollte ihn zwingen, thätig zu werden, verschloß seine Kleidungstücke und Wäsche – er, zornig, machte eine Scene und verließ das Haus. Wir sahen ihn sechs Monate nicht." (Therese's Memoirs, in La Mara 1909, p. 103.) This entry does not mention the exact year that it relates to, and it is in fact mixed up with reports of events after Minona's birth (in 1813). However, the fact that nothing at all is mentioned by Therese about July 1812 suggests that it belongs to the earlier period. It is a fitting continuation, matching the diary entries (by both sisters) in June 1812 and the preceding conflicts. The remark "six months" refers to Therese and the children (who were not with Josephine for that period). Stackelberg returned to Josephine (most likely) in August 1812 (or even earlier), after having rented a room somewhere in Vienna to confer with God.

[15] "Er erzählte später, er hatte ein kleines Zimmer gemiethet, sich auf sein Bett geworfen, in Thränen und Ringen nach Erleuchtung und Hilfe innigst zu Gott gebetet, und siehe da, es ward ihm Hilfe von oben – der Herr selbst mit seiner Gnade kehrte ein in dies von allem irdischen Hoffen und Wünschen baare Herz und erfüllte es mit Trost, mit Liebe und Glaube. Von diesem Augenblick an gehörte es aber auch dem Herrn allein. Er verließ Wien ... und bereitete sich so vor zu der großen Mission, die ihm ward, ... an Esthlands, seines Vaterlandes, Vervollkommnung zu arbeiten." (Therese's Memoirs, in La Mara 1909, p. 103.) Stackelberg's religious ambitions were rewarded in 1819 when he finally settled back in Estonia, becoming a school principal responsible for **religious** education.

My angel, my everything, my very self! ... Is not our love a true edifice in heaven but also as firm as the firmament... You know my faithfulness to you, never can another own my heart, never – never... Angel, you – my life – my everything ... never misjudge the most faithful heart of your Beloved L.
Forever thine – forever mine – forever us.[1]

The Month of July: Encounter

On 1 July 1812, Ludwig arrived in Prague, to stay at the inn "Zum schwarzen Roß" – not far from Count Deym's last residence (probably still accessible to Josephine) and also near to Deym's sister Victoire Golz's place (who was at the time in Nemischl, 70 km south of Prague, but Josephine could stay here any time).

On the same day, the Emperor[2] and his entourage left Prague suddenly. This must have been a further blow to Josephine, if she had planned to see him – remember how he had been consoling her after his friend and her husband Deym's death? And promising (but not giving) her money? Maybe a promise on which Josephine wanted to take him up now...

Beethoven intended to meet his patron Prince Kinsky. On 3 July, he missed a planned meeting with Karl August Varnhagen in the evening – as he explained later in a letter, apologizing:

> Of Teplitz there is not much to tell, few people and among their small number nobody outstanding, therefore I am living alone – alone! alone! alone! Dear Varnhagen, I am sorry that I could not spend the last evening in Prague with you, and I myself found it impolite, but a circumstance that I could not foresee prevented me – please consider this in my favor – verbally more about it.[3]

It appears that on 3 July 1812, on a mild summer evening, both Josephine and Beethoven, unbeknownst to each other, went for a walk, and – suddenly crossed paths.

In this totally unexpected but extremely happy encounter, all the accumulated tension, grief, turmoil, suffering of both their lives were suddenly relieved! (We should also not be surprised that nine months later Minona was born.)

* * *

During the afternoon of 4 July, Beethoven went, as planned, to Teplitz (about 100 km to the west of Prague), where he arrived early the following morning, after an arduous journey.

On 6 July 1812, in the morning, Ludwig wrote the first part of what has become known as the **Letter to his "Immortal Beloved"** (continued in the evening and the following day). It was, most likely, never sent.[4] It was not even really a "letter". It was an outpouring of feelings, thoughts and impressions on the spur of the moment (albeit a few days after the event), more like a diary entry, comparable in character to his "Heiligenstadt Testament" ten years before – which was also written in the form of an unsent letter (to his brothers), at a time of severe desperation (the experienced inevitability of becoming deaf).

Interestingly, these two "letters" and a short note from 1807 (about "the M" looking sternly at him) were found in Beethoven's desk after his death.

On 19 July, Beethoven met Goethe, who was not very impressed. On 25 July, Beethoven left Teplitz for Karlsbad, where he stayed (as planned) in the Brentanos' guesthouse until the beginning of August, when they traveled together to Franzensbrunn.

* * *

A very interesting and revealing document was discovered and published by Steblin (2007, pp. 163–169): Thought so far to have been part of Therese's Diary (of 1812), there was a page headed "**Table of Rules**" and dated 5–12 July [1812]. However,

surprisingly, this one sheet was unquestionably in the handwriting of – Christoph Baron von Stackelberg! (Steblin 2007, p. 164.)
At the top, it reads:
> From 5 to 12 July. – Resolution. Be resolved to do what you must, and do without fail what you have resolved.[5]

Below there was something we would today call a spreadsheet (or a matrix), with columns headed by the days of the week (5 to 11), and the rows labeled with ethical categories:
> Resolution, Order, Cleanliness, Tranquility, Chastity, Justice, Economy, Moderation, Humility, Sobriety.[6]

Sure enough, what we find here is a clear confirmation of Therese's characterization of Stackelberg being away to seek "enlightenment" from above with the help of prayer, in order to become even more virtuous:
> Thus this whole document, dated at the time when ... he ... was deliberating about his future, is surely further proof that Josephine was left alone ... in June and July 1812 (Steblin 2007, p. 169).

---

[1] "Mein Engel, mein Alles, mein Ich! ... Ist es nicht ein wahres Himmels-Gebäude unsre Liebe – aber auch so fest, wie die Veste des Himmels. – ... da du meine Treue gegen dich kennst, nie eine andre kann mein Herz besizen, nie – nie – ... Engel, ... du – mein Leben – mein Alles ... verken[n]e nie das treuste Herz deines Geliebten L. – Ewig dein – ewig mein – ewig unß." (Beethoven to Josephine?, 6/7 July 1812, draft, in Pichler 1994, pp. 370–372.)

[2] This was in any case a bad time to try to contact the Emperor of Austria in a personal matter: Just when Napoleon had embarked on his ill-fated campaign to conquer Moscow, various Emperors, Kings and Dukes of Central Europe were busy discussing measures with regard to the French General's expected failure, in Prague as well as in Teplitz.

[3] "Von T[eplitz] ist nicht viel zu sagen, wenig Menschen und unter dieser kleinen Zahl nichts auszeichnendes, daher leb ich allein – allein! allein! allein! es war mir leid, lieber V. den letzten Abend in Prag nicht mit ihnen zubringen zu können, und ich fand es selbst für unanständig, allein ein Umstand den ich nicht vorhersehen könnte, hielt mich davon ab – halten sie daher zu gute – mündlich näher darüber –." (Beethoven to Varnhagen, 14 July 1812, in Goldschmidt 1977, pp. 33, 74, 271.) Here "den letzten Abend in Prag" [the last night in Prague] does not refer to the preceding day (13 July), but to the period when Beethoven and Varnhagen were both in Prague (up to 3/4 July).

[4]   Strictly speaking, there is no proof – neither that it was sent nor that it wasn't. Therefore some have speculated that it might have been sent (as there was some mention of finding out about postal delivery times), but then returned (because Josephine did not go to Karlsbad). This then opens the door to even more speculations – like the recipient returned it (one wonders why?), or there was a copy made by Beethoven (that was sent), and he kept only the original draft (extremely unlikely), etc. I prefer to apply the philosophical principle called "Occam's Razor", meaning that if there are two competing hypotheses of roughly equal merit and explanatory power, then the one should be chosen which is simpler and/or requires fewer assumptions. What is important here is the outcome: Beethoven kept this "Letter", and there is no indication that Josephine ever received it (nor anybody else, for that matter).

[5]   "Depuis 5 Juillet jusqu'au 12. – Résolution. Soyez résolu de faire ce que vous devez et, faites sans manquer ce que vous avez résolu." (in Steblin 2007, p. 163 f.)

[6]   "Résolution, Ordre, Propreté, Tranquillité, Chasteté, Justice, Économie, Modération, Humilité, Sobriété." (in Steblin 2007, p. 164.) It is intriguing that these categories can be found in the famous "*List of Virtues to Achieve Moral Perfection* by Benjamin Franklin" (http://living-smartly.com/2010/07/moral-perfection-virtues-benjamin-franklin, 14 May 2011). Therese, like her father, had always been a great admirer of the "Founding Fathers of the United States". And she and Stackelberg probably had talked about them…

> *Many horrible things happened ... Terrible suffering... Betrayal, slander, the saddest, most horrible period of our lives. ... All morals are sinking ... Destruction ... Complete dissolution.*[1]

August to December: Aftermath

In August, when Therese was in Dornbach near Vienna with the children, she began to write her diary again (or rather, there were again surviving parts of it). She painted a rather dismal picture:

> Many horrible things happened ... Terrible suffering ... Loss of the estates, destruction of all happiness, and discord, separation of our minds. Dissolution ... and hardships without end. Betrayal, slander, the saddest, most horrible period of our lives. Through poverty and want for the whole year. At this moment, there is hardly any cheerful dawn gleaming of a happy future. All morals are sinking, and all health, destruction ... Complete dissolution...[2]

Josephine decided to make an attempt to somehow fix her marriage again, to make peace with Stackelberg and – most importantly – to let him believe (or pretend to believe, as a face-saving measure) that he was the father of her next child. Given the nasty scenes that had happened not too long ago, this must have been quite a sacrifice for her![3]

During their brief encounter in Prague, Josephine had no choice but to tell Beethoven, once and for all, that she could not bring herself to sacrifice her children in order to marry him: Even though Stackelberg's departure could have been a starting point for her to get a divorce, all her six children would have been taken from her in such a case!

On 13 August 1812, Josephine and Stackelberg were together again to sign a new marriage contract, apparently with the assistance of Baron Hager, the police chief, and Baron Traun.[4] In this contract, Stackelberg was no longer guardian of the Deym children:

> Stackelberg takes over the gallery set-up ... Josephine leads the administration ... Josephine being the house mother and the guardian ... the house father is understood to be protector, assistant, guide, instructor of improvements ... The journey to Italy, and if possible the trip to Carlsbad as well as the carriage and horse-riding lessons, necessary for health reasons, Stackelberg assures to Josephine ... Jos. Stackelberg.
>
> ... I declare with the knowledge of Josephine, that if she does not follow these points, I am free of all charges when I return to my home country. Christoph Stackelberg.[5]

Josephine's unborn child was meanwhile "presented" by her to sister Therese:

> Josephine's child I will not look at as mine, but I will raise it on behalf of its parents with the utmost self-denial and a sense of duty.[6]

In October 1812, Therese and the children returned from Dornbach. The plans for a trip to Italy were abandoned; instead

> in late fall [autumn] 1812 the six children moved with their mother, who was pregnant, and Stackelberg to ... Hernals, where they lived frugally with only a maid and a cook. Their finances were completely ruined, the remaining three horses were sold (Steblin 2007, p. 173).

The financial situation was so precarious that Therese even considered offering herself as a maidservant to her brother Franz, with her earnings to be sent to Josephine. On 21 November 1812, Stackelberg was in Budapest to see Franz von Brunsvik, hoping for some assistance with the disastrous financial situation. In December, he returned from a fruitless trip to Brünn (Goldschmidt 1977, p. 216). Josephine's entire fortune (mainly her father's inheritance and what little was left her by Deym) was lost forever.[7]

* * *

On 7 September 1812, Beethoven left the resort of Franzensbrunn alone, traveling back to Karlsbad. On 15–16 September, he returned again to Teplitz in a state of despondency. He spent much of the remainder of his vacation in bed.

In October, Beethoven suddenly appeared in Linz, to see his brother Johann, who planned to marry his housekeeper, Therese Obermayer. Ludwig was opposed to this marriage because Therese was an unmarried mother. He demanded she should leave the house, and he even tried to get the police and the bishop involved! Ludwig's intention was to enforce current police regulations, according to which a person with "immoral conduct" had to leave the city. But all was in vain, because on 8 November Johann and Therese married – to the chagrin of Ludwig the moralist.

Meanwhile, another disaster struck when Prince Kinsky, one of his major patrons, died after falling from a horse. Beethoven had to implore Kinsky's heirs for years until they finally agreed to continue paying him his annuity.

---

[1] "Viel Grässliches geschah … Schreckliches Leiden … Verrath, Verläumdung, die traurigste, schrecklichste Epoche unseres Lebens. … Herabsinken alles moralischen … Zerstörung … Gänzliche Auflösung..." (Therese's Diary, 8 October 1812, in Tellenbach 1983, p. 106 f.)

[2] "Viel Grässliches geschah … Schreckliches Leiden … Verlust der Güter, Zerstörung alles … Glücks[,] und Uneinigkeiten, Trennungen der Gemüther. Auflösung … und Bedrängnisse ohne Ende. Verrath, Verläumdung, die traurigste, schrecklichste Epoche unseres Lebens. Durch Armuth und Noth ein volles Jahr. Kaum glänzt in diesem Augenblick eine heitere Morgenröthe einer glücklichen Zukunft. Herabsinken alles moralischen, der Gesundheit, Zerstörung … Gänzliche Auflösung..." (Therese's Diary, 8 October 1812, in Tellenbach 1983, p. 106 f.)

[3] It is also conceivable that Stackelberg (who had rented a room somewhere in Vienna to spend a week in prayer) returned around 12 July 1812 to Josephine, who had just returned from her eventful trip to Prague. It is possible that they then engaged in "make-up sex" with the result that to this day no one knows for sure who Minona's father was … meaning that even a DNA test could not "prove" anything this way or the other.

[4] "Le Comte de Traun étant arrivé hier soir, Madame la Comtesse, nous devrons avoir l'honneur de vous faire notre cours aujourd'hui à 11 heures avant Diné, espérant y trouver aussi Monsieur Stackelberg." [Count Traun arrived last night, Madame la Comtesse, we will have the honor to meet you today at 11 o'clock before dinner, and we hope to meet Mr Stackelberg, too.] (Hager to Josephine, 13 August 1812, in Goldschmidt 1977, p. 216.) This letter does of course not imply that Stackelberg was present – it only expresses the hope that he was **expected** to be there. – Two years later, we will meet Hager again (as the Police President, acting on behalf of Stackelberg). – Note how Hager (himself a Baron) respectfully addresses Josephine Baroness von Stackelberg as "Madame la

Comtesse" [Countess], using her title by birth, whereas he refers to her husband Baron von Stackelberg simply as "Monsieur" [Mister], that is, omits even his lower title. The differences in class, rank and station – between as well as within – were very subtle (but nevertheless important) in those days...

[5] "Stackelberg übernimmt die Galerie-Einrichtung ... Josephine führt die Verwaltung ... Josephine der Hausmutter u. der Vormünderin ... Unter Hausvater versteht sich, Beschützer, Helfer, Anführer, Anweiser des Besseren ... Die italiänische Reise und wenn möglich die Karlsbader Reise so wie die Equipage u. Reitstunde, weil es für die Gesundheit nötig ist[,] versichert Stackelberg an Josephine ... Jos. Stackelberg – ... Ich [er]kläre mit dem Wissen von Josephine, dass, wenn sie diese Pünkte nicht hält, ich von allen Vorwürfen frei bin, wenn ich in mein Vaterland zurückkehre. Christoph Stackelberg." (Draft Contract between Stackelberg and his wife Josephine, 13 August 1812, in Goldschmidt 1977, p. 529 f.) This incident was the closest to a formal separation, short of a divorce, that one could imagine at this point in time. Note however how Stackelberg has the right to leave any time (at the slightest pretext) without having to fear any retributions, whereas Josephine "gained" the guardianship of her children by Deym, but also the sole responsibility for their upbringing and education.

[6] "Josephines Kind will ich nicht als das meinige ansehen, sondern es für seine Eltern mit der grössten Verleugnung und wie es Pflicht ist, erziehen." (Therese's Diary, 22 September 1812, in Tellenbach 1983, p. 125.)

[7] "Stackelberg has arrived – again the moment has come where I could be so much to Josephine." [Ankunft St. – ist wieder der Augenblick da, wo ich Josephine so viel sein könnte.] (Therese's Diary, 4 December 1812, in Goldschmidt 1977, p. 214.)

Life is like the trembling of sounds.[1]

Adagio molto e cantabile

---

[1] "Leben gleicht der Töne Beben." (Beethoven's Diary, in Solomon 2005, p. 32.)

I was her godmother; the child was virtually bestowed onto me.[1]

1813: Minona

In March 1813, Josephine wrote to Stackelberg about "the anxious days of giving birth" and made another attempt at reconciliation – though not as his "slave":

> If you restore the house, the gallery, my assets, then you must not be arrogant because you only reduce one blemish... It hurts me that you think it is just grinding out one's life – what is purest delight – in the anxious days of giving birth – and, in any case, your wife – to provide joy and some peace and support for herself and 7 children, husband and wife –
>
> I will never doubt your heart – because in quiet moments, you are capable of noble elevation. ... Until then, have patience with me as I have with you – We cannot yet be perfect, tolerance – and goodness – honesty, forgiveness and noble pursuit – you for me and I towards you until our situation has settled down – until my health again lends me the strength which I will then devote to you. ...
>
> Oh love for love, pious profound feeling, pure sensation of a creature that belongs to you – but not as a slave ... you are free.[2]

It is not clear, when exactly Stackelberg left again (before or after the birth), and we have no indication whether he might have suspected that Josephine's next child was not his.

Therese was of course present when on 8 April 1813

> a little girl, Minona,[3] was born – I acted as midwife at 9 o'clock in the evening. ... From that moment on, the lovely little angel belonged to me, and for one and a half years, she knew no one but me. ... She was served and nurtured by me. I carried her on my arms around the Prater.[4]
>
> I was her godmother; the child was virtually bestowed onto me.[5]

Beethoven, the most likely father, must have heard of this. How else can one explain that he immediately felt the urge to pressure his sick brother into granting him the guardianship of his son, Ludwig's nephew Karl? Brother Carl van Beethoven, although already ill with consumption, still had more than 2 ½ years to live![6]

The following month, Ludwig wrote this into his Diary:
> To forego a great act which could be undertaken, and to remain thus ... oh dreadful conditions which do not suppress my feeling for domesticity, but its execution.[7]

He was a father, but could not claim fatherhood! He could have a family and "domesticity" – but the "dreadful conditions" prevented it.

It is striking that in several letters to friends around that time, Beethoven indicated that he might be forced to leave the country (perhaps even suddenly). Did he fear to arouse Stackelberg's wrath (and consequently, to cause problems for Josephine)?[8]

Therese continues in her memoirs:
> On 3 June, we moved to Hacking. ... My little baby was kept very simple and prospered admirably. ... In late autumn, Josephine took her children, and I spent the winter alone with the lovely Minona.[9]

Note how Minona does not really count as one of Josephine's (i.e., Stackelberg's) children.

Beethoven in his Diary emphasized the importance of keeping his and Josephine's secret, quoting Herder:
> Learn to be silent ... Speech resembles silver, but to be silent at the right time is pure gold.[10]

Interestingly, about the same time, Therese noted in her Diary:
> What you must not talk about, let it be sealed on the tongue.[11]

The quotation by Herder as used by Beethoven is found many years later in Therese's Diary, to which she added:
> This fine proverb has been set to music by Beethoven.[12]

This is an astonishing conclusion, as she surely could not have meant the little canon that Beethoven composed on this text a few years later. Could it be that she (like Josephine), a lifelong admirer of his music, understood that so much of it was communicating, without words, "from the heart to the heart"? I think she understood him perfectly. If you listen to his music, you can hear, feel the message. Only, it **cannot** be expressed in words.

* * *

Beethoven now reminded himself to concentrate on his work:
> The best way not to think of your affliction is some occupation.[13]

And he followed this up with some splendid compositions, some of which employed the British national anthem.
> I must show the English a little what a blessing their *God Save the King* is.[14]

Beethoven summed up this fateful year with the copy of a poem in his Diary:

> *Life is like the trembling of sounds*
> *And man is like the play of the lyre;*
> *If it were to fall hard to the ground*
> *Its proper sound is lost forever*
> *And it can never again recover.*[15]

Something must have been shattered in his life, which was never to be recovered: His beloved gone, his child gone, his deafness was increasing alarmingly, and likewise his isolation was growing.

As if this was not yet enough, another disaster occurred with the effect of reducing his income: Prince Lobkowitz, one of his major patrons, went bankrupt and had to leave Vienna in disgrace.

---

[1] "Ich war Taufmutter und das Kind wurde mir förmlich geschenkt." (Therese's Memoirs, in La Mara 1909, p. 102.)

[2] "Wenn du das Haus, die Gallerie, mein Vermögen wi[e]der her stellest, aufrichtest, so darf dich das nicht hochmüthig machen, weil du nur ein Gebrechen verminderst ... Es thut mir weh, daß Leben abhaspeln dich dünkt – was die reinste Freude – in den bangen Tagen der Gebährung – und überhaupt deinem weibe – Freude und einige Ruhe und Unterhalt für sich und 7 Kinder[,] Mann u. Weib

verschaffen – An deinem Herzen werde ich nie zweifeln – weil in Ruhigen Augenblicken du edler Erhebung fähig bist. ... Bis dahin habe Geduld mit mir wie ich mit dir – Wir kön[n]en noch nicht vollkommen seyn[,] Nachsicht – und Güte – Aufrichtigkeit, Verzeihung und edles Streben – du für mich und ich gegen dich bis unsre Laage ruhiger geworden – meine Gesundheit mir jene Kräfte wieder leiht welche ich so gern dann für dich hingebe. ... O Liebe um Liebe, frommes inniges Gefühl, reine Empfindung eines Geschöpfes welches dir angehört – aber nicht als Sklavin ... du bist frey." (Josephine to Stackelberg, 20 March 1813, in Goldschmidt 1977, p. 217.) There is some doubt about this date – it could also have been written on 20 May 1813, after Minona's birth (Steblin 2007, p. 174, n. 88).

3   It has been noted that "Minona" in reverse reads "anonim" (anonymous). But more intriguingly, it is the name of a character (a musician!) in Goethe's *Werther* (a romantic story of unfulfilled love that ends in much sorrow and suicide). The Brunsvik sisters were familiar with novels like this.

4   "... war ein kleines Mädchen geboren: Minona; – ich machte die *sage femme* um 9 Uhr Abends. ... Von dem Augenblick gehörte das liebliche Engelchen mein, und anderthalb Jahre kannte es Niemanden als mich. ... Es wurde bedient und genährt durch mich. Ich trug es im Prater spazieren auf meinen Armen". (Therese's Memoirs, in La Mara 1909, p. 101.) The Prater was (and still is) the largest public park area in Vienna.

5   "Ich war Taufmutter und das Kind wurde mir förmlich geschenkt." (Therese's Memoirs, in La Mara 1909, p. 102.)

6   "Beethoven's claim to be the legal guardian of his nephew Karl ... he made on 12 April 1813 – four days after Minona's birth. This is surely no coincidence. There were strong psychological reasons for his wanting to replace the child he had lost. ... His brother ... did not die until 15 November 1815." (Steblin 2007, p. 176.)

7   "Eine große Handlung, welche seyn kann zu unterlassen und so bleiben ... o schreckliche Umstände, die mein Gefühl für Häuslichkeit nicht unterdrücken, aber deren Ausübung." (Beethoven's Diary, 13 May 1813, in Solomon 2005, p. 30.) Solomon (2005, p. 30) misinterprets this as: "Offensichtlich ein weiterer Hinweis auf die Beendigung des Liebesverhältnisses mit der 'Unsterblichen Geliebten'." [Obviously, a further hint at the termination of the love affair with the "Immortal Beloved".] He remained fixated on the idea that she must have been Antonie Brentano who, after her brief stay in Vienna, had long since returned to Frankfurt with her husband. Only – there is nothing to indicate why Beethoven should write such a note, and at this particular time, if it were indeed related to Antonie!

8   See Tellenbach (1983, p. 119). It is likely that Stackelberg was present (or still around) when (or shortly after) Minona was born. At least Fritz Deym said so in his memoirs (Steblin 2007, p. 173). In this regard, the recollections of Therese (who seemed to imply that he was already away) are a bit different. However, both their views were filtered if not biased: Therese was very critical of her brother-in-law, whereas Fritz apparently was very fond of his stepfather and teacher (to the chagrin of his mother and his aunt).

[9] "Den 3. Juni zogen wir nach Hacking. ... Mein kleines Kindchen wurde sehr einfach gehalten und gedieh vortrefflich. ... Im Spätherbst ließ Josephine ihre Kinder zu sich kommen und ich blieb den Winter allein mit der lieblichen Minona." (Therese's Memoirs, in La Mara 1909, p. 102.)

[10] "Lerne Schweigen ... Dem Silber gleichet die Rede aber zu rechter Zeit Schweigen ist lauteres Gold." (Beethoven's Diary, in Solomon 2005, p. 31) Quoted from Herder. See also the Canon "Das Schweigen" [Silence] WoO 168#1, 1816. And a later remark by Therese: "... nur in der Stille bildet ein Gemüth sich. Pythagoras: **nicht reden**! Das ist mein Ideal." [... only in silence a mind is formed. Pythagoras: **do not talk**! This is my ideal.] (Therese to Schober, 23 February 1837, in La Mara 1909, p. 49.)

[11] "Was du nicht reden darfst[,] laß auf der Zunge versiegelt." (Therese's Diary, 1813, in Tellenbach 1983, p. 132.)

[12] "Dieser schöne Spruch ist von Beethoven in Musik gesetzt." (Therese's Diary, 15 November 1840, in Goldschmidt 1977, p. 294.)

[13] "Das Beste an dein Uibel nicht zu denken ist Beschäftigung." (Beethoven's Diary, in Solomon 2005, p. 32.)

[14] "Ich muß den Engländern ein Wenig zeigen was in der *God save the King* für ein Segen ist." (Beethoven's Diary, in Solomon 2005, p. 37.) In November 1813, he composed the *Battle Symphony* "Wellingtons Sieg, oder die Schlacht bei Vittoria" [Wellington's Victory, or the Battle of Vittoria] Op. 91. See also the 5 Variations for Piano in *D major* on the English Song "Rule Britannia" WoO 78, 1803, and the English Folksong Setting "God Save the King" WoO 157#1, 1817. Beethoven maintained a life long admiration of all things English; he had several times planned to travel to England. And he used to call Handel the "greatest" of all composers.

[15]
Leben gleicht der Töne Beben
Und der Mensch dem Saitenspiel
Wenn es hart zu Boden fiel
Ist der rechte Klang verschwunden
Und es kann nicht mehr gesunden.

(Beethoven's Diary, in Solomon 2005, p. 32.) Excerpt from Adolf Müllner: "Die Schuld" [Guilt]. Leipzig 1816 – a "fateful tragedy".

> *Believe me, Josephine, you do not know what you are doing, believe me, Therese, that you are crazy.*[1]
>
> *One cannot abandon her. She has a nervous disease, she is always exposed to an inner torture.*[2]

1814: A Kidnapping

Beethoven began (and ended) the year 1814 with his greatest triumphs in public: The performance of *Wellington's Victory* Op. 91, and the Symphonies #7 Op. 92 and #8 Op. 93 on 27 February was an enormous success. He also rewrote his Opera *Leonore* completely. It was performed in May under the new title *Fidelio* and finally won the acclaim it deserved. What an irony, that his celebration of the "Triumph of Conjugal Love", of hope, liberation and exaltation occurred at a time when his private life was in a total mess![3]

* * *

While the composer was at his peak, Josephine had to go through the worst time of her life. Therese reports, how disaster was brewing again:

> They were waiting for Stackelberg ... he was the buyer, he was the owner. But during all these events, he was unable to stay in Austria. He then robbed us of his three young daughters, because Josephine did not release them, and she also did not want to follow him.[4]
>
> After the first 6 months of his endeavors, he came to Vienna to visit his wife, and asked her to accompany him to Russia, where an older brother Gottschall [Gottschalk] had died and left him, Christoph, the estates. Josephine was unable – already sickly and ailing – to leave everything behind. Then he demanded his three daughters – Minona being 1 ½ years

> old. ... Josephine said, "leave me my children, I have borne them with much pain!" ...
>
> The next day he went to Siebert,[5] chief of the police, and notified the case to him. Around noon, six cops were at the door ... and the little ones, including the governess, which Josephine had given them, were abducted without a good-bye, the coach waiting outside! For two years, we had not the slightest news of their whereabouts.[6]

Fritz Deym in his memoirs would later simply state that his stepfather "kidnapped" the girls (Steblin 2007, p. 174). However, Stackelberg did not take the little girls home to Estonia, but brought them to Deacon Franz Leyer in Trautenau, Bohemia. And then he left to travel the world.

* * *

Just before "kidnapping" the children, the concerned father had written a friendly reminder to his beloved wife:

> Therese's letter reminded me that you were getting even more wicked every day, and I was not wrong when I did not want to leave you, my wife, for another 8 weeks in this situation. ...
>
> To reply to this wrong and mendacious drivel in order to convince you that you have no feeling and that you are wrong – this would be like trying to wash a Negro white. Where heart and mind are as cranky as with the both of you, this can only be helped by God if he changes your way of thinking; among mankind, you have lost their respect and trust; you and your words are just empty shells without effect.
>
> Now I want only my children and now only because my conscience compels me. ... If you do not assign the children to me today, then tomorrow morning with a torn heart I must do what I have to do without thinking of myself as a bad man...
>
> Believe me, Josephine, you do not know what you are doing, believe me, Therese, that you are crazy, believe me, that you put yourselves in the pillory, and one day you both will cry tears of blood. Relent ... I cannot wait one hour longer.[7]

Stackelberg, however, enlightened by pious thoughts, did not stop here: Josephine should lose the custodianship of her children by Deym as well! From the police records, it is clear that he had done his best to slander his wife, carefully preparing his case by spreading defamation of her and Therese. Their uncle Joseph Count von Brunsvik tried – in vain – to intervene:

> I found out that the many rumors disseminated about my niece Baroness Stackelberg née Countess Brunsvik have been caused by the fictions and enlargements of some passionate and irritated people, and by corrupt servants, and my honor demands that they do not receive confirmation in public by the removal of the guardianship, and that my niece is not humiliated and depressed in such a sensitive matter –
>
> It is not irrelevant to me whether the children, who are related to me and most worthy, should be deprived of the great influence of their mother and be handed over to a stranger, whom I do not know, and so I ask you, Baron Hager, to do everything to allow my niece to retain the guardianship.[8]

Police President Hager (who was to become Metternich's Gestapo chief, running the same secret police who would also keep records about Beethoven and Schubert) was not impressed:

> Due to total physical neglect in that second marriage and shocked by the danger that the girl would already in childhood be seduced by her stepbrother, Baron Stakelberg had, in accordance with the Land Law [the Law of the Landed Estates], sought police assistance in order to accommodate his children elsewhere, to which the mother could not be brought to consent, even by friendly urging...
>
> In this way, the young Count [Fritz] Deym appears to have been entirely neglected, in fact, unfortunately, he became a fully developed debauchee, who ridiculed religion in the most impertinent manner – and he found his favorite pastime in visiting the lowest taverns, and in this as well as in the former, he was unfortunately endorsed by his mother, as a matter of principle...
>
> On several occasions, I had gained some insight into the Stackelbergs' domestic affairs, and I noticed the simultaneous extravagance, eccentric tendency and apathy, as displayed by your niece, who had demonstrated this already in the choice of her second husband, and all this

> combined in such a way that it was no wonder that all my efforts to improve the situation were bound to fail.
>
> Unfortunately, it seems to be true that it was mainly the influence of your second niece Therese on her sister, which pushed her into this negative direction. ... The other day, Baroness Stackelberg and one Countess [Anna] Brunsvik wished to see me, probably about this same matter – however, I was indisposed and could neither visit nor receive them.[9]

Stackelberg, the pious and learned Pestalozzi-follower had not only successfully educated young Fritz, his favorite stepson, to become a drunkard, swear about religion [!] and – sort of – come to grips with the onset of puberty:

> Stackelberg did not even balk at the suspicion of incest between the stepsiblings.[10]

Therese was furious, and she told her mother:

> Hager should be ashamed, to believe a stranger, like this Stackelberg, and to insult our family thus.[11]

And she implored Hager:

> Those nasty allegations by the vindictive stepfather are slander... Who could hurt a mother, who only wants the best, thus! My dear, dear friend, save this woman from her impending disaster. Bear in mind that nothing can be more harmful to the children than if they had to believe that their mother could not be their guide in this world. They are fatherless, attached to their mother, and they are of an age where they already understand what they love.[12]

Even 14-year-old daughter Viky wrote a letter, begging the police:

> You do not want to make fatherless creatures motherless as well! – Let us be kept by the best of all mothers! ... Do not thrust us among strangers! ... Do not believe the slander![13]

* * *

Beethoven, meanwhile, had things more mundane on his mind, as he found it necessary to remind himself in his Diary:

> Shoe brushes for cleaning, in case someone comes.[14]

Apparently, somebody had pointed out to him his scruffy appearance!

However, continuing ill health caused him much grief and concern:
> Decision by the doctors about my life – – if there is no recovery – I must – – – – – – use –???[15]

Bearing in mind that the state of medicine was still at the level of the middle ages, it is understandable that Beethoven had a deep distrust of physicians. The various cures he had to endure, not to mention the questionable medication, might have done him more harm than good.

As usual, he tried to find solace in concentrating on his work:
> There is still more to do in this world, do it soon! Do not continue my current way of life, my art also calls for this sacrifice – – rest in diversion only to be the more powerful when working on your art – Because patient courage is the gift we received from Destiny.[16]

Beethoven ended this year (on 29 November 1814) with another tremendously successful concert for the opening of the Congress of Vienna at the Redoutensaal, attended by the Empresses of Austria and Russia, the King of Prussia and an assorted number of members of the highest aristocracy. He performed the Cantata "Der glorreiche Augenblick" [The Glorious Moment] Op. 136 – fitting the occasion – and, again, the *Battle Symphony* ("Wellington's Victory") Op. 91 as well as the Symphony #7 Op. 92.

* * *

There is a remarkable entry in Therese's Diary:
> Josephine is Tasso, [so] is Beethoven, **her** beautiful soul raises us to heaven: **we** must give her worldly food...
> Received the letter from Beethoven. Wrote to Beethoven. ...
> Jos[ephine]. Write history. Bet[hoven].[17]

Cryptic though it is, this reveals a few things:

- Josephine and Beethoven are (perceived as) united metaphorically by the figure of Tasso, after a play by Goethe, a tragedy of unfulfilled love, suffering and early death. It is remarkable that Therese made this observation in the year when *Fidelio* was premiered with great success – and Tasso's beloved was called "Eleonore"! (Goldschmidt 1977, p. 319.)

- Her "soul" goes to heaven, but she still needs "worldly food": maybe an allusion that Josephine was either not eating enough because she was so unwell, or simply that poverty was setting in and money – even for food – was becoming scarce.
- Therese was (i.e., remained) **in regular contact with Beethoven via letters** – sure enough, none of them survived. They most likely also saw each other regularly.
- She was contemplating to write a "history" of Josephine **and** Beethoven. Certainly not meant to be published, but once again indicating that their relationship was not just a brief fling a dozen years ago but, in fact, still ongoing – forever.

Therese even contemplated the unthinkable – that a Countess should have to work, when she wrote to Josephine that their mother

> will take care of you – she will ... get you if you wish a job with Empress Louise or the Grand Duke [von Würzburg], she is glad that you are not staying with Stackelberg. ... Franz is furious and morose because she wants money for you. ... She asked wistfully whether it would not be possible [for you] to stay with her.[18]

The dreadful events of the year 1814, the loss of three of her children, and the threat to lose the custodianship of the remaining four, left their marks:

> One cannot abandon her. She has a nervous disease, she is always exposed to an inner torture. I love and appreciate Josephine only all the more, because she is not happy. Lottchen [Charlotte] and I shall not let her down; she has a high degree of individuality. ...
> Josephine's mind is striving for the highest.[19]

* * *

Josephine was desperate to get her life as a mother of four unruly teenagers back on track. Her main concern was the proper education of her oldest son Fritz, who needed a firm hand, after his recent escapades. As fate would have it, she got more than she bargained for when she

> hired the dubious mathematics teacher Andrian [Karl Eduard von Andrehan–Werburg] ... she gradually fell under

his charismatic spell, becoming pregnant and giving birth to Emilie, hiding in a hut (Steblin 2007, p. 174).

Not much is known about this "Andrian", a dubious character, who was to become the fourth man to father a child of Josephine's. Steblin (2007) seems to be the first to mention more details about him (after Tellenbach 1983, pp. 141–189, who thought he had an upstanding character and that Emilie was his sister).

Once again she became weak in a state of despair and illness – a repeat of her being seduced by Stackelberg, albeit this time it was indeed an adulterous affair. Being (still) exceptionally beautiful and attractive, it was no wonder that any man, who came near her, became enraptured. And sadly, unscrupulous gallants and charlatans like Andrian did not hesitate to take advantage of her weakness. Only this time, Josephine had to cover up her "misstep" and went into hiding until the baby – another daughter – was born.

Josephine would have nothing more to do with this charlatan. She abandoned her eighth child when Emilie was seven days, and Andrian was forced to raise the baby alone (Steblin 2007, p. 174).

The girl died two years later of the measles (Skwara/Steblin 2007, p. 187, n. 15).

---

[1]   "... glaube mir Josephine[,] daß du nicht weis[s]t was du thust, glaube mir Therese daß du wahnsinnig bist." (Stackelberg to Josephine, May 1814, in Tellenbach 1983, p. 134.)

[2]   "Man kann sie nicht verlassen. Sie ist nervenkrank, immer einer inneren Marter ausgesetzt." (Therese's Diary, 1814–15, in Goldschmidt 1977, p. 293.)

[3]   Beethoven now used to change his lodgings frequently – a sign of undetermined restlessness. There were reports of him behaving arrogantly in public, not paying his bills in pubs, his clothes being dirty, and his hair long and unkempt...

[4]   "Man wartete auf Stackelberg ... er war Käufer, er war Eigenthümer. Diese ganzen Vorgänge hindurch war er aber außer Stande, in Oesterreich zu bleiben. Er raubte uns seine drei kleinen Töchter, da sie Josephine nicht herausgeben und ihm auch nicht folgen wollte." (Therese's Memoirs, in La Mara 1909, p. 100 f.)

[5]   The police order, dated 8 May 1814, is reproduced in Goldschmidt (1977, p. 531 f.).

[6]   "Nach den ersten 6 Monaten seiner Strebungen kam er nach Wien, besuchte seine Gattin und forderte sie auf, ihn nach Rußland zu begleiten, wo ein

älterer Bruder Gottschall [Gottschalk] gestorben [war] und ihm, Christoph, die Güter vermacht hatte. Josephine konnte nicht – schon kränklich and angegriffen ... alles verlassen. Da verlangte er seine drei Töchter – Minona 1½ Jahr alt. ... Josephine sagte: 'laß mir die Kinder, ich habe sie ja mit Schmerzen geboren!' ... Des andern Tages ging er zu Siebert, der Chef der Polizey war, und zeigte ihm den Fall an. Um [die] Mittagszeit standen sechs Vertraute vor dem Thor ... und die lieben Kleinen wurden ohne Abschied, der Reisewagen vor dem Thor, mit ihrer Gouvernante, die Josephine ihnen gegeben hatte, uns entführt! Zwei Jahre hatten wir nicht die geringste Nachricht von ihrem Aufenthalt." (Therese's Memoirs, in La Mara 1909, p. 107.) Therese's memoirs contain an error here, as the death of this brother actually occurred one year later. As in the case of 1812–1813 (and elsewhere), she tends to contract events that took place at different times, into a single one.

7   "Theresens Brief mahnte mich ... daß du wo möglich von Tag zu Tag noch schlechter wurdest u. ich nicht unrecht hatte wenn ich dich mein weib nicht noch 8 Wochen in dieser laage lassen will. ... Dir alles jenes verkehrte lügenhafte Gewäsch zu beantworten um dich zu überzeugen, daß du ohne Gefühl bist u. dich irrst – hiesse einen Mohren weiß waschen wollen. Wo Herz u. Verstand einmal so verschroben sind wie bei Euch beiden kann nur Gott helfen wenn er den Sinn ändert; für Menschen habt ihr Achtung u. Zutrauen verlohren u. ihre Worte sind euch nur ein leerer Schaal ohne Wirkung. Ich will jetzt nur meine Kinder u. sie jetzt nur weil mein Gewissen mich dazu treibt. ... Wenn du mir nicht die Kinder heute zusagst[,] morgen früh mit zerrissenem Herzen thun muß [ich] was ich nicht lassen kann ohne mich selbst für einen schlechten Menschen zu halten ... glaube mir Josephine[,] daß du nicht weis[s]t was du thust, glaube mir Therese daß du wahnsinnig bist[,] glaubt mir daß ihr euch selbst an den Pranger stellt u. einmal blutige Thränen weinen werdet. Gib nach ... ich kann keine Stunde mehr zugeben." (Stackelberg to Josephine, May 1814, in Tellenbach 1983, p. 133 f.)

8   "Ich habe erfahren, daß die vielen ausgestreuten Gerüchte über meine Nichte B[aronin] St[ackelberg] geb. G[räfin] B[runsvik] von erdichtungen u. vergrößerungen einiger leidenschaftlicher u. gereizter Menschen u. corompirter Domestiquen herrühren u. es liegt meiner Ehre daran ... daß selbe durch die Wegnahme der ... Vormundschaft keine Bestätigung im Publikum erhalten u. auch meine Nichte nicht so empfindlich gedrükt u. betrübt werde – es ist mir auch nicht gleichgültig ob die K[inder,] die mir so werth u. so nahe verwandt sind[,] des größten Einflußes der Mutter beraubt u. einem fremden[,] den ich nicht kenne[,] übergeben werden[,] u. so ersuche ich sie B[aron] Hager ... alles anzuwenden um meiner Nichte die Vormundschaft zu erhalten." (Joseph Count von Brunsvik to Police President Hager, 9 August 1814, in Tellenbach 1983, p. 135.)

9   "Wegen gänzlicher körperlicher Verwahrlosung [in] jener 2ten Ehe u. aufgeschreckt durch die Gefahr daß das Mädchen von dem Stiefbruder schon in Kindesalter verführt werde, hatte B.[aron] Stakelberg mit Beistimmung der Landrechte, Polizei assistenz erwirkt um seine Kindern anderwärtig unterzubringen[,] wozu die Mutter durch keine gütliche Vorstellung zu vermögen war. ... Auf diese Weise stellte sich der junge Graf [Fritz] Deym bald als gänzlich verwahrlost ja leider als ein fast schon ausgebildeter Wüstling dar, der über das Religionswesen auf die frechste Weise spöttelte – u. in dem Besuch niederer

Schenken seine Lieblingsbeschäftigung fand u. leider von der Mutter in dem einen wie in dem anderen grundsatzmässig unterstützt war. ... Ich habe in die St[ackelberg]-schen häuslichen Verhältnisse oft einzudringen Gelegenheit gehabt u. schon damahls überspannung, excentrische Tendenz u. apathie zugleich von Seite der Fr. Nichte[,] von der selbst auch die Wahl ihres 2ten Gemahls zeigte[,] in solchem Maaße vereinigt gefunden, daß es mich nicht befremden konnte alle meine freundschaftlichen Versuche zur Einwirkung einer bessern Ordnung der Dinge scheitern zu sehen. Leider scheint es wahr[,] daß der Einfluß dero 2ten Fräulein Nichte Therese auf die ... Schwester dieser vorzüglich diese ungünstige Richtung gab. ... Jüngst wollten mich B.[aronin] Stakelberg u. eine Gr.[äfin Anna] Brunsvik wahrscheinlich in der selben Sache sprechen – allein ich war schon unpäßlich u. konnte sie weder Besuchen noch empfangen." (Police President Hager to Joseph Count von Brunsvik, 28 October 1814, in Goldschmidt 1977, p. 533 f.)

10 "Stackelberg [war] nicht einmal vor der Verdächtigung des Inzests unter den Stiefgeschwistern zurückgeschreckt." (Tellenbach 1983, p. 135.)

11 "Hager sollte sich schämen, einem Fremden[,] diesen St[ackelberg,] zu glauben und die Familie so zu beleidigen." (Therese to Mother Anna, 20 October 1814, in Goldschmidt 1977, p. 535.)

12 "Jene bösen Beschuldigungen des rachsüchtigen Stiefvaters sind Verläumdungen ... Wer könnte eine Mutter die das Beste will so kränken! lieber theurer Freund retten Sie diese Frau von dem ihr drohenden unglück. Bedenken Sie[,] daß den Kindern nichts schädlicher sein kann, als wenn sie glauben müßten[,] ihre Mutter kön[n]e nicht ihre Leiterin auf dieser Welt sein. Sie sind vaterlos[,] hängen mit ganzer Seele an der Mutter u. sind in dem Alter, wo sie schon begreiffen was sie lieben." (Therese to Police President Hager, 1815, in Tellenbach 1983, p. 136.)

13 "Vaterlose Wesen werden Sie nicht auch Mutter los machen wollen! – erhalten Sie uns die beste aller Mütter! ... Stoßen Sie uns nicht unter fremde Menschen! ... Glauben Sie nicht der lästerung." (in Tellenbach 1983, p. 137.)

14 "Schuhbürsten zum Abputzen, wenn Jemand kommt." (Beethoven's Diary, in Solomon 2005, p. 38.)

15 "Bestimmung der Aerzte über mein Leben – – ist keine Rettung mehr – so muß ich – – – – – – brauchen – ???" (Beethoven's Diary, in Solomon 2005, p. 39.) The dashes probably indicate omissions by the copyist, either entirely illegible or – something better not to make public.

16 "Vieles ist auf Erden zu thun, thue es bald! Nicht mein jetziges Alltagsleben fortsetzen, die Kunst fordert auch dieses Opfer – – in der Zerstreuung ruhn um desto kräftiger in der Kunst zu wirken – Den[n] ausduldenden Muth verlieh den Menschen das Schiksal –." (Beethoven's Diary, in Solomon 2005, p. 41.) The last sentence is a quote from Homer's *Ilias*.

17 "Josephine ist Tasso, [so] ist Beethoven, **ihre** schöne Seele erhebt uns zum Himmel: **wir** müssen ihr die irdische Nahrung reichen... Reçu la lettre de

Beethoven. Écrit a Beethoven ... Jos. Geschichte schreiben. Bet." (Therese's Diary, October 1814, in La Mara 1920, p. 86; Tellenbach 1983, p. 141.)

[18] "[Die Mutter] will für dich sorgen – sie will ... wenn du wünschst eine anstellung bei Kaiserin Louise od. dem Großherzog [von Würzburg] verschaffen, sie ist froh das du nicht bei St[ackelberg] bleibst. ... Franz ... ist wild u. verdrießlich weil sie das Geld haben will für dich. ... Sie frug so wehmütig ob es den[n] nicht denkbar sei bei ihr zu bleiben." (Therese to Josephine, 10 August 1814, in Tellenbach 1983, p. 131.)

[19] "Man kann sie nicht verlassen. Sie ist nervenkrank, immer einer inneren Marter ausgesetzt. Ich liebe und schätze Josephine nur um so mehr, weil sie nicht glücklich ist. Lottchen und ich sollen sie nicht untergehen lassen; sie hat eine hohe Individualität. ... Josephinens Geist strebt nach dem Höchsten." (Therese's Diary, 1814–15, in La Mara 1920, p. 86.)

> *What fights! what scenes were occurring in 1815 and 1816! From then on, her dwindling life was terribly in tatters.*[1]

1815: Tohuwabohu[2]

Beethoven began this year by reminding himself of the need to keep his silence:
> Even the most intimate friend, spare him your secret! – Are you demanding loyalty from him, yet fail yourself?[3]

Again, he tried to concentrate on his art in the face of adversity (despite this, his productivity was to remain very low):
> All what life means is to be sacrificed to the Exalted one, and a sanctuary of Art; let me live, by any expedients if they can be found![4]
>
> Seek the high goal of **self-perfection in creating**! ...
>
> Often, an individual can [achieve] more [alone] than together with thousands, for the intentions of people are difficult to control, and rarely wins the better reason.[5]

His struggle was a lonely one – he was alone.

Beethoven then became immersed in the study of works about Pantheism and Eastern religion:
> He who is free of all lust and desire, that is the Almighty. He alone. No one is greater than He is; His mind is intertwined in Himself. He the Almighty is present in every part of space.[6]
>
> Spirit of spirits ... Goodness without limits! Wisdom without limits! – Oh guide my spirit. Oh lift it out of this heavy depth, delighted by Your power, such that it can fearlessly strive upwards with fiery momentum.[7]
>
> On your wanderings across the earth, where the paths are now high, then low, and the proper one is rarely known, the traces of your steps will not always be uniform; but virtue will drive you forward in the right direction.[8]
>
> Blessed is he who has suppressed all passions and then with his energy handles all affairs of life, unconcerned about

success! Let the motive be in the deed and not in the outcome. Do not be one of those whose drive to act is the hope of reward. Do not spend your life in inactivity. Be busy, do your duty. ... The true sage does not care about good or evil in this world. Thus, take pains to preserve this use of your reason, for such use in life is a precious art.[9]

Virtue, however, leads to a steep path and thus cannot attract people easily and fast.[10]

* * *

On 6 April 1815, one of Stackelberg's brothers died, leaving him a considerable inheritance. At long last, he owned (again) some money, and so he went to Vienna (presumably in a triumphant mood), to fetch Josephine.

Only, she refused to follow him – as before. Apparently, she had just thrown out Andrian, and was understandably not keen to let Stackelberg know of her pregnancy. He then wrote her a long letter (in Skwara/Steblin 2007, pp. 183–187; see below, under "Reflections"), apparently after yet another argument, revealing much of the difficulties that the two of them had with each other.

On 29 April 1815,

> Josephine's aunt, Catherine Dezasse, née Brunsvik, and Uncle Philipp Seeberg tried to help the incensed Josephine and suggested a temporary separation of the spouses for two or three years.[11]

It seems that Stackelberg then left again ... not without telling the police a few things about her. (Andrian possibly did likewise.)

On 30 June 1815, the Viennese Police Department called for spy reports about Josephine from Budapest,[12] according to which

> this Countess had lived for some time only from voluntary donations by her mother. Before that, it is said that she and her spouse Stackelberg had lived glamorously on an estate, and together they used up the entire inheritance by Deym, this way creating not only for herself, but also for her children a difficult situation, and also causing her brother, who had given them a security of 5,000 Ducats, no small embarrassment.

> The morality of this Countess is said to be in no good repute, and it has been stated that she cannot be excused from having given rise to the discord in the marriage.[13]

Stackelberg therefore – despite being for once not short of money – not only managed to extract yet another loan from his brother-in-law Franz (who at the time was still doing all he could to help his sister), he also showed his gratitude by going to the police and slandering Josephine!

> All people, **all** creatures are alike ... People are full of faults, tempers, arrogance and selfishness. ... Andrian is full of distrust and jealousy, like Christoph, **one is like the other**. ... Creatures are acting with selfish intent. –
> Nobody can be trusted, no one can be believed! A fool, who believes and trusts.[14]

Therese, as always, stayed loyally at her sister's side – and she contacted Beethoven as well (by keeping track of his whereabouts):

> She cannot be left to herself. She has a nervous breakdown, all the time she is exposed to an inner torment ... Döbling Beethoven ... Paskolati 94 Mölkerbastey.[15]

> Once again the very sad example of my unfortunate sister tells me that you have to keep all relations with strangers on the basis of friendship only. Taking people into your house and becoming too intimate with them is extremely dangerous and stupid.[16]

> *Beethoven* 1055–56 Seilerstaat.[17]

On 16 September 1815, the day Josephine gave birth to Emilie (in secret, hiding under the pseudonym "Countess von Mayersfeld" in a mountain hut), Therese noted (you can hear her sigh):

> Emilie's birth, at ¼ to 4 o'clock in the morning. Feelings, thoughts, *Oh dieu!* May she remain pure! true and blessed! that is why You let there be creatures, magnificent Almighty![18]

As if all this was not enough pain and suffering, Josephine's mother also began to withdraw her support, causing Therese to lament:

> Poor mother! unworthy mother! You **must** not know, thou shalt not know what is killing your child![19]

The mutual estrangement between the once so happily united members of the Brunsvik family was increasing at a rapid pace:

> How this mother, always narrow-minded and parochial, often bizarre, vulgar in her judgments, conversations and

opinions, spoils my fantasy, bewilders me, tears my thoughts apart![20]

Mother has the audacity to call us reckless, us, who we are dedicating our lives to the most solid efforts with boundless self-sacrifice! Reckless we are not – reckless is she, who gave her noble child away to an old man without fortune ... She disinherited us. ... The spirit of pettiness has made our family so extravagantly unhappy; that's why I hate it.[21]

* * *

On 14 November 1815, the dying Carl van Beethoven's will was set to give his wife Johanna and his brother Ludwig co-guardianship of his then nine-year-old son Karl. Johanna reportedly had had an affair during this time of his final illness. When Ludwig heard of it, he passed the information on to his brother – which most likely motivated Carl's decision to delete Johanna's name. After Ludwig had left, however, Carl added a codicil reinstating Johanna as co-guardian and stipulated that Karl should continue to live with his mother.

This was the beginning of an attempt at fatherhood and family life which Beethoven desperately tried to achieve, followed by protracted and nasty legal battles with his sister-in-law. He ended up looking after a nephew, who ultimately did not reward his efforts; Karl would eventually become so desperate that he attempted to commit suicide, breaking his uncle's heart...

This, however, is a story to be told at some other time (and place), and it is itself full of myths and legends already (see Magnani 1972).

---

[1] "Welche Kämpfe! welche Auftritte 1815 und 16! Von da an war ihr schwindendes Leben eine schreckliche Zerrissenheit." (Therese's Memoirs, in La Mara 1909, p. 96.)

[2] Chaos, Shambles; Mess, Fiasco, Disaster.

[3] "Auch den vertrautesten Freund verschone mit deinem Geheimniß! – Forderst du Treue von ihm, die du dir selber versagst?" (Beethoven's Diary, in Solomon 2005, p. 52.) Quoted from Herder.

[4] "Alles was Leben heißt sey der Erhabenen geopfert und ein Heiligthum der Kunst, laß mich leben, sey es auch mit Hilfsmitteln wenn sie sich nur finden!" (Beethoven's Diary, in Solomon 2005, p. 45.)

[5] "Das hohe Gut der **Selbstvollendung im Erschaffen** suchen. ... Der Einzelne kann öfters mehr als im Verein mit Tausend[,] denn schwer zu lenken sind der Menschen Willen und selten siegt der bessere Verstand." (Beethoven's Diary, in Solomon 2005, p. 55.)

[6] "Was frey ist von aller Lust und Begier das ist der Mächtige[.] Er allein. Kein Größerer ist, als Er, Sein Geist ist verschlungen in sich selbst. Er der Mächtige ist in jedem Theile des Raumes gegenwärtig." (Beethoven's Diary, in Solomon 2005, p. 57.) From "Das brahmanische Religionssystem" [The System of Brahman Religion].

[7] "Geist der Geister ... Güte ohne Grenzen! Weisheit ohne Maaß! – O leite meinen Geist[.] O hebe ihn aus dieser schweren Tiefe durch deine Kraft entzückt[,] damit er furchtlos streb' aufwärts in feurigem Schwunge." (Beethoven's Diary, in Solomon 2005, p. 62.) From the *Hymn to Narayena*.

[8] "Auf Deiner Wanderschaft über die Erde, wo die Pfade bald hoch bald niedrig gehen und der echte selten kenntlich ist, wird allerdings die Spur deiner Tritte nicht immer gleichförmig seyn; aber die Tugend wird dich in gerader Richtung vorwärts treiben." (Beethoven's Diary, in Solomon 2005, p. 61.)

[9] "Selig ist, der alle Leidenschaften unterdrückt hat und dann mit seiner Thatkraft alle Angelegenheiten des Lebens unbesorgt um den Erfolg verrichtet! Laß den Beweggrund in der That und nicht im Ausgang seyn. Sey nicht einer von denen[,] deren Triebfeder zum Handeln die Hoffnung des Lohn[es] ist. Laß dein Leben nicht in Unthätigkeit vorüber gehen. Sey betriebsam, erfülle deine Pflicht. ... Der wahre Weise kümmert sich nicht um [das] Gute oder Böse in dieser Welt. Befleissige dich also[,] diesen Gebrauch deiner Vernunft zu erhalten[,] denn solcher Gebrauch ist im Leben eine köstliche Kunst." (Beethoven's Diary, in Solomon 2005, p. 61 f.) From the *Bhagavad-Gita*.

[10] "Die Tugend aber führt auf einen steilen Pfad und kann dabey nicht so leicht und geschwind die Menschen an sich ziehn." (Beethoven's Diary, in Solomon 2005, p. 64.) A quote from Hesiod.

[11] "Josephines Tante, Catherine Dezasse, geb. Brunsvik, und ... Onkel Philipp Seeberg ... versuchen der aufgebrachen Josephine zu helfen und schlagen eine befristete Trennung der Eheleute von zwei bzw. drei Jahren vor." (Tellenbach 1983, p. 182.)

[12] "Am 30. Juni 1815 forderte die Wiener Polizeidirektion ... Spitzelberichte über Josephine aus Budapest an." (Tellenbach 1983, p. 140.)

[13] "Diese ... Gräfin hatte ... einige zeit ... blos von der freywilligen Spende ihrer Mutter gelebt. Vorher soll sie mit ihrem Ehegatten ... Stakelberg auf einen ... Gut flott gelebt, und zusammen das ganze Deymische Vermögen verthan haben, wodurch sie nicht allein sich selbst, und ihre Kinder in höchst mißliche Lage

versetzt hat, sondern auch ihren Bruder, welcher für sie den Betrag von 5000,– Dukaten Bürgschaft geleistet haben solle, in eine nicht geringe Verlegenheit gebracht hat. Die Moralität dieser Gräfin solle in keinem Vortheilhaften Renomée stehen, und man behauptet Dieselbe von dem Vorwurf der gegebenen Veranlassung zur erfolgten Mißhelligkeit der Ehe, nicht frey sprechen zu können." (Tellenbach 1983, p. 140.)

[14] "Die Menschen[,] die Kreaturen sind sich **alle** gleich ... die Menschen voll Fehler[,] persönlichkeit[,] Dünkel u. Eigennutz. ... a[ndrian] hat mißtrauen u. Eifersucht wie C[hristoph,] **einer wie der andre**. ... Voll eigennütziger Absicht handeln Kreaturen. – Zu trauen[,] zu glauben ist keiner! Thor der glaubt u. traut." (Therese's Diary, July 1815, in Tellenbach 1983, p. 143.)

[15] "Man kann sie nicht verlassen. Sie ist nervenkrank, immer einer inneren Marter ausgesetzt ... Döbling Beethoven ... Paskolati 94 Mölkerbastey." (Therese's Diary, Summer 1815, in Tellenbach 1983, p. 142 f.) Döbling was one of Beethoven's frequent summer holiday destinations (like Baden) – where he therefore could have met Therese. "Paskolati 94 Mölkerbastey" was his (slightly misspelled) address in Vienna. At the very least, there must have been (again) contact by letter.

[16] "Das abermalige höchst traurige Beispiel meiner unglücklichen Schwester lehrt mich[,] daß man mit allen fremden Personen auf dem Freundschaftsfuß bleiben muß. leute ins Haus nehmen u. zu vertraulichkeit brauchen ist höchst gefährlich u. dumm." (Therese's Diary, July/August 1815, in Tellenbach 1983, p. 142 f.)

[17] Therese's Diary, 1816, p. 106 (in Steblin 2007, p. 150, n. 25.) "Seilerstaat" means "Auf der Seilerstadt" (now "Seilerstätte").

[18] "Geburt Emiliens 4 uhr ¼ auf 4. Morgens. Empfindungen[,] Gedanken, *Ohdieu*! Rein bleibe sie! wahr u seelig! darum ließest du Geschöpfe werden, Großes mächtiges Wesen!" (Therese's Diary, 16 September 1815, in Steblin 2007, p. 174, n. 90.)

[19] "Unglückliche Mutter! unwürdige Mutter! Du **darfst** nicht wissen, du sollst nicht wissen was dein Kind tödtet!" (Therese's Diary, 25 October 1815, in Tellenbach 1983, p. 131.)

[20] "Wie diese Mutter, stets kleinlich und beschränkt, oft bizarr, gemein mit ihren Urtheilen, Reden, Ansichten mir die Phantasie verdirbt, verwundert, die Gedanken zerreißt!" (Therese's Diary, 1815–17, in La Mara 1920, p. 85.)

[21] "Mutter untersteht sich, uns leichtsinnig zu nennen, wir, die wir unser Leben den solidesten Bestrebungen weihen mit grenzenloser Aufopferung! Leichtsinnig sind wir nicht – leichtsinnig ist sie, die ihr edles Kind weggab an einen Greisen ohne Vermögen ... Enterbt hat sie uns. ... Der Kleinlichkeitsgeist hat unsre Familie so extravagant unglücklich gemacht; darum ist er mir verhaßt." (Therese's Diary, 5 December 1816, in La Mara 1920, p. 85 f.)

Endurance – acquiescence – submission.[1]

1816: The Last Yearning

Before the year 1815 was out, Deacon Franz Leyer in Trautenau, Bohemia, had written to Josephine, about her three daughters, who had been with him for nearly two years:

> For a long time it should have been my duty to report to you about the well-being of your children, and the heartfelt longing with which they languish for you as their most beloved mother.
>
> However, my enduring hope that Baron von Stackelberg would soon come to pick them up and to lead them into your tender arms, in accordance with his promise, prevented me. But since his departure for Switzerland, we heard nothing at all from him, and his silence and especially the non-arrival of his monetary help caused us all, especially me, the greatest embarrassment.
>
> Already during his stay in Russia, we went into debt. ... But now since he does no longer send us anything, our discomfort is growing every day, and we have not the least resources at our disposal, to provide in the future their food, housing, etc. ...
>
> What should be done with the poor deplorable children? ... Time smoothes out all incongruities, it heals all wounds by and by! I ask you as a stranger, as a priest of a religion preaching peace, reconciliation and love, let the trials of an erring father not be paid for by these poor, naïve and helpless children.[2]

Josephine immediately scraped together some money and sent it to Leyer (Tellenbach 1983, p. 138), who promptly replied:

> Please accept in the name of your noble children our deepest thanks not only for the 800 Gulden but also especially for the sweet comfort that you have the grace to assure us for the future.
>
> When I stepped into the midst of your naïve little ones and told them: Your good mother will now take away all worries about your future supplies, they all wept and cried

> with joy, and they wished their mother would already come tomorrow.[3]

For several months, nothing happened, and Stackelberg apparently could not bring himself to touch his considerable inheritance in order to provide for his own children. Note also, that he obviously lied to the churchman, as he had told Leyer to take care of the children until he would come back to return them to their mother!

Deacon Leyer finally made a reasonable suggestion, having received from Stackelberg

> not even the smallest contribution to provide for the children... The best for the children would be, indeed, if you take them to Vienna, because, as I believe, due to the difficult economic circumstances of their father, no further support will be forthcoming, and there the children can obtain the education that best corresponds to their birth and station.[4]

Therese's memoirs describe vividly what happened next:

> For two years, we had heard not the slightest news of their whereabouts. ... Suddenly, a letter from the Deacon of Trautenau in Bohemia arrived informing us that the children ... had been left with him by Baron Stackelberg for a few weeks, but the money had been used up long ago. ...
>
> He asked us, with their father gone missing, to pick up the children and to send the required money.
>
> The children are already sitting in the carriage – then Baron Otto Stackelberg, the younger brother, appears and protests against the departure of the children. He comes in the name of the father [!], provided with money. – Our money, however, was never returned.[5]

The final parting of Josephine from her husband (though he would return) was described by Therese thus:

> Stackelberg had taken leave of us and Austria. ... However, his newfound dignity as a devout Christian forbade him revenge and lawsuits. He departed ... indignant in his deepest soul![6]

Even though this must have been quite a shock for Josephine, Therese, in her later view, merged these events with the subsequent separation of the Brunsvik sisters:

> Josephine let them [the children] go calmly. ... She was ailing ... We separated.[7]

Josephine was so ill and also burdened with the education of her four Deym children (now in their teens) that she was probably rather happy to be relieved of the care and upbringing of the three Stackelberg girls (given that Therese was now also about to leave her).

* * *

Most likely, there was also another meeting – the last one – between Ludwig and Josephine during their summer holidays (as so often before, in Baden – see Tellenbach 1983, p. 148):

> 1816, they were all in Baden for a wonderful holiday. ... The printed list of spa guests shows Josephine registered there on 30 April 1816 as: "Nr. 7 Frau Gräffin v. Mayersfeld-Dejm, aus Wien". ... Thus, Josephine was in Baden in May 1816, and Beethoven could have gone for a walk with her then, mentioning her as the "one woman" whom he loved in his letter to Ries on 8 May, and pining over her absence later that summer, as Fanny[8] noted in her diary on 16 September 1816 (Steblin 2007, p. 179).

On 2 June, Josephine had made an application for a passport, to travel to the spa in "Pirmont" [Pyrmont] (Tellenbach 1983, p. 148). However, probably due to the upheaval caused by Stackelberg's intervention (and also the continuing lack of money), she had to change plans.[9]

Amazingly, there is an entry in Beethoven's Diary, around August 1816:

> ... not to P - t, but with P. – discuss the best way how to arrange it.[10]

It seems that both had planned secretly (maybe again with the help of Therese as a go-between) to go to (and meet in) Pyrmont, but due to Josephine's change of plans, they met in Baden instead – where it was quite possible to be seen by someone who knew them.

Solomon – in his comment on Beethoven's diary note – did not have a clue:

> "P-t" and "P" cannot be identified. Leitzmann considers "Pt" to be the name of a place and tentatively mentions Bad Pyrmont in Westphalia.[11]

As for the mysterious "P", Beethoven was probably referring (affectionately) to "Pepi", Josephine's nickname, and "but with P[epi]" could be short for either "travel with P[epi]" (to Baden instead of Pyrmont) or "stay (or meet up) with P[epi]" (once in Baden). Needless to say, the sudden change of travel plans (by Josephine) required some efforts to arrange things.

Intriguingly, there was also – years later – an entry by nephew Karl in a conversation book of Beethoven:

> In Helena [Baden], you were walking with a woman arm in arm. Who was **that**?[12]

The answer – if any – is not known. However, we can be certain that Beethoven kept his silence.

In November, Josephine was severely depressed, due to her mounting debts and Stackelberg's announcement to return the next summer. Therese noted:

> Poor Josephine! How I feel sorry for you, how your shattered soul must look like, and how much you have to suffer.[13]

* * *

Andrian, who apparently found it difficult to accept their separation, wrote this to Josephine as his parting shot:

> I repeat that I will love you even from a distance, and that I and Emilie will keep your memory pure and dear ... God be with you, you poor forsaken woman, who suffers from injustice and does wrong only out of – love.[14]

In effect, more tormenting than comforting, one must suppose.

* * *

In February 1816, there was a concert in the Deym villa with only Beethoven's music, where the composer was also present. Most likely, he met the Brunsvik sisters on that occasion (Tellenbach 1983, p. 147). In April, Beethoven composed the Song Cycle "An die ferne Geliebte" [To the Distant Beloved] Op. 98. Was she then, for him, once again, "so nah, so fern" [so near, so far]?

A letter to Ries seems to indicate that he was still (or again) occupied with thoughts about his (only) beloved, and the fading impossibility to marry her:

> My best greetings to your wife; alas, I have none; I have found only one [!], whom I will probably never possess, but that does not make me a woman hater![15]

"**Only one**"! Note also that the qualification "probably" ("wohl" in German) indicates that the woman in question was still potentially available (i.e., she could not have been Antonie Brentano, who was living far away in Frankfurt am Main).

Beethoven was not only ill again, but also in such a desperate mood that he was thinking of death and suicide, as in this letter:

> Now my health has been vacillating for 6 weeks, such that I often think of death but without fear.[16]

He wrote into his Diary morbid remarks like this one:

> He who is afflicted with an evil which he cannot change, but which gradually brings him closer to death and without which his life would have been longer, must think that he could have perished even faster through murder or other causes.[17]

He repeated his decision not to write operas and similar music "popular" at the time, but to continue with his own style (being now almost completely deaf):

> Operas and everything else – let it be, just write in your own way – and then a habit, to conclude your unhappy life.[18]

The "habit" (or "frock") – meaning a monk's dress – here symbolizes the turning away from normal earthly life (by becoming a monk, metaphorically speaking).

What follows, is again the conflict between defiance against the crushing force of fate and resignation, surrender, humility:

> Show me your power, fate! We are not master of ourselves, what is decided must be, and so be it![19]

> Endurance – acquiescence – submission, and thus we can still gain from the greatest misery and become worthy.[20]

Through suffering to salvation.

> Only in your life as an artist, restricted though you are due to your senses, nevertheless this is surely the only reason of being for you.[21]

Per aspera ad astra.[22]

His compositions during this year were again mainly folksong arrangemants and songs (lieder) – among them a second setting of "An die Hoffnung" [To Hope] Op. 94, which is remarkable as it differed from the first one ten years earlier by adding this at the beginning:

> *Is there a God? Will He ever fulfill*
> *That which yearning promises in tears?*
> *Will this our mysterious being be revealed*
> *Before some final judgment?*
> *Man must hope! But he must not ask!*[23]

And yet another (the third) version of a Song in *E major* "Sehnsucht" [Yearning] WoO 146, ending in:

> *Oh, conjure up before my eyes*
> *The lovely woman, who flees before me.*
> *Let me press her to my heart,*
> *So that true love may be kindled!*
>
> *You noble woman, whom I love,*
> *How much I long for you;*
> *Appear, ah, appear,*
> *And let Hope smile upon me!*[24]

Two of the most interesting – and intriguing – diary entries Beethoven wrote about this time were (most likely) about Therese:

> Because of T. there is no other way than to let it be God's decision, never to go where you could commit injustice out of weakness.[25]
>
> However, towards T. be as good as possible, her devotion deserves never to be forgotten, never – even though unfortunately there could never arise any beneficial consequences for you.[26]

He clearly emphasized his gratitude to Therese, who not only continued to support Josephine (and who might have arranged their meeting in Baden),[27] but also showed her unending devotion towards Beethoven.

Only, "beneficial consequences" (union with Josephine) could not be expected. There was "no other way".

* * *

Josephine's situation, her illness in particular, got worse. She still had the continuing support of her sister, but now she had to go through the frustrating experience of losing her mother's love and support.

> It is a heartbreaking sight to see the good but weak Josephine ... her nerves are weak, and in her current situation she is hardly able to cure herself.[28]

Josephine knew

> the true cause of my physical suffering... My body is only sympathizing. It is my soul that is suffering unbearable pain.[29]

as she told her doctor. And she still had Therese's compassion:

> Poor Josephine! How I feel sorry for you, how it must look like in your broken soul, what do you have to suffer! No one can truly be angry with you.[30]

Josephine made a last attempt at reconciliation with her mother:

> I consider it my duty, dear mother, to report to you the embarrassment in which I find myself ... My grief does not permit me to tell my mother about my situation, which it seems she does not want to know anything about.
>
> Not only the loss of the management of my children's assets, but also my life is probably the price I have to pay ... and it aroused in me the feeling of having embraced you probably for the last time. The doctor solemnly declared that with so little peace of mind, joy and serenity ... there is no way to think of any recovery, and nothing but an early death is to be expected. Thus, I am constantly chained to the bed, to an unhappy fate, which will lead me into another world.[31]

Learning that her daughter was about to die, Anna von Brunsvik's reply was rather dispassionate:

> I am sorry about your indisposition, but still more about your sad situation into which you are going to sink deeper and deeper as long as a complete change of mind does not give your actions an appropriate change of direction – you

have only yourself to blame ... but with the serious intention to destroy the source of the evil with all your efforts for ever. –

Who forsakes God, Pepi, will be forsaken by Him! – Return to the merciful Almighty – He will accept you back, enlighten you and assist you visibly. ... Knowledge of ourselves is the very first prerequisite that no one can give to us other than we ourselves; your first husband strove to teach you knowledge of people – your relationship with him could have been your fortune if you had wanted it. –

At his death he left you in pretty good circumstances, if you had not been carried away by your desire for higher indulgences; when I met you then in Baden in melancholy and dissatisfied with your fate, I called you several times: Pepi! do not sin against God! ... I was as young as you when I became a widow ... I stretched myself to the ceiling ... lived by little means ... but always with honor and decency. ... Therefore, I can only regret, but not help – I feel sorry particularly for your poor children and your mother. – [32]

Serves you right! Sin against God!

Therese summed up the torment of those years:

They wanted to take her sons away, to educate them in a common institution like common people. What fights! what scenes were occurring in 1815 and 1816! From then on, her dwindling life was in terrible tatters.[33]

---

[1] "Ertragung – Ergebung – Ergebung." (Beethoven's Diary, in Solomon 2005, p. 68.)

[2] "Schon längst wäre es meine Pflicht gewesen ... Nachricht von dem Wohlbefinden Ihrer liebenswürdigen Kinder, und der herzlichen Sehnsucht zu geben, womit Sie nach Ihnen als ihrer innigstgeliebtesten Mutter schmachten. Allein meine fortdauernde Hoffnung: Herr Baron von Stackelberg würde dieselben seinem Versprechen gemäß bald abholen und in Ihre zärtlichen Arme führen, hinderte mich daran. Doch seit seiner Abreise in die Schweiz erfahren wir auch nicht das Geringste von Ihm, und Sein Stillschweigen und besonders das Ausbleiben Seiner Geldhülfe setzt uns Alle, besonders mich, in die größte Verlegenheit. Schon während seiner Anwesenheit in Rußland gerieten wir in Schulden. ... Allein jetzt da Er gar nicht[s] mehr schickt wird unsere Verlegenheit mit jedem Tage größer, und wir haben nicht ... die geringsten Mittel in Händen, womit wir in Zukunft ihre Kost, Wohnung u. s. w. besorgen sollen. ... Was ist also mit den armen

bedauerungswürdigen Kindern anzufangen? ... Die Zeit gleicht alle Mißverhältnisse aus, sie heilt nach und nach alle Wunden! Ich bitte Sie als Unbekannter, als Priester einer Religion, die Frieden, Versöhnung und Liebe predigt, lassen Sie die Irrungen eines Vaters nicht die armen, unbefangenen hilflosen Kinder entgelten." (Leyer to Josephine, 29 December 1815, in Tellenbach 1983, p. 137 f.)

3   "Nehmen Sie in Namen Ihrer vortrefflichen Kinder unsern innigsten Dank nicht nur für die erhaltenen 800 fl sondern auch insonderheit für den süßen Trost, den Sie uns für die Zukunft zuzusichern die Gnade haben. Als ich in den Kreis Ihrer unbefangenen Kleinen kam, und Ihnen sagte: Ihre gute Mutter würde uns nun alles Kummers um fernere Versorgung entreißen, da weinte und schrie alles vor Freude, und [sie] wünschten, die Mutter möchte morgen schon kommen." (Leyer to Josephine, 22 January 1816, in Tellenbach 1983, p. 138.)

4   "... auch nicht den Geringsten Beitrag für die Verpflegung der Kinder erhalten ... Das Beste für die Kinder wäre freilich, Sie nehmen solche nach Wien, in dem, wie ich glaube, bei den mißlichen ökonomischen Verhältnissen des Vaters gar nicht auf eine solche Unterstützung zu rechnen ist, und dort die Kinder doch die Erziehung erhalten können, die Ihrer Geburt und Ihrem Stande zusagt." (Leyer to Josephine, 26 April 1816, in Tellenbach 1983, p. 139.)

5   "Zwei Jahre hatten wir nicht die geringste Nachricht von ihrem Aufenthalt. ... Plötzlich erscheint ein Brief vom Dechant von Trautenau in Böhmen, welcher uns meldet, daß die Kinder ... bei ihm durch Baron Stackelberg für wenige Wochen zurückgelassen wurden, das Geld aber ... schon längst verzehrt [sei]. ... Er bitte, da der Vater verschollen, die Kinder abholen zu lassen und das nöthige Geld zu senden. ... Die Kinder sitzen schon im Wagen – da erscheint Baron Otto Stackelberg, der jüngere Bruder, und legt Protest ein gegen die Abreise der Kinder. Er kommt im Namen des Vaters [!] mit Geld versehen. – unser Geld wurde aber nicht zurückgesendet." (Therese's Memoirs, in La Mara 1909, p. 105.) Therese's recollection seems to imply that she or Josephine (or both) were in fact in Trautenau to pick up the girls. However, and probably mainly due to Josephine's ill health (again, exacerbated after giving birth to her eighth child), Therese stayed with her in Vienna, and they had sent servants with a carriage (and more money) to Trautenau.

6   "Stackelberg hatte Abschied genommen von uns und Oesterreich. ... Aber seine neue Würde als gläubiger Christ verbot ihm Rache und Prozesse. Er reiste ... davon, indigniert im tiefsten seiner Seele!" (Therese's Memoirs, in La Mara 1909, p. 105.) It seems, Therese is commenting here sardonically on Stackelberg's justification for his reluctance to continue the legal battles to salvage the Witschapp estate.

7   "Josephine ließ sie ruhig ziehen. ... Sie kränkelte ... wir trennten uns." (Therese's Memoirs, in La Mara 1909, p. 105.)

8   Fanny was a daughter of Cajetan Giannatasio del Rio who looked after Beethoven's nephew at the time. She wrote a diary where she reported that Beethoven, when asked by her father, mentioned that several years ago he had been in love with a woman whom he could not marry. "Dennoch ist es jetzt wie den ersten Tag. Ich hab's noch nicht aus dem Gemüth bringen können." [Yet it is now as on the first day. I just cannot get it out of my mind.] (Tellenbach 1983, p. 146; see

also Goldschmidt 1977, p. 309.) It seems as if his recent meeting with Josephine in Baden was still fresh on his mind. Fanny, who was hopelessly in love with the composer, may have asked her father to find out about his availability. His reply was probably evasive, as he clearly was not in love with the then 26-year-old Fanny (who later also noticed a precious ring on Beethoven's hand, see Tellenbach 1983, p. 146 f.).

9   "Josephine ist nicht mehr nach Pyrmont gefahren." [Josephine did not travel to Pyrmont, after all.] (Tellenbach 1983, p. 149.)

10   "... nicht nach P - t, sondern mit P. – abreden, wie es am besten zu machen sey –." (Beethoven's Diary, in Solomon 2005, p. 73.)

11   "'P-t' und 'P' können nicht identifiziert werden. Leitzmann sieht 'Pt' als einen Ortsnamen an und nennt tentativ das westfälische Bad Pyrmont." (Solomon 2005, p. 73.) See Albert Leitzmann: "Ludwig van Beethoven. Berichte der Zeitgenossen, Briefe und persönliche Aufzeichnungen." [Ludwig van Beethoven. Reports by Contemporaries, Letters and Personal Notes.] Leipzig 1921.

12   "In Helena [Baden] bist du mit Einer Arm in Arm gegangen. Wer **das** war?" (Konversationsheft 1824, in Tellenbach 1983, p. 149.)

13   "Arme Jo[sephine]! Wie bedaure ich dich, wie muss deine zerrüt[t]ete Seele aussehen und was musst du leiden." (Therese's Diary, 5 November 1816, in http://www.xs4all.nl/~ademu/Beethoven/.)

14   "Ich wiederhole dir[,] daß ich auch in der Ferne dich lieben werde, und daß ich Emilien, dein Andenken rein und theuer erhalten werde... Gott mit dir du armes verlassnes Weib, das Unrecht leidet und Unrecht thut nur aus – Liebe –." (Andrian to Josephine, ca. 1816, in Tellenbach 1983, p. 175.)

15   "Alles Schöne an Ihre Frau; leider hab ich keine; ich fand nur eine [!], die ich wohl nie besitzen werde, bin aber deswegen kein weiberfeind." (Beethoven to Ries, 8 May 1816, in Goldschmidt 1977, p. 159.) Anderson (1961) translates "wohl" incorrectly with "doubtless" (Tellenbach 1983, p. 249). The German wording clearly indicates that there is still "doubt" – or rather, hope!

16   "Nun ist meine Gesundheit auch seit 6 Wochen auf schwankenden Füßen so daß ich öfter an meinen tod, jedoch nicht mit Furcht denke." (Beethoven to Marie Erdödy, 13 May 1816, in Solomon 2005, p. 66.)

17   "Der mit einem Uibel behaftet wird, welches er nicht ändern kann, sondern welches nach und nach ihn dem Tode näher bringt und ohne welches sein Leben länger gedauert hätte, muß denken, dass er auch so durch Mord oder andere Ursachen hätte noch geschwinder umkommen können." (Beethoven's Diary, in Solomon 2005, p. 66.)

18   "Opern und alles seyn lassen[,] nur für deine Weise schreiben – und dann eine Kutte wo[mit] du das unglückliche Leben beschließest." (Beethoven's Diary, in Solomon 2005, p. 71.)

[19] "Zeige deine Gewalt Schicksal! Wir sind nicht Herrn über uns selbst; was beschlossen ist, muß seyn, und so sey es denn!" (Beethoven's Diary, in Solomon 2005, p. 66.)

[20] "Ertragung – Ergebung – Ergebung[,] so gewinnen wir noch beym höchsten Elend und machen uns würdig." (Beethoven's Diary, in Solomon 2005, p. 68.)

[21] "Nur in deinem Kunstleben[,] so beschränkt du auch jetzt deiner Sinne halber bist, so ist dieses doch das Einzige Daseyn für dich." (Beethoven's Diary, in Solomon 2005, p. 72.)

[22] Through Exasperation to the Stars. See also Goldschmidt (1977), p. 439–443.

[23]
Ob ein Gott sei? Ob er einst erfülle,
Was die Sehnsucht weinend sich verspricht?
Ob, vor irgendeinem Weltgericht,
Sich dies rätselhafte Sein enthülle?
Hoffen soll der Mensch! Er frage nicht!

[24]
O zaubre meinen Blicken
Die Holde, die mich flieht,
Laß mich ans Herz sie drücken,
Daß edle Lieb' entglüht!

Du Holde, die ich meine,
Wie sehn' ich mich nach dir;
Erscheine, ach, erscheine
Und lächle Hoffnung mir!

[25] "Wegen T. ist nicht anders als Gott es anheim zu stellen, nie dort hin zu gehen, wo man Unrecht aus Schwachheit begehen könnte." (Beethoven's Diary, in Solomon 2005, p. 79.)

[26] "Jedoch gegen T. so gut als möglich[,] ihre Anhänglichkeit verdient immer nie vergessen zu werden – wenn auch leider nie davon vorteilhafte Folgen für dich entstehen könnten." (Beethoven's Diary, in Solomon 2005, p. 82.)

[27] There is evidence that Therese stayed in touch with Beethoven, as she once again carefully recorded his latest address: "*Beethoven* 1055–56 Seilerstaat." (Therese's Diary, 1816, p. 106, in Steblin 2007, p. 150, n. 25.)

[28] "Es ist ein herzzerreissender Anblick, die gute aber schwache Josephine zu sehen ... sie ist nervenschwach u. ihre laage ist wohl kaum geeignet um [sich]

selber davon zu curieren." (Therese's Diary, 5 November 1816, in Tellenbach 1983, p. 162.)

29 "... die wahre Ursache mein[es] kör[perlichen] Leidens ... Der Körper n[ä]hmlich ist nur mitleidend. Die Seele leidet unerträglichen Schmerz." (Josephine to her doctor, November 1816, in Tellenbach 1983, p. 162.)

30 "Arme Jo[sephine]! Wie bedaure ich dich[,] wie muß es in deiner zerrütteten Seele aussehen[,] was mußt du leiden! Zürnen kann dir wahrlich niemand." (Therese's Diary, November 1816, in Tellenbach 1983, p. 162.)

31 "Ich halte es für meine Pflicht liebe Mutter Ihnen von der Verlegenheit in welcher ich mich befinde Nachricht zu geben... Wehmut erlaubt mir nicht meiner Mutter von meiner Lage Kunde zu geben welche sie nicht zu wissen scheinen will. Nicht nur der Verlust der Verwaltung des Vermögens meiner Kinder, sondern mein Leben ist wahrscheinlich der Preis dafür ... und erregt in mir das Gefühl Sie wahrscheinlich das letztemal umarmt zu haben. Der Arzt erklärt feyerlich daß ... bey sowenig Gemüths Ruhe, Frohsinn und Heiterkeit ... an keine Genesung zu denken sey, und nichts als ein gewisser Todt vorauszusehen sey. So bin ich beständig an das Bett geschmiedet, an ein unglückliches Loos, welches ... mich in eine andre Welt führt." (Josephine to her mother, 9 November 1816, in Tellenbach 1983, p. 163 f.)

32 "Ich bedaure deine Unpäßlichkeit, noch mehr aber deine traurige Laage, in welche du dich immer tiefer versenken wirst, so lange Eine gänzliche Sinnesänderung deinen Handlungen keine angemeßene Wendung geben wirdt – such Alle Schuld bloß in dir selbst ... aber mit dem ernstlichen Vorsatz, die Quel[l]e des Übels mit aller Anstrengung auf immer zu zernichten. – wer Gott verläßt Pepi, Den verläßt Er auch!!! – Kehre zum Allbarmherzigen zurück, Er wird dich wieder aufnehmen[,] dich erleuchten, und dir sichtbar beystehen. ... Kenntnis unserer selbst ist das aller Erste Bedürfnis, das kann uns niemand als wir selbst uns geben, dir Menschenkenntniß beyzubringen bewarb sich dein Erster Gemahl – deine Verbindung mit ihm hätte dein Glück seyn können wänn du gewollt hättest. – bey seinem Tode verließ Er dich in recht guten Umständen; wänn du dich ... nicht von der Begierde nach höhrem Genuß hättest hinreißen lassen, als ich dich damahls in Baaden melancolisch und Unzufrieden mit deinem Schicksaal fand, rief ich dir mehrmalen zu[:] Pepi! versündige dich nicht an Gott! ... eben so jung als du wurde ich Wittwe ... streckte mich nach der Decke ... lebte überall klein ... aber immer mit Ehre und Anstand. ... Ich kann also nur bedauern, aber nicht helfen – Vorzüglich bedaure ich deine armen Kinder und deine Mutter. – –" (Anna to Josephine, 30 December 1816, in Tellenbach 1983, p. 164 f.)

33 "Man wollte ihr die Söhne nehmen und sie in einem gemeinen Institut zu gemeinen Menschen bilden. Welche Kämpfe! welche Auftritte 1815 und 16! Von da an war ihr schwindendes Leben eine schreckliche Zerrissenheit." (Therese's Memoirs, in La Mara 1909, p. 96.)

Go out, my light![1]

1817: Resignation

Beethoven spent most of this year in deep depression. His deafness was almost total by now, and he once again made plans to travel (which as always came to naught):

> To save you there is no other way than to go away, only then can you float again to the heights of your art, whereas here you are going to sink into vulgarity.[2]

Like Josephine in her letters to him (in 1807), he recognized again the importance of a spiritual union, by quoting Plutarch:

> Sensual pleasure without the union of souls is and will remain brutish, after which one has no traces of a noble sentiment, but only remorse – – –.[3]

> Peace and freedom are the greatest virtues. – True friendship can only be based on the union of similar natures.[4]

His deafness increased his loneliness, and also his suspicion and wariness:

> Living alone is like poison for you in your deaf state; suspicion always must be entertained when there are mean people around you.[5]

* * *

Among his few compositions of this year (mainly songs), there was the Song "Resignation" in *D major* WoO 149:

> *Go out, my light!*
> *What you so dearly need*
> *Has gone forever;*
> *In this place here*
> *You'll find it no more!*
> *Now you must do without it.*

You used to burn so brightly,
Now you are deprived of air;
When this is blown away,
The flame wavers,
Seeks - and finds nothing -
Go out, my light![6]

Therese asked herself
> whether Josephine is not suffering punishment because of Luigi's woe! His wife – what would she not have made of him, the Hero![7]

Too late!

* * *

On 9 March 1817, Stackelberg returned to Vienna, apparently after having "served" two years of separation, as requested by Josephine's relatives in 1815. Again, he tried to convince Josephine to leave Vienna and go with him. Again, she refused, the memory of the shock still fresh in her mind when Stackelberg's brother Otto had wrenched the three little girls from her.

There is also a document signed by Christoph von Stackelberg and dated 23 June 1817, about a bond of money owed to Josephine, indicating the main reason for his being in Vienna again – to scrounge some money:

> About 342 in words three hundred and forty-two Gulden in twenties...[8]

---

[1] "Lisch aus, mein Licht!" (Song in *D major* "Resignation" WoO 149.)

[2] "Dich zu retten ist kein anderes Mittel als [fort] von hier, nur dadurch kannst du wieder so zu den Höhen deiner Kunst entschweben, wo du hier in Gemeinheit versinkst." (Beethoven's Diary, in Solomon 2005, p. 86.)

[3] "Sinnlicher Genuß ohne Vereinigung der Seelen ist und bleibt viehisch, nach selben hat man keine Spur einer edlen Empfindung[,] vielmehr Reue – – –." (Beethoven's Diary, in Solomon 2005, p. 87.) This remark – a quote from Plutarch – is frequently interpreted as an indication that Beethoven might have been with a prostitute – so what? (But see the chapter about "Solomon".)

[4] "Ruhe und Freyheit sind die größten Güter. – Wahre Freundschaft kann nur beruhn auf der Verbindung ähnlicher Naturen." (Beethoven's Diary, in Solomon 2005, p. 89.)

[5] "Das Alleinleben ist wie Gift für dich bey deinem Gehörlosen Zustande, Argwohn muß bey einem niedern Menschen um dich stets gehegt werden." (Beethoven's Diary, in Solomon 2005, p. 92.)

[6] *Lisch aus, mein Licht!*
Was dir gebricht,
Das ist nun fort,
An diesem Ort
Kannst du's nicht wieder finden!
Du mußt nun los dich binden.

Sonst hast du lustig aufgebrannt,
Nun hat man dir die Luft entwandt;
Wenn diese fort geweht,
Die Flamme irregeht,
Sucht, findet nicht;
Lisch aus, mein Licht!

[7] "Ob Josephine nicht Straffe leidet wegen Luigis Weh! Seine Gattin – was hätte sie nicht aus dem Heros gemacht!" (Therese's Diary, 12 July 1817, in Schmidt-Görg 1957, p. 31.)

[8] "Ueber 342 sage drei Hundert und zwei und vierzig Gulden in Zwanziger..." (Stackelberg to Josephine, 23 June 1817, in Tellenbach 1983, p. 171.)

You are dying, my noble soul.[1]

Finale

---

[1] "Du stirbst edle Seele." (Therese to Josephine, 27 December 1819, in Tellenbach 1983, p. 187.)

> *Melting into one can happen
> only when first we have been
> melted with Eternity – this alone
> is union – forever.*[1]

1818: The Last Letter

Beethoven continued to struggle with his fate, his deafness and his loneliness – and the additional problems he had (brought upon himself) with his recalcitrant nephew. His resolution was once more to concentrate on his art:

> Sacrifice once again all the trifles of social life to your art.[2]

The only major composition of this time period was the Piano Sonata #29 in B flat major "Hammerklavier" Op. 106, which took him the better part of the last three years – but what a monumental achievement it was!

The last words in his Diary, completing half a decade of misery, before embarking on the final and ultimately most successful period of his creative life, with the first germinating seeds of the Ninth Symphony, the glorious *Missa Solemnis* and the all-transcending late String Quartets already in his mind:

> At peace, let me then be subjected to all changes, and I put all my trust only in Your unwavering kindness – Oh God! You, Immutable one, my soul shall rejoice in You. Be my Rock, my Enlightenment, forever my Faith and my Trust! – –
> [3]

* * *

And so we are back again with Josephine, who, mortally ill and delirious, wrote a long letter on 8 April 1818, Minona's fifth birthday – maybe to Ludwig?

The last one.

> I can only speak in a few words of that which the Spirit tells me in moments of calm ... Our friendship can also only be assumed to exist in such moments ... In so far as the soul speaks – it does not speak any more. – Spirits are silent.
>
> I would not have written these fragments, had I not believed this way to answer a request by you which must be dear to me after your last words – What your appearance arouses in my feelings – I cannot describe – – – – – – We all do not know, what we are doing, talking, what we are – the universe in our heart ... is the starry sky ... It seems to break within us, the axis, shattered, torn from its hinges, destroyed are we standing here – opposite each other ... what we mutually destroyed within us – – – – – – it is standing before our inner eye...
>
> Happy you are not – – – – – but deaf [!] – – – busy with a stern glance beyond – and so calm – serene ... in a state of negative happiness – the Book of Memories has many colors – you have browsed it frequently – viewed it – judged it – yourself – too...
>
> Melting into one can happen only when first we have been melted with Eternity, with true sincerity this true desire, the more it purifies itself – this alone is union – forever – everything is like a shell; a form; a casing which ... moves in a continuous line up to the last point – If the Spirit could reveal itself to you completely, due to its deficiencies it cannot – – – – – – – – –.[4]

* * *

Intriguingly, like Beethoven in his Letter of 1812, Josephine inconveniently neglected to name the addressee. We can only assume that due to the date being Minona's birthday, and Beethoven being most likely her father, Josephine was thinking of him. She even calls him "deaf"! Of course, the confused mental state in which she was by now explains this letter's fragmented and obviously incoherent content. But who can blame her?

Josephine's ongoing misery, her poverty, grief, loneliness, frailty, and the continuing conflicts with her family (who wanted her to leave Vienna and go back to Hungary) was summed up by Therese:

How many things had to happen and how often did I hurt Josephine and did not understand her at all.[5]

---

[1] "In eins zusammen schmelzen kann nur dan[n] geschehen, wenn zuerst in eins geschmolzen wir sind mit dem Ewigen ... ist allein Vereinigung – für ewig." (Josephine to Beethoven?, 8 April 1818, draft, in Tellenbach 1983, p. 195.)

[2] "Opfere noch einmal alle Kleinigkeiten des gesellschaftlichen Lebens deiner Kunst." (Beethoven's Diary, in Solomon 2005, p. 104.)

[3] "Gelassen will ich mich also allen Veränderungen unterwerfen und nur auf deine unwandelbare Güte o Gott! mein ganzes Vertrauen setzen. Dein[,] Unwandelbarer[,] Deiner soll sich meine Seele freuen. Sey mein Fels, mein Licht, ewig meine Zuversicht! – – –." (Beethoven's Diary, in Solomon 2005, p. 105.) Quoted from Christian Sturm: "Betrachtungen über die Werke Gottes im Reiche der Natur." [Reflections on the Works of God in the Realm of Nature.] Reutlingen 1811.

[4] "Ich kann nur mit wenig Worten von dem sprechen was der Geist zu mir spricht in den Augenblicken der Ruhe ... Unsere Freundschaft kann auch nur in solchen Augenblicken als existierend angenommen werden ... Indem die Seele spricht – spricht sie nicht mehr. – Geister sind stumm. Ich hätte diese Bruchstücke nicht geschrieben, glaubte ich nicht hiedurch einem Wunsch von dir zu begegnen, der mir nach deinen letzten Worten theuer seyn muß – Was deine Erscheinung in mein[en] Empfindungen weckt – kann ich nicht schildern – – – – – – Wir wissen keines, was wir thun, sprechen, sind – das Weltall in der Brust ... ist der Sternenhimmel ... – – – Sie scheint zu brechen in uns die Axe, aufgelöst, aus den Angeln gerissen, zerstört stehen wir da – uns gegen über ... was wir an uns gegenseitig, was wir in uns selbst zu Grunde richteten – – – – – – es steht vor unsrem innern Auge ... glücklich bist du nicht – – – – aber betäubt – – – mit einem ernsten blick hinaus beschäftigt – u. so ruhig – gelassen ... in einem zustande von negativen Glück – das Buch der Erinnerung zeigt mancherlei Farben – du hast es durchgeblättert oft – durchgesehen – gerichtet – auch dich – selbst... In eins zusammen schmelzen kann nur dan[n] geschehen, wenn zuerst in eins geschmolzen wir sind mit dem Ewigen, mit wahrer innigkeit dieses reine Verlangen, je mehr es sich reinigt – ist allein Vereinigung – für ewig – alles andere Schaale; Form; Gehäuse welche ... in einer fortlaufenden Linie sich bewegen bis an den letzten punkt – Kön[n]te der Geist sich dir ganz offenbaren[,] seine Mäng[e]l sind es, das[s] er es nicht kann – – – – – – – – –." (Josephine to Beethoven?, 8 April 1818, draft, in Tellenbach 1983, p. 195.)

[5] "Was hat alles geschehen müssen u. wie habe ich Josephine oft wehgethan u. sie gar nicht verstanden." (Therese's Diary, 1818, in Tellenbach 1983, p. 183.)

> *An unusually harsh fate is our lot ... A wide gulf is between us. The mother's heart has no sympathy for her child – the sister's love is extinguished.*[1]

1819: Final Visit

Josephine's oldest son was again causing her trouble:
> Fritz Deym the son had not learned anything ... and he did not want to learn anything. He showed an interest in the military – to the horror of his mostly bedridden mother.[2]

Therese was also shocked; her view of the army was all too realistic:
> They are supposed to be for our protection but on command they turn against their own people![3]

During the summer of 1819, Fritz's gambling debts caused more financial problems for Josephine. This resulted in a definitive break with her mother – and her brother, who was no longer willing to support her:
> Franz was determined and unshakable to make no more sacrifices for Josephine.[4]

Mother Anna declared that she would withdraw any further support unless Josephine sold the Deym villa, separated formally from Stackelberg and returned to Hungary. Josephine, knowing that she could not keep the children after a divorce, refused to the despair of Therese, who in turn admonished their mother (alas, only in her Diary!) – because all the money was given to Franz:
> Oh Mother, how cruel, how unfair are you dealing with us, how unscrupulous! The heart of a mother, who prefers **one** child in a distribution where only law and justice should reign, is rejected by the Deity. Are you not trembling before the remorse on your death bed?[5]

* * *

> After another 2 ½ years, Stackelberg finally came back to Vienna with Minona, who was already six years old, and her sisters. It was remarkable how the child had developed. Without being beautiful, she was strong and commanded her older sisters so much that we used to call her the governess. It was also evident that she had the most genius among the sisters.[6]

While Josephine was too sick and delirious to be interested in anything anymore (not even her children), Therese was excited to note how "her" Minona had developed.

* * *

But … there was also Beethoven, who must have heard about it (probably from Therese):

> [When] Stackelberg was in Vienna with Minona, Beethoven talked continually about a woman whose husband might become suspicious that one of his children, the one with musical talent, might be Beethoven's. There is in fact evidence that Minona was musical (Steblin 2007, p. 180).

This was based on the following entry in Beethoven's Conversation Book of mid December 1819 by his friend Oliva:

> Because you are always talking about that woman, the husband should recognize among his children **yours** as the one, who possesses musical talent.[7]

"That woman": Did Beethoven mention her name? Certainly not (otherwise Oliva could have referred to her). Most definitely, Beethoven kept his silence. But the knowledge that his daughter Minona was nearby – for the first time after six years – must have stirred him up so much that he could not refrain from making a few remarks about a child of his by an unknown woman in a conversation with Oliva (who did not know him well, and in any case like everybody else knew **nothing** about Josephine). We may also assume that Beethoven could trust Oliva (who handled his delicate financial affairs) not to make a fuss about the matter.

* * *

Josephine concluded the year by writing a farewell letter to her sister Therese that was full of bitterness:
> It really seems to me that in your abundance you do not see the dark shadows over our life. You know nothing of the dark hours that are our companions every day. ... An unusually harsh fate is our lot – Modesty and self esteem must be silenced. A wide gulf is between us. The mother's heart has no sympathy for her child – the sister's love is extinguished – profane reality is triumphant – here four children and a mother are wailing – and there, parties are the order of the day – They seek reasons not to believe – what is. – Farewell – even departing, dying, I will love **those** who hate me.[8]

Therese, as the older sister, could not resist the urge to castigate her:
> You are dying, my noble soul – out of obstinacy and a wrong view of life and virtue – you are dying by your own choice, and thus you are fulfilling your fate ... I know that no one can help you if you do not help yourself – namely by submitting to the law of necessity. ... Therefore, not our hearts are separated, but our views; your **view** is going to kill you. ... You know that I would lay down my life in every sense of the word to save you.[9]

---

[1] "... ein ungewöhnlich hartes Schicksal ist unser Loos ... Eine weite Kluft liegt zwischen uns. Der Mutter Herz hat keinen Anklang für ihr Kind – die Schwesterliebe ist erloschen." (Josephine to Therese, December 1819, in Tellenbach 1983, p. 187.)

[2] "Fritz Deym, der Sohn, hatte nichts gelernt ... und wollte nichts lernen. Er zeigte Lust zum Militär – der Mutter, die schon viel bettlägerig war, ein Gräuel." (Therese's Memoirs, in La Mara 1909, p. 105.)

[3] "Sie sollen unser Schutz sein und sind auf Commando gegen ihr eignes Volk!" (Therese's Memoirs, in La Mara 1909, p. 106.)

[4] "Franz war eisern entschlossen, keine Opfer mehr für Josephinen ... zu bringen." (Tellenbach 1983, p. 190.)

[5] "O Mutter, wie grausam, wie unbillig verfährst du mit uns, wie gewissenlos! Das Mutterherz, welches **ein** Kind vorzieht in der Austheilung, wo nur Recht und Gerechtigkeit herrschen soll, ist von der Gottheit verworfen. Zitterst du nicht vor der Reue auf dem Sterbebett?" (Therese's Diary, 1818–19, in La Mara 1920, p. 85.)

145

[6] "Nach 2 ½ Jahren kömmt endlich Stackelberg mit der nun schon sechsjährigen Minona und ihren Schwestern nach Wien. Merkwürdig hatte sich das Kind entwickelt. Ohne schön zu sein, war sie stark und imponierte dermaßen ihren ältern Schestern, daß wir sie immer die Gouvernante nannten. Es zeigte sich auch später, daß sie das meiste Genie unter den Schwestern hatte." (Therese's Memoirs, in La Mara 1909, p. 105.)

[7] "Oliva: Weil Sie immer von der Frau sprechen, so wird der Gemahl an jenem seine[r] Kinder das Musiktalent besitzt **Ihr** Kind erkennen." (Conversation Book, mid December 1819, in Steblin 2007, p. 179.)

[8] "Mir scheint wirklich, daß du in deinem Überfluß die dunkeln Schatten unsres Lebens gerne übersiehst. Du weißt nichts von den trüben Stunden[,] die Gefährten jedes unsrer Tage [sind.] – ... ein ungewöhnlich hartes Schicksal ist unser Loos – Bescheidenheit und Selbstgefühl g[e]bieten zu schweigen. Eine weite Kluft liegt zwischen uns. Der Mutter Herz hat keinen Anklang für ihr Kind – die Schwesterliebe ist erloschen – Profane Wirklichkeit triumphiert – Hier jammern 4 Kinder und eine Mutter – und dort sind Feste an der Tagesordnung – Man sucht Gründe, um nicht zu glauben – was ist[.] – Lebt wohl – auch scheidend, sterbend, werde ich **die** Lieben, die mich hassen." (Josephine to Therese, December 1819, in Tellenbach 1983, p. 187.)

[9] "Du stirbst edle Seele – aus Eigensinn, aus falscher Ansicht des Lebens u. der Tugend – du stirbst u. erfüllst dadurch dein selbstgewähltes Loos; ... ich weiß daß dir kein Mensch helfen kann, wenn du dir nicht selbst hilfst – nehmlich dadurch daß du dich dem Gesetz der nothwendigkeit ... unterwirfst. ... Nicht die Herzen sind also getrennt, aber die Ansichten; deine **Ansicht** tödtet dich. ... Du weißt daß ich meine existence in jedem Sinn des Wortes hingebe[,] um dich zu retten." (Therese to Josephine, 27 December 1819, in Tellenbach 1983, p. 187 f.)

> *No one can help! ... only One*
> *Man, but He must not know!*[1]

1820: Final Illness

The split in the family was by now final and irreparable:

> Josephine was too proud to ask her mother once more to help her.[2]

All Therese could do was to lament her fate:

> My sister is passing away in fear and grief! I cannot save her![3]
>
> Josephine, my high-spirited sister became weaker and weaker ... nervous consumption was setting in – and she was snatched away from us, the beautiful woman.[4]
>
> Her fate was extremely tragic.[5]

Exasperated, she wrote to Josephine:

> At last, I must believe that you are really insane!! ... and if you perish this time, it happens just as I foresaw three years ago.[6]

Towards the end of the year, already on her deathbed, Josephine wrote to her son Fritz:

> My soul has been longing only for matters of the Spirit, and above all I will not fail in faithfulness ... She who lived only for her loved ones, may also die for them, share the last penny with her children...
>
> If your grandmother does not send me the so often requested 10 Marks [200 Gulden] before the New Year, then I cannot tell what the outcome will be – in the worst case, I have calculated that our assets will be gone in January 1821, and not enough will be left to cover even the most basic necessities for a decent living. My sufferings and my exertions have been too much for me to cope with, for a long time, as you know.[7]

Once again, and for the last time, she exclaims her sacrifice for the love of her children.

Therese expressed her desperation about Josephine's final days:
> My sister is perishing in fear and grief! I cannot save her! ... I am shackled in body and soul ... and finally, everything is rotting and breaking down because no one can help – ! ... only One Man, but He must not know, and One Woman – She knows already![8]

"Only One Man"? Could that have been Beethoven? Because – "He **must not** know"! And the "One Woman", who knew only too well (but did not care), must have been her mother...

* * *

Beethoven (who was actually doing well financially) kept bugging his friend Franz Brentano, asking him for more money:
> My circumstances are so tough and pressing ... though I am not to blame for this, thank God. It is my excessive devotion to others.[9]

One might think his "devotion" to his nephew Karl could be the main reason for this (but then he could have said so – the Brentanos knew about his nephew). However, it seems that he might have sent money – secretly – to Josephine, via a straw man:
> On 17 December, he thanked Artaria [the publisher] for an advance of 150 Gulden and at the same time asked for a further one hundred and fifty.[10]
>
> I beg you very much, please, do not delay the matter assigned to you. The man is ill, he is living in the Adlergasse ... opposite Count Deym's house.[11]

It was too late.

---

[1] "... niemand helfen kann – ! ... nur Einer, doch der darfs nicht wissen!" (Therese's Diary, 1820, in Tellenbach 1983, p. 194.)

[2] "Josephine war zu stolz, die Mutter selbst noch einmal um Hilfe anzugehen." (Tellenbach 1983, p. 192.)

[3] "Meine Schwester vergeht in Angst u. Kummer! ich kann sie retten nicht!" (Therese's Diary, 1920, in Tellenbach 1983, p. 193 f.)

[4] "Josephine, meine geistvolle Schwester ... wurde schwächer und schwächer ... die Nervenschwindsucht bildete sich aus – und sie ward uns entrissen, die herrliche Frau." (Therese's Memoirs, in La Mara 1909, p. 110 f.)

[5] "Ihr Loos war höchst tragisch." (Therese's Diary, 1820, in Tellenbach 1983, p. 183.)

[6] "Zuletzt muß ich auch noch glauben du seist wirklich verrükt!! ... u. wenn du dießmal zu Grunde gehst[,] so geschieht nur etwas, daß ich 3 Jahre vorausahnde." (Therese to Josephine, 18 November 1820, in Tellenbach 1983, p. 191 f.)

[7] "Es sehnt mein Gemüth sich ... nur allein nach den Gütern des Geistes u. vor allem an Treue soll es mir nicht gebrechen ... Wer leben mag für die seinigen, soll auch für sie sterben[,] den letzten Pfennig mit ihren Kindern theilen ... Wenn unsere Gr[oß]M[utter] mir bis zum neuen Jahre die so oft gebetenen 10 M[ark] nicht sendet[,] so kan[n] ich für keinen Ausgang stehen – im entgegengesetzten Falle ist meine Rechnung so gestellt, daß wir im Januar 1821 nicht nur das Vermögen geendet[,] sondern [nicht einmal] einen sicheren, zur Nothdurft anständigen Unterhalt haben werden. Mein Leid und meine Anstrengungen überfordern wie Du weißt schon lange das Maß meiner Kräfte." (Josephine to Fritz, end of 1820, in Tellenbach 1983, p. 193.)

[8] "Meine Schwester vergeht in Angst u. Kummer! ich kann sie retten nicht! ... Ich bin gefesselt an Leib u. Seele ... u. endlich bricht es morsch zusammen da niemand helfen kann – ! ... nur Einer, doch der darfs nicht wissen u. Eine – die weiß es schon!" (Therese's Diary, 1820, in Tellenbach 1983, p. 193 f.)

[9] "Meine Lage ist dermalen hart und bedrängt; ... schuld bin ich, Gott sei dank, nicht daran. Meine zu große Hingebung für andere ist es." (Beethoven to Franz Brentano, 28 November 1820, in Tellenbach 1983, p. 194.)

[10] "Am 17. Dezember dankte er Artaria für einen Vorschuß von 150 Gulden und bat zugleich um weitere einhundertfünfzig." (Tellenbach 1983, p. 194.)

[11] "Ich bitte Sie recht sehr, die Ihnen übertragene Angelegenheit nicht aufzuschieben. Der Mann ist krank, wohnt in der Adlergasse ... gegenüber dem gräflich Deymschen Haus." (Beethoven to Artaria, 17 December 1820, in Tellenbach 1983, p. 194.)

> *Beethoven! Josephine's intimate friend, her soul mate! They were born for each other.*[1]

1821: Death and Oblivion

Therese remembered the final illness and death of her sister Josephine:

> She developed nervous consumption. She suffered from want, was lacking food and assistance of any kind – and she was torn away from us, this wonderful woman, who even on the edge of the abyss was playing with flowers, like a naïve child. My sister, so much loved by me, had been everything to me: Friend, Mother, Example, Leader![2]

* * *

Josephine von Brunsvik died on 31 March 1821 in her own home, only accompanied by Viky, her oldest daughter. She was buried without any ceremony at Währing cemetery.

> No memorial stone marks her grave ... Once again, the Brunsvik family has applied their *damnatio memoriae* with full severity. Exactly six years later, Breuning and Schindler would choose there, "where he always liked to stay", a burial place for Beethoven.[3]

She was to be forgotten almost like she never existed. Except by one man, who "always liked to stay" at her grave.

But no one ever knew why.

* * *

At the beginning of the year 1821, Ludwig fell seriously ill with rheumatic fever; by July, hardly recovered, he developed jaundice. In the autumn, Beethoven suffered the ignominy of being arrested as a vagrant and taken to a police station just outside Vienna where he was identified on the following morning by Herzog, the musical director in Wiener Neustadt. The policemen could not believe that this man, who looked like a tramp, was the famous composer Beethoven, as he repeatedly claimed!

Even his musical output had a low point. But the most remarkable composition of this year was the Piano Sonata #31 in *A flat major* Op. 110, clearly a Requiem for Josephine (Tellenbach 1983, p. 259 f.). It was originally planned to be dedicated to Antonie Brentano (Goldschmidt 1977, p. 118), whose husband Franz had generously supported Beethoven with money.

Beethoven may have used some of this money to keep Josephine going – until the bitter end.

* * *

Twenty years later, Therese reflected in her Diary about Beethoven:
> How unhappy, with such intellectual talent. At the same time Josephine was unhappy! *Le mieux est l'ennemi du bien* – both together they would have been happy (perhaps). What he needed was a wife, that's for sure.[4]

"Perhaps" indeed. The saddest irony of their tragic lives is, that by not being together as a married couple, they avoided a lot of trouble they might have caused each other, as they were both difficult personalities. Who knows how they might have got along...

At least Ludwig was able to sublimate the loss of his beloved (in 1812), after a long drought in his productivity that lasted nearly six years (the "Diary Years"), when he had to remind himself repeatedly to concentrate on his art. And he concluded his life as an artist – especially after Josephine's death – by composing his greatest works: The Ninth Symphony, the *Missa Solemnis* and – after a break of 13 years – the last five (and most outstanding) of his 16 String Quartets. These compositions transcended and surpassed everything that had ever been heard before, and they were justifiably called "absolute Music".

While Beethoven, from humble beginnings, rose to become a world star, albeit at pains of becomng deaf and isolated, without a loving wife, and increasingly ill and suffering, Josephine's life had started on the bright side: She was born as a wealthy Countess, brought up and educated according to the standards of her class, and, after marrying the (supposedly) wealthy Count Deym, she was looking forward to "life as a ball" – with star pianist Beethoven, among others, providing the entertainment.

Or so it seemed. Josephine's major "fault" was certainly – and ultimately, tragically – her beauty, her charm and her grace. Men who saw her fell for her. We know this of Deym, Wolkenstein, Stackelberg, Andrian – all fell in love with her at first sight. Beethoven, too, initially; only he had to suppress his feelings for five years, and then he could express himself only in secret love letters – and in music. Ludwig & Josephine's love was **a love made in Heaven**, built on mutual **spiritual** understanding, from the very beginning.

And on **Music**.

Both struggled – each in their own idiosyncratic way – to come to terms with the implications: Josephine was from the beginning "enthusiastic" about his music; Ludwig was not so much attracted by her "sex appeal" as by **all** her characteristics as a **person**, by her "whole Self". **Music** was the language by which he expressed himself, the language they both understood.

And – their love was always a **secret**; in fact, this was a precondition. It was always their mutual understanding that a "normal" union via marriage was not (and would never be) possible. And any publicity (or even gossip) would have been fatal. Thus, it was really only sister Therese, who knew everything. And, most likely, her brother Franz with whom Beethoven was "per Du". But, strangely, almost all the letters between Franz (as well as Therese) and Beethoven are lost, also all – if any – entries by Franz in conversation books!

* * *

In 1848, Therese reminisced:
> I was so lucky to have been acquainted with Beethoven, intimately and intellectually, for so many years! Josephine's intimate friend, her soul mate! They were born for each other, and if both were still alive, they would be united.[5]

[1] "Beethoven! ... Josephinens Haus- und Herzensfreund! Sie waren für einander geboren..." (Therese's Diary, March 1848, in Goldschmidt 1977, p. 296.)

[2] "Die Nervenschwindsucht bildete sie aus. Sie litt Mangel, entbehrte Nahrungsmittel und Hilfe aller Art – und sie wurde uns entrissen, diese herrliche Frau, die noch am Rande des Abgrunds wie ein unbefangenes Kind mit Blumen spielte. Meine so sehr geliebte Schwester war mir alles gewesen: Freundin, Mutter, Vorbild, Leiterin!" (Therese's Memoirs, in La Mara 1909, p. 111.)

[3] "Kein Gedenkstein bezeichnet ihr Grab ... Auch hier hat die Familie Brunswick ihre *damnatio memoriae* in aller Strenge betätigt. Genau sechs Jahre später wählten Breuning und Schindler dort, 'wo er stets gern weilte', eine Grabstätte für Beethoven." (Tellenbach 1983, p. 198.)

[4] "Wie unglüklich bei so grossen Geistesgaben. Zu gleicher Zeit war Josephine unglüklich! *Le mieux est l'enemi du bien* [The best is the enemy of the good] – sie beide zusammen wären glüklich gewesen (vielleicht). Ihm hat eine Frau gefehlt[,] das ist gewiß." (Therese's Diary, 22 December 1846, in Goldschmidt 1977, p. 296.)

[5] "Ich Glückliche hatte Beethovens intimen, geistigen Umgang so viele Jahre! Josephinens Haus- und Herzensfreund! Sie waren für einander geboren[,] und lebten beide noch, hätten sie sich vereint." (Therese's Diary, March 1848, in Goldschmidt 1977, p. 296.)

Reflections

> *What yearning with tears for you – you – you my life – my everything!*[1]

The Letter

The so-called "Letter to the Immortal Beloved" Beethoven wrote on 6/7 July 1812 has puzzled many ever since it was discovered after his death by Schindler, together with the letter from 1802, to be called the "Heiligenstadt Testament", and a brief note about "the M", made in 1807.

This note from 1807, expressing Beethoven's despair about the impossibility of finding the one who is "**allowed**" to be his when faced down by the stern look of the mother ("the M") of his beloved Josephine, together with the two long "letters" from 1802 and 1812, most aptly describe his state of mind at three decisive stages during this central decade of his life.

Incidentally, the "Heiligenstadt Testament" was also written like a letter (to his two brothers), but obviously never sent. Never meant to be sent, that is. Because it was really a "letter to himself", or a diary note, written in letter form. Like the note about "the M", on a sheet of paper.

The "Testament" of 1802, because of its character, was always understood not to have been a letter. The same applies to the draft letter to the "Immortal Beloved", which is really a misnomer, as he does **not** address her like this (at the beginning) – the term "Immortal Beloved" appears only once, almost like an aside, in the third part of this document. It probably stuck because it was unique in Beethoven's vocabulary.

The term by which Beethoven did address his "Immortal Beloved" first of all (at the very beginning of the Letter and again towards the end) was

My angel.

And this is really where we should start our search (or "hunt") for this – supposedly – "mysterious" woman. Schindler (1840) thought she was Julie Guicciardi – probably after talking to Franz von Brunsvik, who was only too happy to distract any suspicion away from Josephine (Tellenbach 1983, p. 17).
Therese immediately knew that such a letter (it was in three parts) could not have been written to Julie ["Giulietta"]:
> Three letters by Beethoven, allegedly to Giulietta. Could they be hoaxes?

And soon after she noted in her Diary in no uncertain terms:
> Three letters by Beethoven ... they must have been to Josephine whom he loved passionately.

And to no one else.

However, Therese's Diary was never fully published (except for the first part in a Hungarian book),[4] and her memoirs when published (in German)[5] did not mention anything about the love between Josephine and Beethoven. And his love letters were kept under lock until 1957.[6] **No one outside the Brunsvik family ever knew anything** – the only exceptions were Beethoven's close friends Lichnowsky and Zmeskall, who never said a word about Ludwig & Josephine.

The mystery remained until 1920 when La Mara (pseudonym of Ida Maria Lipsius) published a short book based on documents she discovered.[7] Her conclusion was that Josephine was most likely the "Immortal Beloved", based on the secret dedication of the song "An die Hoffnung" [To Hope] and letters by Charlotte and Therese that expressed concern about Ludwig seeing Josephine so often alone.

However, La Mara still thought the Letter was written around 1806/7. After it had been established that the Letter must have been written in 1812 (based on watermarks), it was Kaznelson (1954), who added one and one together to find out that it was indeed two: He concluded that Josephine's daughter Minona, born nine months later, must have been Beethoven's child. Because, Stackelberg had been away.

This was – or rather, should have been – resoundingly confirmed, when Schmidt-Görg published 13 of the so far unknown love letters in 1957. However, he incorrectly concluded that the love affair was over in 1807, due to Josephine's apparent (but clearly forced) withdrawal.

Not only did the last exchange of love letters actually occur in 1809 (when Josephine was already pregnant with Stackelberg's first child), maybe even as late as 1810, but it was in these last letters that Beethoven emphasized in particular and repeatedly his "eternal faithfulness" to Josephine – despite (or because of) her withdrawal!

The very act of contemplating even the possibility that Beethoven's moral stance was such that he did not care about Josephine dumping him, but just went on to date some other girlfriend, as if nothing had happened, and then **to write a Letter like this to someone else – this is beyond comprehension**.[8]

True, he was briefly in love with Julie Guicciardi, but he knew only too well that he would never be able to marry her, and he got over her marriage to Count Gallenberg very quickly. (And he threw in the dedication of his "Moonlight" Sonata to her, for good measure.)

True, he made a clumsy proposal to Teresa von Malfatti (which her noble family would not have accepted anyway). He soon realized that it was a "foolish" step – really just an impulsive act out of frustration after Josephine got married again.

And true, indeed, Ludwig's love of Josephine – especially after she had become a widow and was "available" – was unlikely, no, **impossible**, ever to result in marriage. Like in the case of Julie, he could never hope to marry a Countess. Not only was the Brunsvik family's consent not to be expected – his fame as a composer and his sincere friendship with brother Franz notwithstanding – but Josephine would have been forced to give up the custodianship of her children (whom Beethoven also liked very much).

This was known to both, and they were all too painfully aware of it. That is why they made every attempt (successfully, as it turned out) to keep their relationship **secret**. And it is for that very reason – a "normal" love relationship, with marriage as the legal basis and pre-condition for physical union, being unobtainable – that Ludwig and Josephine both drifted, together, into the realm of the Spirits. A world where they both felt at home, with a language they both understood – the world and the language of **Music**. In this world, and in the next.

Their love was – now and forever – an "edifice in **Heaven**".

That is why Ludwig repeatedly emphasized his inability to express his feelings in words – it was only in **Music**, which was willing to obey him, where he was the undisputed master. He knew it, and so did she.

They understood each other – in Music.

That is why Ludwig never bothered to publish a composition with a dedication to her – not only was there no need, as both knew exactly which compositions were written for Josephine. It would also have been a violation of their **agreement about total secrecy**.

That is why Ludwig assured Josephine that it was not the "drive to the opposite sex" that attracted him to her, but her "whole Self with all its characteristics".

They loved each other as like-minded spirits.

That is why Josephine kindly warned him not to love her too "sensually" – we may assume that he obtained (or maybe just asked for) a kiss from her, but she did not want to go any further, to avoid an unwanted (and most inconvenient) pregnancy.

Of course, in the intense situation that surrounded their unexpected encounter on 3 July 1812, Josephine had just been abandoned by her husband, and she was extremely desperate. But after three days of reflection, Beethoven became slowly aware that a lasting union with her in this world was more and more unlikely, if not impossible, after all.[9]

Theirs was now, finally and irrevocably, a love to be transcended (for him, via music) – until he could send his "soul embraced by you into the realm of the spirits".

Several compositions (especially many of those that were conspicuously left undedicated) can be identified as having been composed specifically for Josephine or with her in mind (see the more comprehensive discussions in Tellenbach 1983, pp. 205–267; and Goldschmidt 1977, pp. 343–431):[10]

-   The 3 Piano Sonatas Op. 31 (1801–1802) were the first of Beethoven's major works without dedication (he sent the printed autograph straightaway to Josephine).
-   In 1803, he thought it appropriate to publish the Song in *G major* "Ich liebe dich so wie du mich" [I love you as much as you love me] WoO 123, a.k.a. "Zärtliche Liebe" [Tender Love], composed in 1795. Undedicated.

- The *Andante favori* in *F major* WoO 57, "Josephine's Theme": he sent this to her together with a love letter ("here – **your – your *Andante***"). Undedicated.
- The Piano Sonata in *F major* Op. 54 was without dedication, and the Sonata in *F minor* Op. 57 "Appassionata" was dedicated to Franz von Brunsvik. The sketches of both are mixed up with those of the Opera *Leonore* (Le–o–no–re = Jo–se–phi–ne), composed in 1804 after she became a widow.
- In 1807, Josephine's withdrawal was reflected in four versions of the Song "Sehnsucht" [Yearning] WoO 134, and in 1808, the Cello Sonata in *A major* Op. 69 with the heading "Inter Lacrimas et Luctum" [Amidst Tears and Sorrow].
- In 1809, the Piano Sonata in *F sharp major* Op. 78 was dedicated to Therese, and in the Piano Sonata in *E flat major* "The Farewell" Op. 81a he mourned her absence and expressed his joy at her return (and a brief rekindling of Hope again).
- In 1810, after her marriage to Stackelberg, the Song "Wonne der Wehmut" [The Bliss of Melancholy] Op. 83#1. And the String Quartet #11 in *F minor* "Quartetto serioso" Op. 95 was so personal that it would not be published until 1816, after Beethoven had met Josephine again, for the last time, and then he dedicated this composition to Nikolaus Zmeskall – the man who had been their common friend since their very first meeting in May 1799.
- The Symphony #8 in *F major* Op. 93 of 1812, exuberant and full of joy, was the only symphony without dedication; similar feelings are expressed in the last Violin Sonata in *G major* Op. 96.
- In 1817, the Song in *D major* "Resignation" WoO 149 – after their last meeting – all too clearly expressed the situation (Josephine being increasingly, indeed mortally ill). Undedicated.

It was only in 1818 – when the aftermath of 1812 was finally absorbed – that Beethoven found his footing again and embarked on the composition of the three major, gigantic works of his entire life: The "Hammerklavier" Sonata in *B flat major* Op. 106 (completed in 1818), and then the Symphony #9 in *D minor* Op. 125, and his greatest work, the *Missa Solemnis* Op. 123.

In between, the saddest of news, of Josephine's early death in 1821, prompted Beethoven to compose the Piano Sonata in *A flat major* Op. 110 as her Requiem – and to remove the original dedication.

It was originally dedicated to Antonie Brentano.

* * *

In order to dissect this now so famous "Letter to the Immortal Beloved", we need to analyze the **words and phrases** being used, and we have to recall what Beethoven wrote only a few years before to Josephine in (at least) 15 love letters (and several known letters she wrote to him),[11] and the circumstances that surrounded their relationship, from the beginning until July 1812.

The relevant text of this letter will now be given, in the original German (see also Goldschmidt 1977, pp. 21–23; photocopy of the original opp. p. 240) on the left, and in English on the right, immediately followed by some comments (indicated by subscript references).

Mein Engel[1], mein alles[2], mein Ich[3]. –	My angel[1], my everything[2], my very self[3]. –
nur einige Worte heute, und zwar mit Bleijstift (mit deinem)[4] ... warum dieser tiefe Gram, wo die Nothwendigkeit spricht – Kann unsre Liebe anders bestehn als durch Aufopferungen, durch nicht alles verlangen[5]. Kannst du es ändern, daß du nicht ganz mein, ich nicht ganz dein bin ... blick in die schöne Natur[6] und beruhige dein Gemüth über das müßende[7] – die Liebe fordert alles[8] und ganz mit Recht, so ist es **mir mit dir, dir mit mir** – nur vergißt du so leicht, daß ich **für mich und für dich** leben muß, wären wir ganz vereinigt du würdest dieses schmerzliche	only a few words today, and with a pencil (with yours)[4] ... why this deep grief, where necessity speaks – Can our love exist but by sacrifices, by not demanding everything[5]. Can you change it, that you are not completely mine, that I am not completely yours ... Look upon beautiful Nature[6] and calm your mind about what must be[7] – Love demands everything and completely[8] with good reason, that is how it is **for me with you, and for you with me** – Only you forget too easily, that I must live **for myself and for you** as well, if we were wholly united, you would not feel

eben so wenig als ich empfinden – meine Reise war schrecklich … Esterhazi₉ hatte … dasselbe Schicksal ... nun geschwind zum innern vom aüßern, wir werden unß wohl bald sehn₁₀, auch heute kann ich dir meine Bemerkungen nicht mittheilen, welche ich während dieser einigen Tage über mein Leben machte ... die Brust ist voll dir viel zu sagen₁₁ – Ach – Es gibt Momente, wo ich finde daß die Sprache₁₂ noch gar nichts ist – erheitre dich – bleibe mein treuer einziger schatz₁₃, mein alles₁, wie ich dir[;] das übrige müßen die Götter schicken, was für unß sejn muß und sejn soll. – dein treuer₁₅ ludwig. –	this as painfully, just as little as I would – my journey was terrible … Esterhazi₉ had … the same problems ... Now quickly from the exterior to the interior. We will probably see each other soon₁₀, only, today I cannot convey to you my observations which I made during these few days about my life ... My heart is full with so much to tell you₁₁ – Oh – There are moments when I feel that language₁₂ is nothing at all – Cheer up – Remain my faithful₁₃ only darling, my everything₁₄, as I for you; the rest is up to the Gods, what must be for us and what is in store for us. – your faithful₁₅ ludwig –
Abends Montags am 6ten Juli –	Monday evening on 6 July –
Du leidest mein theuerstes Wesen₁₆ – eben jetzt nehme ich wahr … die einzigen Täge wo die Post von hier nach K.₁₇ geht – du leidest₁₈ – Ach, wo ich bin, bist du mit mir, mit mir und dir rede ich[,] mache daß ich mit dir leben kann₁₉, welches Leben!!!! so!!!! ohne dich … wie du mich auch liebst – stärker liebe ich dich doch₂₀ – doch nie verberge dich vor mir₂₁ – Gute Nacht ... Ach Gott	You are suffering, you my dearest creature₁₆ – Only now do I realize … the only days when the mail is delivered to K.₁₇ – You are suffering₁₈ – Oh, wherever I am, you are with me, I talk to myself and to you[,] arrange [it] that I can live with you₁₉, what a life!!!! as it is!!!! without you ... As much as you love me – I love you even more deeply₂₀, but – but never hide yourself from

– so nah! so weit!₂₂ ist es nicht ein wahres Him[m]els-Gebäude unsre Liebe₂₃ – aber auch so fest, wie die Veste des Himmels₂₄. –	me₂₁ – Good night ... Oh God – so near! so far!₂₂ Is not our love a true edifice in Heaven₂₃ – but also as firm as the firmament₂₄. –
Guten Morgen am 7ten Juli –	Good morning on 7 July –
schon im Bette drängen sich die Ideen zu dir meine Unsterbliche Geliebte₂₅, hier und da freudig, dann wieder traurig. Vom Schicksaale abwartend, ob es unß erhört – leben kann ich entweder nur ganz mit dir oder gar nicht₂₆, ja ich habe beschlossen in der Ferne so lange herum zu irren₂₇, bis ich in deine Arme fliegen kann, meine Seele von dir umgeben in's Reich der Geister schicken kann₂₈ – ja leider muß es sejn₂₉ – du wirst dich fassen um so mehr, da du meine Treue gegen dich kennst₃₀, nie eine andre kann mein Herz besizen, nie – nie₃₁ –	while still in bed my thoughts turn towards you my Immortal Beloved₂₅, now and then happy, then sad again, waiting whether fate might answer us – I can only live either wholly with you or not at all₂₆, yes, I have resolved to stray about in the distance₂₇, until I can fly into your arms, and send my soul embraced by you into the realm of the Spirits₂₈ – Yes, unfortunately it must be₂₉ – You will compose yourself, all the more since you know my faithfulness₃₀ to you, never can another own my heart, never – never₃₁ –
O Gott warum sich entfernen müßen, was man so liebt und doch ist mein Leben in V[ienna] so wie jezt ein kümmerliches Leben – Deine Liebe macht mich zum glücklichsten und zum unglücklichsten zugleich₃₂ - in meinen Jahren jezt bedürfte ich einiger Einförmigkeit[,] Gleichheit des Lebens – kann diese bei unserm Verhältniße bestehn?₃₃	O God why do I have to separate from someone whom I love so much, and yet my life in V[ienna] as it is now is a miserable life – Your love makes me at once most happy and most unhappy₃₂ – At my age, I would now need some conformity[,] regularity in my life – can this exist in our relationship?₃₃

–	–
Engel$_{34}$ ... sej ruhig, nur durch Ruhiges beschauen unsres Dasejns können wir unsern Zweck zusam[m]en zu leben erreichen – sej ruhig$_{35}$ – liebe mich – heute – gestern$_{36}$ – Welche Sehnsucht mit Thränen nach dir – dir – dir – mein Leben – mein alles$_{37}$ – leb wohl – o liebe mich fort – verken[ne] nie das treuste$_{38}$ Herz deines Geliebten L. ewig dein ewig mein ewig unß$_{39}$.	Angel$_{34}$ ... be patient, only through quiet contemplation of our existence can we achieve our purpose to live together – be calm$_{35}$ – love me – today – yesterday$_{36}$ – What yearning with tears for you – you – you my life – my everything$_{37}$ – farewell – oh continue to love me – never misjudge the most faithful$_{38}$ heart of your Beloved L. Forever thine forever mine forever us$_{39}$.

Observations:

[1]   "My **angel**": The love letter by Beethoven to Josephine in April 1805 concludes with "leb wohl **Engel** – meines Herzens" [farewell **angel** – of my heart], which is also the only time (before 1812) that he uses the intimate "**Du**" form! The following letter in April/Mai 1805 concludes with "leben sie Wohl **Engel** meines Herzens" [farewell **angel** of my heart], this time sticking again to the conventional "Sie" form of addressing.

[2]   "my **everything**": "mein **alles**" can also be translated as "my **all**". In his love letter at the beginning of 1805, he calls her "mein **Alles** meine Glückseeligkeit" [my **everything**, my happiness] and "Meine Erquickung – mein **Alles**" [my solace – my **everything**], concluding that she is "**everything**" to him. In his letter from 20 September 1807, he asserts "liebe J. **alles** – **alles** für sie" [dear J. **everything** – **everything** for you].

[3]   "my very **self**": "Mein **Ich**" can also be translated as "My **Self**" or "My Other **Self**" (or perhaps "My Ego" or "My **Alter Ego**"). It is yet another variation on the theme of Ludwig & Josephine being "like-minded spirits".

[4]   "with a **pencil** (with yours)": It has been noted that around this time Josephine had started to use a **pencil** for writing her diary (Steblin 2007, p. 162). It is intriguing to think that the very pencil with which she wrote of herself wanting to be an "**Angel**" (see the quotation at the beginning of this book) was then given by her to Ludwig.

[5]   "why this deep **grief**, where **necessity** speaks – can our love exist but by **sacrifices**, by not demanding everything": Beethoven refers to their love relationship

that since its beginning in 1799, and especially since it entered its most intense phase in 1804/5, could never be consummated (at least not in marriage). Among the **sacrifices** they had to make was the need to keep their love **secret** all the time.

~6~ "look upon beautiful **Nature**": A reminder of the times they had spent together on summer holidays in the countryside. Beethoven's ***Pastoral*** Symphony (of 1807/8, begun in 1803) in particular can rightly be described as Josephine's.

~7~ "calm your mind about what **must** be": "What **Must** Be" would become a recurring theme in Beethoven's life – and it is also reflected in his music (see the note he wrote on the fourth movement of his last String Quartet #16 in *F major* Op. 135: "**Must** It Be? – It **Must** Be!"). Interpreted as his defiantly coming to grips with a merciless fate. (Etc.)

~8~ "love demands **everything and completely**": Perhaps the clearest allusion to the fact that on the night of 3 July 1812 their love was finally consummated.

~9~ "my journey was terrible ... – **Esterhazi** had ... the same problems": Prince Paul Anton Esterházy was of course well-known to his fellow Hungarians, the Brunsviks. Beethoven's casually referring to him clearly indicates that both writer and addressee knew him well. (The Mass in *C major* Op. 86 was first performed in the Esterházy castle in 1807.) This alone should rule out the possibility that Antonie Brentano (or anybody else) might have been the "Immortal Beloved", because even if she had known this name (**and** had known that Beethoven knew him), it is unlikely that Beethoven would have mentioned him in this casual manner.

~10~ "We will probably see each other soon": Here the German "wohl" is – given the context – more like a hopeful "maybe". It is like an appeal to arrange another meeting, but not at all certain at the time. Again this actually rules out Antonie Brentano (in particular): Even though Beethoven and the Brentanos were indeed to meet soon after (in Karlsbad), this had already been planned by both parties well ahead, and it is not at all clear why Beethoven should then express it here like a meeting he was **hoping** for but which could possibly **not** happen (as it did indeed in the case of Josephine, who most likely returned to Vienna immediately).

~11~ "Only, today I cannot convey to you my observations, which I made during these few days about my life ... My heart is full with so much to tell you": Again, with reference to the next hoped-for meeting, there is much left to be said.

~12~ "There are moments when I feel that **language** is nothing at all": In a letter of the first quarter of 1805, Beethoven complains "why is there no language expressing what is more than respect – far more than everything – which we can name – oh, who can call **you**, and not feel no matter how much he talks about you – that all this can hardly – reach **you** – – only in *music* – Oh, I am not too proud when I believe that notes are more willing to me than words – **you**, you, my everything, my happiness – Oh no – not even in **my musical notes** can I express it, even though nature gifted me with some talents in this respect, it is still too little for **you**." In his love letter of March/April 1805, Beethoven writes "what else I would like to tell you – how I am thinking of you – what I am feeling for you – but how weak, how paltry is this **language** – mine at least".

~13~ "Cheer up – **Remain** my **faithful only** darling": Ludwig mentions (appeals to) Josephine's faithfulness; to ask her to **"remain"** faithful clearly refers to a **pre-existing and long** relationship. It is therefore extremely unlikely to think of Antonie Brentano (or anybody else) to be perceived as "faithful" to Ludwig, after just a few months of (supposed) "intimate" acquaintance. More even than the preceding appeal to her being **and** remaining "faithful" – who else but Josephine could have been asked to remain his "**only**" darling? Unless, one postulates that Beethoven was insincere, a liar…

14 "my **everything**, as I for you": Or "my **all**", as before, repeated as yet another reminder of what used to be said in the earlier love letters, with the additional thought that he will remain equally faithful to her.

15 "your **faithful** Ludwig": It seems Beethoven first wanted to conclude this letter already on the morning of 6 July (signing off once more with his "faithfulness").

16 "You are **suffering**, you my dearest creature": Beethoven was only too aware of Josephine's desperation, and her illness (probably another reason why she wanted to go to a spa like Karlsbad or Franzenbrunn – as she had already planned at the beginning of the year).

17 "the only days when the mail is delivered to **K**.": "K" is most likely **Karlsbad** where Josephine probably said she wanted to go. It does not matter whether she actually went there (and managed to stay there without being registered which is not entirely impossible) or not – Beethoven did (most likely) not send the Letter, after all (or if he did, it could not be delivered, and he got it back). On the other hand, it is not conceivable that he would have attempted to send such a Letter to Antonie Brentano (who was on her way to Karlsbad, with husband and child), as they were soon to meet again in Karlsbad anyway. And what about the possibility that Antonie's husband could intercept such a letter? Is this really a likely scenario?

18 "you are **suffering**": The repetition indicates the importance of Josephine's misery and desperation, most likely increased by the fact that she could not be united with Ludwig, because of her children, and her financial situation (which in case of a divorce would have become even more disastrous). On the other hand, Antonie's situation was very comfortable, by comparison. She was soon after to return to Frankfurt, Brentano's hometown, and even though she often felt a little homesickness, at the time in question she was actually very much "in good hope" or "expecting": She had been pregnant for one month.

19 "Oh, wherever I am, you are with me, I talk to myself and to you[,] arrange [it] that I can live with you": it is up to Josephine to "arrange" a way to live together (by seeking a divorce). See Steblin (2007, p. 147, n. 2).

20 "as much as you love me – I love you even more deeply": Probably a hint that he did not stop loving her when she withdrew from him, a few years before.

21 "but never **hide** yourself from me": A very strong reminder that Ludwig had not forgotten Josephine's going into **hiding** when he tried to visit her in 1807. This alone should be sufficient to **prove** that she, and **only** she, must have been the addressee – **no other woman** could possibly be accused of having been "**hiding**" from him!

22 "Oh God – so **near**! so **far**!": A reminder that Ludwig and Josephine were both living in Vienna, but she was – metaphorically – "**far**" away from him, i.e., **unreachable**.

23 "Is not our love a true edifice in **Heaven**": Again an allusion to their love being possible only in the realm of the Spirits.

₂₄ "but also as **firm** as the firmament": In German, "fest wie die Veste des Himmels", via a wordplay (aptly translated as "firm like the firmament") another hint at the **eternal** (immortal) nature of their relationship.

₂₅ "while still in bed my thoughts turn towards you my **Immortal** Beloved": "**Unsterblich**" is also sometimes translated as "**Eternal**" (not quite correct as "immortality" has a beginning – birth – whereas "eternity" has neither beginning nor end). It is certainly not referring to the person endowed with this attribute (she died only too soon); rather it is Beethoven's love that is "**Immortal**". Meaning it will never die (and it never did). This alone should make it clear once again that **only one** woman could ever have been the object of such a love – to advocate any other woman as the addressee of this Letter presupposes that Ludwig's love of Josephine had indeed died. And to prove it!

₂₆ "I can only live either wholly with you or not at all": This is not a suicide note (as it is sometimes misinterpreted). It just means "I can only live either wholly with you or not at all **with you**". Meaning of course the sad fact that they had to continue living separately.

₂₇ "yes I have resolved to stray about in the distance": It seems that Beethoven made plans to travel, as stated again in the first entry of his "Diary" soon after.

₂₈ "until I can fly into your arms, and send my soul embraced by you into the realm of the Spirits": Once again the main theme of their "eternal" love, to be consummated eventually in the "realm of the Spirits".

₂₉ "yes unfortunately it **must** be": The "It **Must** Be"-theme once more.

₃₀ "you will compose yourself all the more since you know my **faithfulness** to you": Sure enough – she knew about this his pledge for at least eight years.

₃₁ "never can another own my heart, never – never": What else do we need to conclude that "eternal", "immortal" or "forever" relate to the future as well as to the past (and to **only one** woman)!

₃₂ "Your love makes me at once most happy and most unhappy": "Happy" because his love is reciprocated; "unhappy" because they cannot stay together.

₃₃ "at my age I would now need some conformity[,] regularity of my life – can this exist in our relationship?": Being now 41, he is missing the domesticity of married life…

₃₄ "**Angel**": That is how he calls her. And again, that is why we should call this document the "Letter to his **Angel**", because that is how it begins and how it is concluded, and it clearly shows the continuity with the previous 15 letters.

₃₅ "be patient – only through quiet contemplation of our existence can we achieve our purpose to live together – be calm": He tries to comfort her as she is clearly upset about the latest developments in her marriage.

₃₆ "love me – today – yesterday": "Yesterday" here is of course metaphorical, relating to earlier times of their love.

₃₇ "What **yearning** with tears for you – you – you my life – my **everything**": Indication that Ludwig had been waiting (hoping and longing) for this; again she is his "**everything**".

₃₈ "farewell – oh continue to love me – never misjudge the most **faithful** heart of your Beloved L.": As so often before, he stresses his **faithfulness** at the end of the letter.

[39]   "**Forever** thine – **forever** mine – **forever** us": This triad at the end matches the beginning of "My **angel**, my **everything**, my very **self**". And "Ewig" = "Forever" or "Eternally" – is it conceivable that such a pledge could be given to a person he knew or had been acquainted with for a short time, as opposed to Josephine, for whom he had languished for more than 10 years?

* * *

You can analyze this letter to death, but there is no way to escape the impression that the choice of words (including those deliberately signaling to the addressee what only they both knew about) is so similar to those of the previous 15 love letters (all to Josephine – there are no others), that even without any further corroboration one is forced to conclude that, even though not named, **only Josephine** could have been the "Immortal Beloved".

Let it be emphasized again, the woman addressed repeatedly in this letter as "My **Angel**" and "My **Everything**" must be the same as the recipient of the previous love letters. It is just not conceivable that Beethoven could have been driven to this choice of words and phrases with regard to any other woman with whom he had been acquainted, no matter how closely.

---

[1]   "Welche Sehnsucht mit Thränen nach dir – dir – dir – mein Leben – mein alles!" (Beethoven to Josephine?, 6/7 July 1812, draft, in Pichler 1994, p. 371 f.)

[2]   "Drei Briefe von Beethoven, angeblich an Giulietta. Sollten es Machwerke sein?" (Therese's Diary, 12 November 1840, in Tellenbach 1983, p. 15.) Given that Beethoven had briefly been in love with Julie ("Giulietta") Guicciardi (as revealed in his letter to Wegeler in 1801), and this was known at the time (to Therese and Franz at least) – if Therese ruled out the possibility that such a Letter allegedly to Julie must have been a "hoax", what might she have said if someone had suggested Beethoven's Letter was instead to one Antonie Brentano? Or to anybody else, for that matter? For more interesting details about "Giulietta", see Steblin (2009). As for Schindler (1940), he not only falsified but also destroyed letters and many conversation books, and his – still widely quoted – biography of Beethoven (the first one) is full of errors, mainly an attempt at self-aggrandizement.

[3]   "3 Briefe von Beethoven ... sie werden wohl an Josephine sein, die er leidenschaftlich geliebt hat." (Therese's Diary, 15 November 1840, in Goldschmidt 1977, p. 295.) The German term "wohl" in this context could also be rendered as "probably" or "certainly". However, it sounds very much as if Therese was pretty sure.

[4] Therese's Diary and other notes (in German and French), up to 1813, were first published by Czeke (1938), with a lengthy introduction in Hungarian. Marianne Czeke could not find a publisher for the second part which is now kept in Budapest and (on film) in the Beethoven-Archiv in Bonn. Rolland (1928) saw part of it and came close to identifying Josephine, but he then tended towards Therese. Kaznelson (1954) used Therese's Diary as a source, and sure enough, he came to the conclusion that the "Immortal Beloved" must have been Josephine. Goldschmidt, Tellenbach and Steblin also spent considerable time and effort to locate, examine and verify various documents (see Steblin 2007, p. 162).

[5] La Mara (1909) first published Therese's Memoirs, believing that she was the one. But later she became convinced, after analyzing letters she found in the Brunsvik estate, "that Josephine widowed Countess Deym was Beethoven's 'Immortal Beloved'." [… drängte sich mir die Überzeugung auf, daß … Josephine verwitwete Gräfin Deym die "unsterbliche Geliebte" Beethovens … sei.] (La Mara 1920, p. 1.) La Mara's valuable books are not only in German, but also printed in the old, difficult to read German Fraktur typeface.

[6] Beethoven's "13 Letters" were first kept in the estate of Fritz Deym in Nemischl, and after the Second World War they ended up in the Beethoven-Archiv in Bonn – well before 1957.

[7] La Mara found letters by the Brunsvik sisters in Charlotte's estate in Siebenbürgen (Romania), now lost.

[8] In the chapter about *Solomon*, we shall investigate in detail the claim that Antonie Brentano was the "Immortal Beloved" and the associated (lack of) corroberation.

[9] This is not to be misunderstood as Beethoven having given up all hope – on the contrary, the central theme of **"Hope"** stayed with him for at least another four or five years (also reflected in his music) until he finally gave in to Resignation. In the Letter of 1812, he was still expressing his intention to "wander around in the distance"…

[10] "Wherever one looks, one single continuous stream of emotions from Op. 96 to Op. 111!" [Wohin man blickt, ein einziger ununterbrochener Gefühlsstrom von op. 96 bis op. 111!] (Goldschmidt 1977, p. 376.)

[11] Schmidt-Görg (1957) published 13 love letters by Beethoven to Josephine, plus one note by Josephine that appears to be a copy of another letter by Beethoven (between what he numbered as letters 4 and 5). Another (the 14th or 15th) letter was later published by Schmidt-Görg (1969). See also Goldschmidt (1983), pp. 187–189.

There is no proof that Beethoven and Antonie met in Prague.[1]
There is still room for a reasonable doubt.[2]

The Wisdom of Solomon

Beethoven's so-called "Letter to the Immortal Beloved" appeared to many, even to this day, like
> an uncontrolled outburst of passionate feeling, dithyrambic in tone, confused in thought, ridden with conflicting emotions (Solomon 1972, p. 572).

Although there has been a lot of speculation, due to the lack of firm evidence, this Letter is obviously important for an assessment of Beethoven's life and personality. The stony silence that the Brunsvik family[4] maintained most of the time did not help either.

Therefore, when Maynard Solomon suggested in 1972 that Antonie Brentano could have been Beethoven's "Immortal Beloved", this was like dropping a bombshell. So far, no one had ever thought of her – even though, according to Solomon, the facts necessary to come up with this conclusion had been staring us in the face all along: She was in Prague and in Karlsbad at the time (like Beethoven), and she was acquainted with him, even on friendly terms. Although, unfortunately, there is **not a single document or letter by anyone** indicating that this relationship was ever anywhere close to what might be called "love", given the time and circumstances – apart, of course, from this one fateful Letter.

Solomon had first made a name for himself as a record producer, then as a Marxist writer,[5] and finally by publishing works about Mozart, Schubert and Beethoven – characterized by "bold" psychoanalytic speculations.[6] He won some acclaim for his works, mainly in North America but now increasingly in Europe as well, probably because those who initially praised his writings had little experience in conducting scholarly research in Europe, or indeed with foreign languages: the most relevant scholarship on this topic was published usually in German, sometimes in French.

Nowadays, there is also an avalanche of Internet websites that often propagate, if anything, even more misinformation.[7]

* * *

Before embarking on a detailed discussion of Solomon's "claim to fame" in the context of the enigmatic "Immortal Beloved", it is perhaps appropriate to present some of the most glaring examples of his numerous misrepresentations by way of **incorrect translations from the German** – incorrect not only in the sense of making sometimes an honest mistake by misinterpreting certain words or phrases. No, he chose consciously and deliberately (and insisted, even after corrections were offered, in the second edition of his *Beethoven* book) very suggestive wordings.

Given that we are dealing here with Beethoven's "love life" in some sense, it should be noted that the insinuation that he was – ever, occasionally or even regularly – visiting prostitutes is actually not supported by any conclusive evidence (Tellenbach 1983, pp. 285–287). A typical example is Beethoven's response to a letter by his friend Zmeskall, who had made a remark about "fortresses" – slang at the time for women that could easily be "conquered" (i.e., bought with money):

> Thank you very much, my dear Z., for your explanations. Regarding the fortresses, I thought you had the view of me that I do not wish to dwell in sultry places.[8]

This is, if anything, a very clear denial (and an honest one – to a dear friend). It is also well-known that Beethoven lived most if not all his life like a monk (i.e., celibate). And how he was at odds with his brothers because they had married women of "questionable" (i.e., immoral – in Ludwig's view) character!

After dwelling extensively on some gossip that Beethoven might have visited prostitutes (in his fifties – the man was frequently ill and bedridden, close to his death!),[9] Solomon then relates this rather juicy story:

> "Would you like to sleep with my wife?" asked Karl Peters in a Conversation Book of January 1820. ... Peters was about to leave on a trip and generously offered his wife ... to Beethoven for a night. Beethoven's reply ... was apparently affirmative, for Peters wrote that he would go and "fetch his wife." (Solomon 1998, p. 340.)

Translating "Would you like to sleep **with** my wife?" back to German results in "Möchten Sie **mit** meiner Frau schlafen?" In a footnote, Solomon (1998, p. 475, n. 37) even provides the original German text of what Peters wrote:

> "Wollen Sie bey [!] meiner Frau schlafen? Es ist so kalt."

Here, "bey" ("bei" in modern German) translates first as "**at**" (and then maybe as "in", "with", etc., depending on context). And why was "Es ist so kalt" [It is very cold] omitted?

Solomon (1998, p. 475, n. 37) then adds the – astonishing – comment:

> One authority implausibly [!] suggests the entry could be read, "Would you like to sleep over at my wife's place?"

In case you know some German, you might be inclined to think (quite plausibly!) the same as this "one authority" (why not named?): The context, unfortunately, does not fit the picture of Beethoven the notorious fornicator (nor the – respected – Peters[10] couple being habitually promiscuous). According to Tellenbach (1983, p. 285), it went like this (on the left in the original German, on the right in English – my translation):

Hofrat Peters: "Ich muß mit meiner Frau um 5 nach Gumpendorf. Wollen Sie bey meiner Frau schlafen? Es ist so kalt."	Court Councilor Peters: "I have to go to Gumpendorf with my wife at 5 o'clock. Do you want to sleep at my wife's [place]? It is very cold."

So, Beethoven's (and Prince Lobkowitz's) old friend Peters offered his wife's house (being vacated but well heated – it's January!) to him to stay there for a night... After which Peters had to excuse himself, as he wrote into the deaf man's book:

> I need ... to pick up my wife.[11]

– for their journey. **Not** to "fetch" her and lead her into Beethoven's bed!

* * *

Antonie von Birkenstock was born in 1780 in Vienna and had spent most of her youth (from the ages of 7 to 15 years, after the death of her mother) in a cloister. Like Josephine (but here the similarities end), she was married early (in 1798) to a rich (and much older) man whom she did not know (a common practice in those days): Franz Brentano (born in 1765), a banker and merchant, who took her to his hometown of Frankfurt am Main.

Contrary to Joseph Count Deym, Franz Brentano was indeed very rich and successful in his business; therefore, his lack of a title was no obstacle to marrying a noblewoman.[12] His young wife bore him six children, and apart from Antonie becoming a little homesick, they seem to have got on with each other reasonably well.

In late 1809, Antonie's father became terminally ill, and the Brentanos returned to Vienna, where von Birkenstock died soon after. Antonie had to spend much time – indeed, the better part of the next two years – managing the execution of her inheritance (the villa and enormous art collections to be sold or auctioned), with her husband frequently away in Frankfurt to attend to his business.

During the year of 1810, Beethoven became acquainted with the Brentanos, including – and first of all – Franz's sister Bettina. In Teplitz, Goethe was surprised to see the latter walking with Beethoven hand in hand. Bettina would become notorious because later in life – after Beethoven had become a "celebrity" – she tried to imply there was a love affair, by forging letters.[13]

Beethoven developed a deep, mutual friendship with Franz and Antonie. He visited them frequently in Vienna, and he played the piano to comfort Antonie when she was sick, even in Franz's absence. Both spouses were very thankful for this. There were never any signs of jealousy on the part of Franz, who became a lifelong friend of Ludwig (like the other Franz, Count von Brunsvik).

Could it be that there was simply no reason for jealousy, in fact, there never ever was, until the end of Beethoven's life? Just like there was never any reason for Count Deym to be jealous, even though Beethoven came almost daily to give Josephine piano lessons?

The only explanation – regarding Josephine's first and second marriage, as well as Antonie's – is that Beethoven resolutely respected the married status of any woman, as is (and was) well-known. There was a famous incident in 1807 when Beethoven naïvely invited his beautiful pupil Marie Bigot to an outing when she was alone. Her over-jealous husband was not impressed, and Beethoven wrote a letter of apology, emphasizing his moral stance regarding his respect of marriage (Tellenbach 1983, p. 54).[14]

This, together with Beethoven's musical celebration of conjugal love and fidelity in the Opera *Leonore* (a.k.a. *Fidelio*), and his explicit admission to Josephine that he had suppressed any upcoming feelings of love during her marriage to Count Deym, should more than rule out any suggestion that he might have contemplated a relationship with Antonie, his best friend's wife, that was beyond mere friendship.

Antonie's admiration, indeed adoration, of Beethoven (as a composer) was **no secret**, however, as she indicated in January 1811, in a letter to her brother-in-law Clemens Brentano:

> … and place the original into Beethoven's sacred hands, whom I deeply admire, he is walking divinely among mortals, his elevated stature opposed to the world beneath.[15]

Solomon (1998, p. 237) admits:

> Thus far there was no sign of a romantic attachment between Beethoven and Antonie Brentano.

But even a "romantic attachment" (which Beethoven undoubtedly felt towards Bettina for a while) is not really the same as "love". However, what then follows is speculation:

> At what point this worship was transformed into love is not yet known. My estimate is ... in the fall [autumn] of 1811. … The love affair was under way by late 1811 (Solomon 1998, p. 238).

He proves this "estimate" retrospectively by her letter to Clemens – which if anything does not testify to a "romantic" attachment Antonie's, but just to the fact that she "deeply admired" Beethoven as a composer.

It is astonishing that Solomon wants us to believe that there could have been anything like a "love" relationship – the only reason to do so is that he thinks the Letter of 1812 was to Antonie, therefore there **must** have been something going on between the two of them. Not the other way round, as in the case of Josephine where a passionate (but secret!) love lasting over a decade was briefly rekindled.

And whose "worship was transformed into love"? Obviously only Antonie's. If you want to go that far, given that single letter to Clemens – who apparently did not get the point. And what about Beethoven? Is there anything at least vaguely similar to his many love letters to Josephine?

Yes, there is (sort of): Beethoven presented Antonie with two compositions, one of them the revised Oratorio *Christ on the Mount of Olives* Op. 85 (not exactly one with overly erotic content, but the cloister-educated Antonie must have appreciated it).

Sure enough, Franz Brentano knew all about it:

> I am longing for Vienna, because Toni has not been well all winter, which caused me some hours of grief here; Beethoven is cheering her up sometimes by his beautiful piano playing.[16]

Franz certainly also knew all about the Song "An die Geliebte" [To the Beloved] WoO 140, an autograph of which contains in Antonie's handwriting the remark: "Requested by me from the author on 2 March 1812":[17]

> *Your silent eye has shed a tear*
> *That glistens lovingly,*
> *Oh, may I suck it from your cheek,*
> *Before the earth imbibes it.*
>
> *It lingers, hesitating, upon your cheek,*
> *Ardently longing to devote itself to constancy.*
> *Now that I have received it in a kiss,*
> *Your anguish has become mine!*[18]

The background to this can be found in Goldschmidt (1977, p. 138):

> In November 1811, we see Beethoven writing a newly composed song with the heading "An die Geliebte" [To the Beloved] into the album of the Bavarian Court singer Regina Lang.[19]

"Dilettante verses" by a "clumsy author, a real dilettante, a coffeehouse poet", as Goldschmidt adds, sardonically.[20] Beethoven had also expressed his dissatisfaction with the text – but then, why shouldn't he do a pretty (and talented) girl a favor, if he was in the mood?

It looks like Antonie somehow came across this little song, and upon hearing that it had been composed by Beethoven, asked him for a copy. So the facts are: Beethoven composed a (not very deep, mind you) love song for some singer and even wrote the words into her album – does this now constitute yet another entry in our long list of "candidates" for a possible "Immortal Beloved"? In any case, Beethoven did **not** compose this for Antonie (nor for Josephine; sure enough, poems he set to music for **her** were usually written by the likes of Goethe). And can composing music to such a simpleton's lyrics constitute an expression of deep affection for an educated woman?

Solomon, however, does not mention the original history of this third-rate, second-hand song's creation. Instead, he lets us believe that Beethoven had composed it specifically as "requested by" his beloved Antonie! Confidently, he then wraps up his "Solution of the Riddle":

> The threads in a powerful [!] fabric of evidence ... make it all but certain that Antonie Brentano was the woman to whom Ludwig van Beethoven wrote his impassioned letter of July 6–7, 1812 (Solomon 1998, p. 231).

* * *

Two more examples of Solomon's misinterpretations (and misrepresentations) that show how he deals with evidence (or the lack thereof) when it suits him.

First, he quotes Beethoven's note of 1807 about "**the M**", claiming it was made in 1817. However, his major serious mistake (once again) is a significant translation error. The original German text by Beethoven:

> Baaden am 27 Juli[.] Als die M. vorbeifuhr und es schien als blickte sie auf mich (in Goldschmidt 1977, p. 57).

is given by him as

> Baden, 27 July, when M. passed by and, I think, looked at me.[21]

My own translation again:
> Baden, 27 July [1807.] When the M. drove by and it appeared as if she looked at me.

The important point here is to notice that Solomon renders "**die M.**" [**the** M.] simply as "M." – implying that it must have been a **name**, as opposed to "**the** M."[22] where "M." should be interpreted as the abbreviation of a person's **role**. It is also well-known that Anna von Brunsvik, **the** Mother, was usually referred to simply as "[the] M." by her children – and wasn't Beethoven part of the family?

Solomon (1998, p. 229) correctly observes:
> The sight of "[the] M" again ... tore open a half–healed wound.[23]

(namely Beethoven realizing that "**the** M." = **the** Mother, Anna von Brunsvik, would never allow him to marry Josephine), but then he speculates
> "M" to be her [Antonie's] daughter Maximiliane, the sight of whom (thought Thayer) revived in Beethoven the image of her mother (Solomon 1998, p. 229).

Pure fantasy (see Goldschmidt 1977, pp. 90–92)! It had already been proved, by comparing watermarks (Schmidt-Görg 1966), that this note by Beethoven had been written in 1807. There is no proof that the Brentanos (who moved to Frankfurt in 1812) were anywhere near Baden in 1817, but there is evidence that Anna von Brunsvik was in Baden in 1807.

* * *

The second example is full of convoluted reasoning. It involves the long since revised or at least corrected conjectures by Thayer,[24] this time regarding Beethoven's references to "**T**" in his Diary in late 1816 (where he most likely expressed his gratitude to Therese, who kept him in contact with Josephine, whom he had just met in Baden). Solomon (1998, p. 228) begins with the unsubstantiated claim that
> Thayer knew [!] of the existence of a love affair between Beethoven and Antonie Brentano.

Only, he never told anyone! And as proof, Solomon (1998, p. 228) offers a strange quote from Thayer:
> One of Beethoven's transient [!] and intense passions for a married woman, known to have occurred in this period of his life, has its precise date fixed by these passages in the so-called 'Tagebuch' [Diary] from the years 1816 and 1817. ... As the family name of this lady ... is known [?], it is certain that the T ... is not Therese Malfatti.[25]

From this, Solomon (1998, p. 228 f.) concludes:
> Thayer's words precisely [!] describe Antonie and Franz Brentano. ...
> "Toni" Brentano was the woman whose family Thayer attempted to shield from harmful publicity.

Thayer really knew very little about Antonie Brentano, let alone of her ever having had an "affair" with Beethoven. And even though – or just because – no name was named by Thayer in his interpretation of Beethoven's Diary notes from 1816, apart from **excluding** one name (Teresa von Malfatti), one is even more puzzled by the fact that what Thayer clearly identified (though did not elaborate) as a "**transient**" passion (and in 1816 – not 1812!), for Solomon it is just another piece in the puzzle that frames Antonie Brentano as Beethoven's "Immortal" (not really "transient") Beloved! And sure enough, Thayer, who published just about everything about Beethoven he could get hold of, kept mum about this "harmful" secret.

* * *

In June 1812, the Brentanos planned a trip to Prague and later to Karlsbad, to find a teacher for their children (among others). As Beethoven had also been "ordered" by his doctor to go to the spas in Teplitz and Karlsbad, the three of them agreed to meet up in Karlsbad – which they subsequently did.

As his "Solution to the Riddle", Solomon (1998, p. 218) proclaims
> requirements ... first, that the Immortal Beloved be a woman closely acquainted with Beethoven during the period in question.

Why is this a "requirement" (or a pre-condition)? Is it sufficient to assume that a "close" acquaintance could trigger such a letter – as opposed to a woman like Josephine with whom Beethoven was evidently passionately in love for many years?

Then he goes on to rule out Josephine (and all other "candidates"), simply because there is indeed (so far) **no proof** of Josephine having been in Prague – as well as in Karlsbad, as Solomon demands (the Letter makes a reference to "K"), even though it appears that she left Prague immediately after her encounter with Beethoven. However, there is nothing about Josephine's whereabouts at all, in particular, nothing to **disprove** her presence in Prague. (In fact, for all the other "candidates" except Josephine and Antonie, there does exist evidence that they were **not** in Prague on 3 July 1812, but elsewhere.)

And that Antonie was supposedly in love with Beethoven is later desperately corroborated by Solomon's (re)interpreting of the most cryptic remarks by and about Beethoven and others in letters and diaries – by **presupposing** that she **must** have been the "Immortal Beloved".

Josephine's possible "candidacy" for the "role" of Beethoven's "Immortal Beloved" is dismissed by assuming that once it was "over" (in 1807 or 1809, or whenever), it was – over:

> The disclosure in 1957 of the 1804–1807 correspondence between Beethoven and Josephine Brunsvik-Deym indicated an early [!] (and chilly [!]) end to an unconsummated romance, and although there is no certainty that the affair was not momentarily rekindled a half-decade later, neither is there any affirmative evidence that this indeed took place (Solomon 1972, p. 572).

So, he dumped her (or she dumped him), and then just moved on to the next date… However, what is really needed here is **convincing** evidence that the "romance" between Beethoven and Josephine was (1) indeed over and (2) in such a **final** way that it could **not** be "rekindled".

Here we have to observe that in reality there was no "chilly" end at all (if we care to actually read the letters and take into account the mounting pressure by the Brunsvik family),[26] that Josephine even in late 1809 when pregnant with Stackelberg's child was thinking of and writing to Beethoven, that Beethoven from 1804 through to 1809 repeatedly and tirelessly assured Josephine of his never ending faithfulness, his "**eternal**" (= "immortal") love – with the **same** words and phrases we find again in the Letter of 1812, addressed to his "**Angel**". But no such words or anything even remotely similar is anywhere to be found by or to Antonie.

* * *

After Solomon's "bold" suggestion was published, there appeared thoughtful and well-researched evaluations and refutations (in German) by Goldschmidt (1977) and especially Tellenbach (1983). By bringing to light more recent research and documents (from archives in Czechoslovakia and Hungary), they demonstrated conclusively that Josephine always was – and remained – the "one and only".

Solomon reacted (or over-reacted) with an article titled "Recherche de Josephine Deym",[27] as he consistently referred to (but thought was not)

> The woman Beethoven called "my immortal beloved" in his letter of 6–7 July 1812, but whose name he inconveniently [!] neglected to provide (Solomon 1988, p. 157).

First, she was not "Josephine Deym", but "Josephine von Stackelberg" at the time – that is, in 1812. In fact, from her second marriage in 1810 until her death in 1821. And she was not a "Countess" but **only** a "Baroness" – an important difference in those days of aristocratic stratification; remember how her family had been reluctant to allow her to marry below her station.[28]

Second, and much more important, what Solomon – pretending to be scornful – deplores, that Beethoven "inconveniently **neglected** to provide" the name – well, that is exactly what we would like to know: **Why?** Knowing the very reason why everything that might be relevant to identify this mysterious (?) woman was kept **secret**, is solving half the "riddle": As with **all** the letters between Ludwig and Josephine, plus the personal dedication of the Song "An die Hoffnung" [To Hope], this letter of 1812 was likewise **not** for anyone else. And Beethoven (most likely) did not (intend to) send[29] it, after all, but kept it in his possession, and this implied for him – mindful of the earlier mishap when Prince Lichnowsky spotted the Song with the dedication to Josephine on his desk – to omit any naming or otherwise identification of the addressee.

Or did he? Here it is perhaps appropriate to pause and spend a thought about the endless repetition of this story, usually starting with these ominous words: "In July 1812, Beethoven wrote a letter to an unnamed woman…"

"**Unnamed**"? Sure enough, he did not "name" her in the sense of calling her by first name, surname, nickname or even initial (in his previous love letters he usually called her just "J"). But how **did** he address her? **Not** as "My Immortal Beloved" – this phrase occurred only once near the end of the letter (though it has stuck ever since).

No – Beethoven called her

My Angel!

That is how the letter famously starts. And **who could that be**? Is it really so difficult to start the search from here and look for clues in his/her/their past?

* * *

> Countess Deym's supporters [!] … have been unable to provide a single item of direct [!] evidence that she and Beethoven sustained any kind of relationship … after 1808 … or that she was in Prague … during the first part of July 1812 (Solomon 1988, p. 157).

One should be careful assuming the absence of evidence to be evidence of absence – what if something turns up tomorrow out of those archives in the Czech Republic, Slovakia and Hungary (or even Estonia)? Indeed, much more evidence did turn up in the meantime, as discovered recently by Steblin (2007, 2009).

"Evidence … **she was in Prague**": at least **indirect evidence** is clearly provided by her diary entry of June 1812 that she intended to "**see Liebert in Prague**" – so there **were** plans. And nowhere is there any indication that this (secret) plan was changed. Moreover, there were many reasons to keep the trip a secret – especially afterwards.

In 1808, Josephine had been traveling for a year and then got married again. Contrary to her first husband Count Deym[30] (who had also been a friend of Mozart and Haydn), Baron von Stackelberg, with whom she soon fell out, was obviously not one with whom Beethoven should (or would have wanted to) become acquainted. Also, Josephine had two more babies to look after, six children in total (in 1812). They were neglected by Stackelberg – whom she had been forced to marry mainly because of the illegitimate birth of his first daughter, and he was supposed to be the teacher and educator of the Deym children.

Thus, there was little chance of any contact – especially as Beethoven's abhorrence of adulterous relations is well documented (he refrained from any advances during her marriage to Deym). Incidentally, this alone should rule out any suggestion that he might have had any intention to get involved with Antonie, his best friend's wife (even when alone with her).[31]

Likewise, they had every reason to keep their – sudden and unexpected – encounter a secret, especially Josephine, as she had been traveling incognito to Prague.

> At that time, traveling almost inevitably [!] left traces: ... newspapers reported the comings and goings of notable – especially aristocratic – visitors. ... The prominent [!] Countess Deym would very likely have been noted somewhere (Solomon 1988, p. 158).

"The **prominent** Countess Deym": was she moving around like Princess Diana, with hundreds of Paparazzi in her wake? Was she really a famous Bohemian Countess or just a little Estonian Baroness? And how difficult would it have been to travel incognito in a private coach with curtains drawn? Staying in private mansions and villas, not in public hotels? Moreover, members of the nobility were not always and not everywhere required to report to the police (here her privilege comes into play), or simply got away with not doing it, especially when they did not stay at hotels. And there were several of Deym's and the Brunsviks' relatives living in Prague or nearby.

Thus, Solomon (1988, p. 158) convincingly rules out

> the "possibility" that Countess Deym was in Bohemia in early July 1812, where she could meet or plan [!] to meet Beethoven.

Only, there was **never**, could never have been, such a "**plan**". The very words used in the Letter from 6/7 July 1812 indicate that the encounter of 3 July was totally unexpected – even though it was written three days later and, especially the second and third parts, after some more time of reflection.

> On 14 June 1812, her husband wrote to his mother... This letter is ... establishing that the Stackelbergs were living together as a family [!] in Vienna during the period surrounding [!] the Immortal Beloved letter. ... It also suggests that the problems leading to the couple's eventual separation in 1813 had scarcely reached a critical point in mid-June 1812 (Solomon 1988, p. 159).

From various diary entries of the Brunsvik sisters, we know how "critical" the situation had been already – and for two years at least. There had been a big row between Josephine and her husband, after a less than amicable year 1811 of being "separated together" (in the bedroom, at least), and Stackelberg had just left in a huff – most likely before the end of June 1812.

The quoted letter to his mother in Estonia (it is not even confirmed whether it was ever sent) demonstrates, if anything, the hypocritical character of Stackelberg, who obviously had reasons to dissemble and to picture his marriage as a happy one.

Solomon then quotes Franz von Brunsvik's letter to Josephine of 25 July 1812:

> I haven't heard a syllable from Stackelberg.[32]

and concludes:

> Franz's references to an ongoing [!] correspondence with the Stackelbergs about financial issues ... make it obvious that the couple was in Vienna ... during most, if not all [!], of July (Solomon 1988, p. 160).

If anything, it sounds as if Franz was referring to the fact that **Stackelberg was still away** ... that is why he (as well as Josephine) did **not** hear anything from him. Even if we admit, that Stackelberg must have been in Vienna (but - not necessarily together with Josephine!) on 25 July, how does this **prove** (like his letter from 14 June) that he was there **all the time**? Not to mention the fact that Stackelberg's "financial issues" had been "ongoing" for more than two years, and Franz helping out with money every now and then...

There is simply **no proof at all** that "both" Stackelbergs were **in their home** in Vienna[33] **between** 14 June and 25 July 1812, let alone "happy together". One cannot help noticing that Solomon's way of arguing is dictated by wishful thinking.

> Her deeply troubled marriage did not altogether disintegrate until April 1813, when the homesick [!] and debt-ridden

Stackelberg left her to "begin a new life" in the "service of the Lord" (Solomon 1988, p. 161).

Solomon reminds us that Stackelberg, far from being a scoundrel (as Therese so vividly described him), was really a pious man, for whom we should feel pity and compassion that his selfish wife, not willing to follow him (and to leave four of her children behind), had forced him instead to endure so much "homesickness".[34]

Worst of all, he suffered so much from being "debt-ridden" (an affliction he brought upon himself, due to his ineptitude in financial dealings – i.e., he took all his wife's money and huge loans from her relatives, but forgot to pay them back), so he wisely decided to leave his debts behind, for his wife to deal with. She surely deserved no better, having caused all the "trouble". What we do know is that Josephine, all alone and lonely, eventually ended up in poverty and on occasion may even have received (secretly) monetary donations from – Beethoven.

* * *

After pontificating that

> The lurid [!] speculation that Beethoven fathered Minona ... should at last be laid to rest (Solomon 1988, p. 160).

and sensing how unconvincing this sounds, he resorts to more special pleading:

> Other circumstances speak against Countess Deym's candidacy ... Beethoven made ... no separate dedications [!] to her ...; there are no presentation copies to her of his autographs or publications ... no gifts [!] to her ... no exchange of portraits, and not even an expression of condolence to any member of her family upon her premature death in 1821 (Solomon 1988, p. 160).

Indeed, Beethoven **never dedicated anything** to Josephine![35] Simply because their love was and had to be kept secret – dedications on published works (especially love songs) were out of the question. On the other hand, there is a considerable number of excellent compositions, not dedicated to anyone, revealing various connotations to Josephine[36] – and one must suspect they were left undedicated for that very reason: Beethoven (and by implication, Josephine) knew, who it was for.

The one composition he did dedicate to her privately, Beethoven was most anxious to keep a **secret**, especially when it was detected by his patron Prince Lichnowsky. As for gifts – wasn't the Music they shared more then enough? Don't we recall his stammering in a letter: "Here – **your** – **your** – *Andante*"[37] (the *Andante favori* WoO 57, a musical declaration of love)? Lastly, bearing in mind how the two lovers always, consistently and ultimately successfully, kept their relationship a secret, shouldn't we **expect** that little – no nothing – was ever known publicly?

However, a **dedication** – of which there were indeed also two (or rather, one and a half) to Antonie (eleven years later!)[38] – was usually **not** necessarily an expression of tender affection or even love: It was simply part of a business transaction. It was sold for money.[39] Franz Brentano, Antonie's husband, showed repeatedly his gratitude by not demanding repayment of considerable "loans" he had made to Beethoven.

To claim that "there are **no presentation copies to her**" of his autographs" is simply not true. (What about Op. 31, Op. 32, WoO 57, WoO 74 – there are probably more than we know of.)

"Condolence"? What about the Piano Sonata in *A flat major* Op. 110,[40] which clearly sounds like a **Requiem** for Josephine? And why should Beethoven express his condolences to the Brunsvik family (let alone the Stackelbergs), when all of them had long since deserted the ailing, prematurely ageing and suffering woman, leaving her alone to slowly waste away?

* * *

> Beethoven neglected [!] her when it suited him: "I would have gone to you today – but – only an overwhelming amount of work prevented me." (Solomon 1988, p. 160.)
>
> Beethoven's habit [!] of taking back his love offerings [!] to her: "Please send me the Andante and the two songs – I promise that you will have all three compositions back the day after tomorrow." ... "Please send me back the book in which I enclosed my lines to you – I was asked for it today." (Solomon 1988, p. 164.)

So, there **were** "love offerings" (gifts?), after all!

> By the summer of 1805, Beethoven's letters took on an aloof [!], and somewhat false, character. He asked for the

return of music he had given or lent her, and when "An die Hoffnung," op. 32, which he composed for her, was published in September, her name had been removed from the dedication (Solomon 1998, p. 199).

Would you believe it – asking back a borrowed item is like being "false" to your beloved! La Mara knew better already in 1920:

> The omission of the dedication of the Song "An die Hoffnung" [To Hope] upon its publication in the autumn of 1805 can easily be understood as intended to keep the secret of their relationship.[41]

After this, Count Wolkenstein's brief infatuation with Josephine occurred thus – in Solomon's imagination:

> By the winter of 1805–6, Josephine had turned away [!] from Beethoven to Count Wolkenstein (Solomon 1998, p. 199).

No matter that it was Count Wolkenstein, who "turned" to Josephine (courting her – unsuccessfully), which made Beethoven understandably jealous. Josephine reacted by reassuring him of her love (as can be seen from her letters in 1806, provided they are read – and translated – carefully).

Solomon (1988, p. 164) discovered

> a curious issue: Countess Deym's advocates read fanciful allusions to their heroine [!] into a vast number of Beethoven's compositions – as though music were a composer's private [!] cipher rather than an aesthetic structure. They seek – and invariably find – "secret" dedications to Josephine.

If music is **not** "a composer's private cipher rather than an aesthetic structure", then Mozart's "Don Giovanni" has nothing to do with his father's death, the tormented lives of Schubert, Chopin, Schumann, Tchaikovsky, Mahler, Berg – nowhere reflected in their "aesthetic structures"? If this is meant to be honest, and not – again – overshooting the target, then one can only conclude that by making such a statement, **Solomon disqualifies himself** from being a serious musicologist.

It leaves a bitter taste after reading that this "leading" American musicologist finds it necessary and appropriate to cynically refer to Josephine as a "heroine", adding insult to injury in a context where her fateful love of the equally unhappy and suffering Beethoven had just been transfigured into the beginning of her end, a long and painful journey into terminal illness, delirium, misery, poverty and oblivion. A journey where, at least occasionally, Beethoven's music brought her comfort and consolation.

Solomon's final words are just polemics:
> By elaborating the assumption that all [!] music is concealed autobiography, Josephine Deym advocacy comes close to the most extreme [!] speculations ... those who resort to deciphering secret codes and hidden texts in Beethoven's instrumental music ... The pursuit of Josephine Deym threatens to convert the works of Beethoven into a new "great cryptogram," whose mysteries may be plumbed only by the initiate (Solomon 1988, p. 165).

* * *

Solomon continued (or rather repeated) his attacks in the second edition of his *Beethoven* biography – including his way to "prove" that Antonie was the one.

He now starts, setting the scene, by gleefully quoting:
> A police report on Josephine dated July 12, 1815, reads, "The morality of the Countess does not appear to enjoy a good reputation, and it is stated that she cannot be absolved from having given ground for conjugal quarrels." (Solomon 1998, p. 198.)

The background to this was most likely denunciations by Stackelberg or Andrian (or both). But then, we know already whose side Solomon is on.

> The Karlsbad police required formal registration of all arrivals (Solomon 1998, p. 217).

> The sine qua non [!] for identification of the Immortal Beloved is that she must have been in Karlsbad during the week of July 6, 1812 (Solomon 1998, p. 219).

Yes, but:
> Clearly, there is no possibility of absolute certainty here... It is possible [!] that the letter arose from a ... meeting with a woman who informed Beethoven that she was going to Karlsbad and then failed to carry out her declared intention (Solomon 1998, p. 219 f.).

So, there is the "possibility" that – as Josephine did – the woman was **not** going to Karlsbad, after all. Why then was this condition a "**sine qua non**"?

Because Solomon (1998, p. 223) knows already that

> the Immortal Beloved ... is Antonie Brentano. ... The weight of the evidence in her favor is so powerful that it is not [!] presumptuous to assert that the riddle of Beethoven's Immortal Beloved has now [!] been solved.

Still, he cannot but admit:

> There is still room for a reasonable doubt (Solomon 1998, p. 461, n. 48).

Nevertheless, he has

> ... in order to follow the implications of my proposed identification somewhat further ... acted on the assumption [!] that Frau Brentano has been proved [!] to have been the Immortal Beloved (Solomon 1998, p. 461, n. 48).

Notwithstanding that

> There is no proof that Beethoven and Antonie met in Prague (Solomon 1972, p. 577).

So, is it "proof" or only a conjecture? Or just an "assumption"? And is there any "**doubt**"? (Yes: "reasonable doubt".) It is mystifying how Solomon's wavering between absolute certainty and "proof" on the one hand and qualifying remarks allowing "doubt" on the other can be hailed as having solved the (supposed) "Riddle of the Immortal Beloved".[43] He is clouding the issue so much with confusing and contradictory remarks, speculations and facts mixed up, that many who read this cannot be blamed for not being able to see through it – and just take his word for it.[44]

* * *

Finally, we need to comment on Solomon's audacity to claim that

> [Josephine's] letters [to Beethoven] speak ... rarely [!] of her love (Solomon 1998, p. 198).

Let us see what she wrote to him as early as February/March 1805:

> My heart you have won already, my dear Beethoven ... the greatest proof of my love – of my esteem you receive through this confession, by this my trust! ... I love you unspeakably.

And later in the same year:
> I love you, and I appreciate your moral character – You have shown so much love and kindness to me and my children, I will never forget it, as long as I live.[46]

Given that this was written just one year after her husband's death, in reply to letters by Beethoven, where he called her his "only beloved", his "everything", his "happiness" – his "**Angel**", in short, rather passionate outbursts of declarations of love, what else do we need to conclude that Josephine responded in kind?

However, the pressure of the Brunsvik family was already being exercised: After Charlotte the chaperone's warnings about Beethoven's all too frequent visits, Therese decreed in January 1805 that Josephine's

> **heart must have the strength to say no**, a sad duty.[47]

It is significant, that it took **two more years until Josephine began to give in**, and only then did she write to Beethoven that she could not "break sacred bonds", i.e., she had to sacrifice her love of him for the love of her children - as Therese was later to confirm:
> She would have been happier with him than with Stackelberg. Maternal affection made her forgo her own happiness.[48]

Josephine also emphasized repeatedly how Beethoven's music had made her "enthusiastic" for him.

And that is, indeed, the main point: Theirs was a relationship in spirit, or "in Heaven", with no chance of physical union (i.e., via marriage). And Beethoven's response in his last letters was to stress once again his never ending **faithfulness** – this despite the fact that Josephine had become inaccessible to him.

Who can seriously imagine that his assertion on 7 July 1812 that
> since you know my faithfulness to you, never can another own my heart, never – never[49]

was now all of a sudden directed to any other woman, let alone to Antonie Brentano, wife of his best friend, whom he both liked and respected – as friends?

* * *

Let us conclude this discussion with the measured judgment passed by Goldschmidt (1977), who had not only consulted with his fellow Marxist Solomon at the time, but did also try his best to give his friend's hypothesis some credence. First, Goldschmidt was aware that **absence of evidence is no evidence of absence**, as there was simply no reason to assume that Josephine's presence in Prague **must** have been documented by the authorities, simply because

> Josephine during her frequent visits to Prague never stayed in a hotel, but with her sister-in-law, Countess Golz. This justifies the assumption that the reunion with Beethoven took place in her house in Prague's Neustadt.[50]

Tellenbach (1983) then provided a thoroughly researched biography of Josephine (in German). Meanwhile, much more information has come to the surface, in documents, letters and diaries, found in archives in the Czech Republic, Slovakia and Hungary, with interesting results.[51]

The best that Goldschmidt could say about Solomon's conjecture, after discussing its many inherent inconsistencies:

> In order to possibly verify the Antonia-Hypothesis with its inherent factual contradictions once and forever, it is necessary to falsify the other hypotheses that have been offered.[52]

In other words: Only if one could falsify, disprove or otherwise make extremely unlikely the "Josephine Hypothesis", only then would it make sense to even begin and try to find someone else – not just start with someone who was around[53] at the time and/or was a friend of Beethoven (and nothing more, really).

After his subsequent and very detailed analysis and evaluation of the "Josephine Hypothesis", Goldschmidt's verdict is:

> Without conclusive [!] proofs of the opposite one should no longer want to part prematurely with the increasingly justified assumption that the "Immortal Beloved" could hardly be anyone else but the "Only Beloved".[54]

Steblin (2007, p. 180) sums up convincingly her own comprehensive analysis:

> All of the puzzling aspects about Beethoven's affair with the "Immortal Beloved," including his various cryptic comments, can be explained in terms of his one known

Only one! beloved – Josephine. Why do we doubt his word that there was only one woman who had captured his heart?

* * *

The trouble with Solomon is that he comes across as haughty and arrogant, that he uses eloquent sounding language (often based on questionable – but really only superficial – "psychoanalytic" concepts), obviously with the aim to impress and intimidate readers, rather than to educate and enlighten them.

The striking difference between the approach taken by Solomon, compared to most European (and some dissenting American) researchers, is that he first ignored them altogether, and then dismissed them summarily as "Deym advocates" or "Josephine supporters", as if they were a bunch of fanatics supporting a football team. In general, he ignored or did not deal in sufficient detail with the arguments and the reasoning of alternative approaches.

On the other hand, almost all books, articles and Internet contributions by European authors acknowledge, quote and/or recognise Solomon's conjecture as a possible, if not even probable alternative to Josephine, despite the overwhelming evidence in favor of the latter and the more than obvious **lack** of any conclusive evidence (let alone proof) in favor of Antonie – the **lack of any proof whatsoever that Beethoven even met Antonie in Prague**, in particular.

The best example for a proper and balanced approach to this is the one taken by Goldschmidt (1977), who not only communicated personally with his friend Solomon but gave him considerable room and every benefit of the doubt possible, to come to the **tentative** conclusion:

Solomon's Antonia hypothesis looks promising.[55]

This sentence has often been quoted – but it is out of context. Because this was only a **preliminary** summary, based on initial investigations. Goldschmidt followed this up by listing its many contradictions, and then he embarked onto the "Brunsvik plane". He summarized his results with a final conclusion that was rather devastating to Solomon's conjecture.

Remarkably, after the "13 Letters" were first published in 1957 (though rarely read), hardly anyone bothered to follow up the trail of these earlier love letters (from 1804 to 1809, maybe even 1810 – certainly not 1807) up to 1812, given that no other meaningful and reliable clues really existed pointing to any other woman whom Beethoven might have loved passionately. It is also most astonishing that his repeated pledges to Josephine of his never-ending **faithfulness** – especially at the very moment when she had to withdraw from him – were not taken seriously.

It was this vacuum into which Solomon threw his "bombshell" by proposing the hitherto almost never-heard-of Antonie. And he took full advantage of the fact that almost nothing of the research literature (being mainly in German) was known in the USA; and by posing like a Sherlock Holmes, who had solved the "riddle" by way of supposedly "logical" reasoning and "proof", he soon created (and reinforced) a myth that has become enshrined, mainly in Anglo-American thought, ever since.

Goldschmidt (1977) and especially Tellenbach (1983) published thoroughly researched refutations of Solomon's untenable conjecture – in German. They were widely ignored in America,[56] but Solomon (1988) found it still necessary to reply with a polemical article defaming the "Deym advocates", scolding the error of their ways. Even Beethoven's most beautiful compositions, many of which can be shown to have been composed for Josephine, were dismissed coldly by Solomon as "deciphering secret codes" hidden in music.

During the last two decades, archives in Eastern Europe became much more available to researchers. And while Solomon obstinately reissued his *Beethoven* biography (adding gleefully, for good measure, the quote from a police report stating that Josephine's "morality does not appear to enjoy a good reputation"), Rita Steblin tirelessly waded through literally mountains of letters, diaries and documents in Czech, Slovakian and Hungarian archives (it is said she did not meet Solomon there). She was not only able to correct many wrong dates and details that kept (and keep) permeating the literature (and, sadly, the Internet) – like the exact date of Josephine's first marriage or Julie Guicciardi's (much earlier) date of birth. She also found more evidence (like the Deyms' love letters or Fritz Deym's diary) which confirmed what should have been more than clear and evident all along:

A new way of looking at old evidence confirms that Josephine was Beethoven's one and only "Immortal Beloved" (Steblin 2007, p. 180). Isn't it time that Beethoven scholars everywhere should take note by now?

* * *

I would have preferred to end this chapter on a more positive note. However, it recently came to light that Solomon can also play hardball, if he does not have his way: William Meredith, Director of the *Ira F. Brilliant Center for Beethoven Studies*, San José State University, reports (in Walden 2011, p. xxx, n. 1) about

> an extended review article by Marie-Elisabeth Tellenbach titled "Psychoanalysis and the Historio-Critical Method: On Maynard Solomon's Image of Beethoven," which was published in ... *The Beethoven Newsletter* in 1993-94. ... I foresaw – correctly – there would be a significant backlash to its publication. ... Solomon ... declined the invitation to respond in the *Newsletter* and subsequently resigned from the Center's advisory board ... The resignation of one of the most popular Beethoven scholars in the United States from the Center's advisory board was hardly a fortuitous event in the history of the fledgling Center.

---

[1] Solomon (1972), p. 577.

[2] Solomon (1998), p. 461, n. 48.

[3] "A wildly enthusiastic speech or piece of writing is still occasionally described as *dithyrambic*." (http://en.wikipedia.org/wiki/Dithyrambic, 8 Mar 2011.)

[4] On their current (6 Feb 2011) German website http://brunswicks.de/ under the heading "Schloss Brunswick – Martonvásár", the following is revealed (or claimed): "Beethoven visited the Brunsvik family several times between 1800 and 1820. Here he composed several of his works (such as the *Moonlight* Sonata). He even dedicated the Sonata 'Appassionata' to his friend Franz Brunsvik. The Count's sisters, Therese, Josephine and Charlotte, turned out to be gifted piano students of Beethoven. The master's letters to the "Immortal Beloved" are evidence of a passionate romance between Beethoven and presumably Josephine." [Beethoven war zwischen 1800 und 1820 mehrmals bei der Familie Brunswick zu Besuch. Er komponierte hier mehrere seiner Werke (z. B. die Mondscheinsonate). Die Sonate '

"Appassionata" widmete er gar seinem Freund Franz Brunswick. Die Schwestern des Grafen, Therese, Josephine und Charlotte, erwiesen sich als begabte Klavierschülerinnen Beethovens. Die Briefe des Meisters an die "Unsterbliche Geliebte" zeugen von einer leidenschaftlichen Romanze zwischen Beethoven und vermutlich Josephine.] Strangely, on the previous page the link to this page is preceded by the sentence: "Furthermore, it is alleged (but not, after all, according to scrupulous research) that certain entanglements occurred between the composer Ludwig van Beethoven and the sisters of his friend Count Franz Brunsvik: Therese and Josephine Brunsvik." [Weiterhin soll es angeblich (laut gewissenhafter Forschungen nun doch nicht) zu gewissen Verwicklungen zwischen dem Komponisten Ludwig van Beethoven und den Schwestern des mit ihm befreundeten Grafen Franz Brunswick gekommen sein: Therese und Josephine Brunswick.] An email request to reveal more details of this "scrupulous research" was not answered by Familie@Brunswicks.de. It is also obvious that on this website the Brunsvik family displays some wishful thinking: They wish to participate in the now so famous composer's glory by claiming that he was often their guest, or composed certain music at their palace.

[5]   "Solomon's belief in Marxism was a driving force in these early years, but it wasn't until 1973 that his writings explicitly reflected this. His 1973 book *Marxism and Art* is one of the books on Marxism from this period that has been continuously in print." (http://en.wikipedia.org/wiki/Maynard_Solomon#cite_ref–1, 19 Dec 2010) He is still listed as an "American Marxist" in http://en.wikipedia.org/wiki/Category:American_Marxists (19 Dec 2010).

[6]   "Most boldly [!], Solomon has not hesitated to offer specific psychological analyses and diagnoses of his subjects. He has, however, been criticized for anachronistic assumptions and a lack of understanding of eighteenth- and nineteenth-century German." (http://en.wikipedia.org/wiki/Maynard_Solomon#cite_ref–1, 19 Dec 2010) - See also the many examples of serious mistranslations by Solomon in Tellenbach (1983), pp. 23, 37, 47, 53, 248, 283–285; p. 296, n. 57; p. 299, n. 29; p. 311, n. 13, etc.

[7]   Notable exceptions are http://www.lvbeethoven.com/ (multilingual) and the very comprehensive http://www.beethovensite.eu/ (unfortunately, almost exclusively in Dutch).

[8]   "Ich danke Ihnen herzlich, mein lieber Z., für Ihre mir gegebenen Erörterungen. Was die Festungen anbelangt, so dächte ich, daß Sie von mir die Meinung hätten, mich nicht in sumpfigen Gegenden aufhalten zu wollen." (Beethoven to Zmeskall, 1816, in Tellenbach 1983, p. 286.)

[9]   In a Conversation Book entry of 1820, one Janitschek was teasing Beethoven: "Wohin sind Sie heute gegen 7 Uhr beym Haarmarkt auf dem Strich gegangen?", which could be translated as "Where did you go today around 7 o'clock on the Haarmarkt near the *Strich*?", where "Strich" – literally "Line" – is German slang for the "red-light district" (probably derived from a line drawn on the footpath that these ladies were not to cross). Solomon (1998, p. 339 f.) – after making the outrageous claim that "Beethoven's sexual activity seems [!] to have continued during this period [1822!]" – continues, relying on a jumbled translation:

"In a Conversation Book of 1820, Janitschek explicitly [!] referred to the composer's having been seen looking for prostitutes: he wrote, 'Where were you going about 7:00 o'clock today hunting [!] for girls (auf dem Strich gegangen) in the district near the Haarmarkt?' The phrase 'auf dem Strich gehen' ... is fairly unambiguously [!] a reference to the pursuit of prostitutes. Beethoven's unrecorded response apparently elicited Janitschek's further remark, in Latin: 'Culpam transferre in alium (Blame it on someone else)'." The phrase "auf dem Strich gehen", by the way, in German usually refers to those who sell their services – not the ones who "hunt" them (so here is at least some ambiguity). However, it seems fairly clear from the response by Janitschek (a man of rather loose morals – probably he was himself there, "hunting") that Beethoven must have denied it (whatever the supposed insinuation was).

[10] "Court Councilor Peters, who was now co-guardian [of Beethoven's nephew Karl], ... was the teacher of [Prince] Lobkowitz's children and a close friend of Beethoven since 1816 at least... Beethoven calls him knowledgeable and morally respectable; the court must also have found him reliable. 'Peters belongs to the most noble people', wrote someone into the C[onversation] B[ook], apparently J. Czerny... His wife had a good voice and was a great admirer of Beethoven who presented her also with a copy of the *Song Cycle* ['To the Distant Beloved']." [Hofrat Peters, welcher also jetzt Mitvormund [Karls] war, ... war Erzieher der Lobkowitzschen Kinder und mit Beethoven mindestens seit 1816 näher befreundet... Beethoven nennt ihn kenntnisreich und moralisch achtbar, auch das Gericht muß ihn doch als zuverlässig erkannt haben. "Der Pet. gehört unter die edelsten Menschen", schreibt jemand im K. B., wie es scheint J. Czerny... Seine Frau hatte eine gute Stimme und war eine große Verehrerin Beethovens, der ihr auch ein Exemplar des Liederkreises ["An die ferne Geliebte"] schenkte.] (Alexander Thayer: "Ludwig van Beethovens Leben." [Ludwig van Beethoven's Life.] Vol. 4, Leipzig: Breitkopf & Härtel (1907), p. 188. See also Forbes (1967), p. 755.

[11] "Ich soll noch ... meine Frau abholen." (in Tellenbach 1983, p. 285.)

[12] The Brentanos, although without a formal title, were descendents of old Italian nobility (Tellenbach 1983, p. 37) and belonged to the city class of so-called "Patricians" in Frankfurt: "Beginning in the 11th century, a privileged class which much later came to be called *Patrizier* formed in the German-speaking imperial cities. Besides wealthy merchant burghers, they were recruited from the ranks of imperial knights ... belonging to certain families or 'houses', as documented for Cologne, Frankfurt am Main and Nuremberg... The use of the word *Patrizier* to refer to the most privileged segment of urban society dates back ... to the Renaissance." (http://en.wikipedia.org/wiki/Patrizier, 8 Mar 2011)

[13] Walden (2011) is trying to propagate the lurid conjecture that Bettina Brentano was Beethoven's "Immortal Beloved", based on the assumption that her forgeries (see Goldschmidt 1977, pp. 536–538) are true (and Beethoven's pledge of "eternal faithfulness" to Josephine is thus not to be taken seriously). It helps that Walden did not read (or quote) any of the relevant German research in this matter.

[14] Sure enough, Marie Bigot was in due course elevated to (yet another) "candidate" for the "role" of Beethoven's "Immortal Beloved". One gets the uncanny feeling that **any** woman who could be shown to have been in contact with

Beethoven even in the most superficial way is eligible to be "advocated" – as long as she is **not** Josephine von Brunsvik!

[15] "... und das original in Beethovens heilige Hände legen[,] den ich tief verehre, er wandelt göttlich unter den Sterblichen, sein höheren Standpunkt gegen die niedere Welt..." (Antonie to Clemens, 26 January 1811, in Goldschmidt 1977, p. 524.)

[16] "Mich sehnt's nach Wien, denn Toni ist den ganzen Winter nicht wohl, das mir hier manche kummervolle Stunde verursachte, Bethhoven erheitert sie zuweilen durch sein schönes Clavier Spiel." (Franz Brentano to Bettina, 7 May 1811, in http://www.xs4all.nl/~ademu/Beethoven/.)

[17] "Den 2tn März, 1812 mir vom Author erbethen." (in Solomon 1998, p. 229.)

[18]
Oh, daß ich dir vom stillen Auge
In seinem liebevollen Schein
Die Träne von der Wange sauge,
Eh' sie die Erde trinket ein.

Wohl hält sie zögernd auf der Wange,
Und will sich heiß der Treue weihn;
Nun ich sie so im Kuß empfange,
Nun sind auch deine Schmerzen mein!

Solomon (1998, p. 229) quotes only the first stanza, translated by him as:

The tears of your silent eyes,
With their love-filled splendor,
Oh, that I might gather them from your cheek
Before the earth drinks them in.

This is, by the way, a(nother) good example to show how being biased can result in a biased translation: (1) The German "**liebevoll**" (literally "full of love") is normally used in the sense of "kindly", "friendly" or – as here by me – "**lovingly**"; its use in German could be exemplified by a sentence like "The nurse lovingly wiped off the sweat from the patient's forehead" – now does this (in itself) constitute a love relationship? For Solomon it does (because he has presupposed it): his rendering "**love-filled**" is also much closer to the (incorrect) "literal" translation, but its **meaning** is obviously much more on the erotic side. And (2) "**splendor**" (synonyms "magnificence", "glory", "grandeur", "brilliance") for the German "**Schein**" – which simply translates as "shine", "gleam" or maybe "sparkle". I think "**glisten**" is good enough here. Note also that Solomon renders the single tear (as well as the one eye) in the plural.

[19] "November 1811 sehen wir Beethoven ein neuverfaßtes Lied mit der Überschrift 'An die Geliebte' der bayerischen Hofsängerin Regina Lang ins Stammbuch schreiben."

[20] "Die dilettantischen Verse haben ebenfalls Stammbuchcharakter. Als den linkischen Verfasser ... von einem wirklichen Dilettanten, dem Kaffeehaus-Literaten Joseph Ludwig Stoll." (Goldschmidt 1977, p. 139.)

[21] Solomon (1998), p. 229. It is interesting to compare the various translations of this not entirely unimportant note by Beethoven that are floating around (and bearing in mind that it was definitely written in 1807, not 1817!). First, the original German: "Nur liebe – ja nur Sie vermag dir ein Glücklicheres Leben zu geben – o Gott – lass mich sie – jene endlich finden – die mich in Tugend bestärkt – die mir **erlaubt** mein ist – Baaden am 27. Juli [1807.] Als die M. vorbejfuhr und es schien als blickte sie auf mich –." My translation: "Only love – yes, only love can give you a happier life! Oh God – let me find her – finally find her – who will strengthen my virtue – who is **allowed** to be mine. Baden, 27 July [1807.] When the M. drove by and it appeared as if she looked at me." Thayer (or maybe Deiters, who translated it for him; in Forbes 1967, p. 685): "Love alone – yes, only love can possibly give you a happier life – O God, let me – let me finally find the one – who will strengthen me in virtue – who will *lawfully* [!] be mine. Baden on July 27 when M drove past and seemed to give a glance at me –." Compare this to Solomon (1998, p. 229): "Love – yes, love alone can make your life happy! O God, let me find someone [!] whose love I am allowed. Baden, 27 July, when M. passed by and, I think, looked at me." It really pays to read this carefully and take note of the differences: While Thayer/Deiters at least conveyed this whole note rather truthfully, one wonders why Solomon chose his particular wordings – and omitted not only the "the" before the "M.", but also truncated the phrase "let me find her – finally find her – who will strengthen my virtue" (clearly full of desperate longing) to "let me find someone"! And he did **not** emphasize the all-important word "**allowed**".

[22] Contrary to English, in German it is indeed possible – even common – to refer to a person by name prefixed by a definite article. However, this is usually in the context of using the name in a disparaging manner. In fact, referring to a third person using this kind of colloquialism in their presence is often seen as an insult.

[23] Quoting Thayer (in Forbes 1967, p. 686).

[24] Alexander Thayer spent all his life tirelessly accumulating every bit of information about Beethoven that he could find (in the 19th century – he died in 1897). His work, thousands of pages, was edited and amended after his death by Deiters and then by Riemann in Germany and by Krehbiel and later Forbes (1967) in the USA. Of course, Thayer was limited by the documents available at the time, and occasionally he made mistakes – most famously (and not surprisingly) with regard to the interpretation of the "Letter to the Immortal Beloved". And this note (its dating and interpretatin) about "the M".

[25] In Forbes (1967), p. 686.

[26] La Mara (1920, p. 62 f.) bluntly observes: "Letters from Therese's estate reveal ... that, due to the pressure by the Brunsvik family, the relationship between

Josephine Deym and Beethoven was terminated." [Briefe aus Thereses Nachlaß verraten, ... daß zufolge Drängens der Familie Brunsvik die Beziehungen zwischen Josephine Deym und Beethoven abgebrochen wurden.]

27   Probably meant as a cheap pun on "Recherche de Beethoven" (Massin 1970) who also concluded (in French) that Josephine was Beethoven's only one.

28   After her "separation" from Baron von Stackelberg (i.e., after he had left her), Josephine occasionally reverted to the surname "Deym" and/or the title "Countess". However, this was strictly speaking not legal (her marriage to Stackelberg was not divorced). Once a passport she had requested under the name of "Deym" was soon after cancelled by the police and reissued as "Stackelberg". However, let's not worry about names too much; as long as we know who we are talking about – for simplicity, why not just call her "Josephine"?

29   There is some doubt whether he did send it or at least planned to do so. The main point here as everywhere in the relations between Josephine and Beethoven is that everything between them was kept **secret**. We should be extremely grateful that Josephine kept at least 15 love letters by him (to be published for the first time 150 years later), whereas he kept this one to himself – but nothing else. And **why did she keep his letters** if her love had – supposedly – cooled down?

30   See Rita Steblin: "Joseph Deym and His Wax Museum: A Transitional Artist Important to Mozart and Beethoven." *International Musicological Society Meeting*, Zürich 2007.

31   Beethoven certainly (and obviously) disliked Stackelberg. And when he met Josephine in July 1812, her husband had just abandoned her, and her marriage was in such a disastrous state, that one can understand that – in her utter desperation – she did not feel like being bound by her vow. Certainly, the content of the Letter (like the consistent use of the intimate "Du") and the birth of Minona nine months later fit into this picture.

32   "Von Stak: habe ich noch keine Sylbe." (Franz Brunsvik to Josephine, 25 July 1812, in Goldschmidt 1977, p. 215.)

33   Strictly speaking, Stackelberg was probably still in Vienna (a big city), where he had rented a room away from home, in order to confer with God. His "Table of Rules" – covering the crucial week from 5 to 11 July – is clear evidence for this (Steblin 2007, p. 169).

34   As for the suggestive assumption that Stackelberg was struck by "homesickness" in 1813, and that this was therefore the reason for the break-up, one should recall that this man had been away from his home country for most of the time between ca. 1800 (probably earlier) and 1819: He first went to Germany to study, then to Pestalozzi in Switzerland, in 1809 to Austria-Hungary with Josephine, and even after his return in 1814 (to "kidnap" his children), he again went away to travel for at least two years (see also Nathalie Stackelberg 1882).

35   That is, to Josephine alone. Beethoven dedicated the Song "Ich denke dein" [I Am With You] with Variations WoO 74 to both Therese and Josephine,

which on formal grounds alone cannot be assumed to be a declaration of love – to two women at once? This does not rule out the possibility (most likely indeed) that Beethoven was in love with Josephine, but for well known reasons he suppressed his feelings, and he used this dedication also to express his gratitude to the Brunsvik (and the Deym) family.

[36] A few compositions by Beethoven without dedication that can be related to Josephine, apart from WoO 57 and Op. 32: Three Piano Sonatas Op. 31, 1802; Piano Sonata in F major Op. 54, 1804; Songs Op. 75, 1809; Symphony #8 in F major Op. 93, 1812; and her "Requiem", the Piano Sonata #31 in A flat major Op. 110, 1821.

[37] In Schmidt-Görg (1957), p. 17.

[38] The two compositions by Beethoven dedicated to Antonie Brentano are the Piano Sonata #32 in C minor Op. 111 (only the English edition), 1821–1822, and the 33 Variations for Piano in C major on a Waltz by Diabelli Op. 120, 1819–1823 – both published in 1823, two years after Josephine's death. The Allegretto for Piano Trio in B flat major WoO 39, 1812 (unpublished), a minor work, and the Piano Sonata #30 in E major Op. 109, 1820, were dedicated to her daughter Maximiliane. At least the later instances can clearly be interpreted as repaying the debts he incurred by "borrowing" money from Franz Brentano. – As for the *Diabelli Variations*, "she [Antonie] was not Beethoven's first choice. His original plan was to have the work sent to England where his old friend, Ferdinand Ries, would find a publisher. Beethoven promised the dedication to Ries's wife (Letter, 25 April 1823). A delay in the shipment to England resulted in confusion. Beethoven explained to Ries in a later letter, 'The variations were not to appear here until after they had been published in London, but everything went askew. The dedication to [Antonie] Brentano was intended only for Germany, as I was under obligation [!] to her and could publish nothing else at the time'." (http://en.wikipedia.org/wiki/Diabelli_Variations#Dedication, 22 Feb 2011)

[39] As Thayer already observed, early on, "[Beethoven's] dedications were but half disguised petitions for favor." (in Forbes 1967, p. 71). And later: "Beethoven's dedications of important works throughout his life were, as a rule, made to persons from whom he had received, or from whom he had hopes of receiving, pecuniary benefits." (in Forbes 1967, p. 107).

[40] The Piano Sonata Op. 110 was originally intended to be dedicated to Antonie Brentano (Goldschmidt 1977, p. 118) – i.e., before Josephine's death. A more than appropriate requiem – just listen to it!

[41] "Das Unterbleiben der Widmung des Liedes 'An die Hoffnung' bei dessen Veröffentlichung im Herbst 1805 ist unschwer als beabsichtigte Wahrung des Geheimnisses der Beziehungen beider zu verstehen." (La Mara 1920, p. 63.)

[42] The Bohemian town Karlsbad (now Karlovy Vary) was also often spelled "Carlsbad", which subsequently caused some to speculate that the "K" in the Letter could have referred to some other place. In the end it does not matter (see the chapter about "The Letter").

43   Not everywhere are Solomon's conjectures and speculations received as ultimate wisdom: "Regarding Solomon, I find him highly **dubious**. You can make a case for anything and **twist** the evidence to fit. For example the Immortal beloved – yes you can point to dates and places and come up with Antonie Brentano, providing you **ignore** Beethoven's character and his own often stated comments on adultery. Beethoven's religious views are well known so is he likely to have described the affair as 'truly founded in **heaven**' – and what is more, 'as strongly cemented as the firmament of heaven' if it were adulterous? Franz Brentano was a personal friend of Beethoven's and is it likely that he would have written to him in 1817: 'I greatly miss your company and that of your wife and your dear children', if he had been having an affair with his wife 5 years earlier? Nor could Beethoven have been discussing the prospect of marriage with her since the Austrian government would not have granted a divorce – her husband had no criminal convictions, and there is no evidence of adultery in either case. Having children made it even more unlikely they would have received a divorce. Solomon chooses to **ignore** these facts." (http://www.gyrix.com/forums/showthread.php?t=3114, 26 Dec 2010)

44   Meredith (in Walden 2011, p. xxi) informs us that "a major Beethoven scholar" told him that "those who refuse to accept the Antonie theory are 'impervious' to the facts [!] of the case".

45   "Mein Herz haben Sie schon längst, lieber Beethoven ... den größten Beweis meiner Liebe – meiner Achtung empfangen Sie, durch dieß Geständniß, durch daß Vertrauen! ... Ich liebe Sie unaussprechlich." (Josephine to Beethoven, ca. February/March 1805, draft, in Tellenbach 1983, p. 74.)

46   "Ich liebe Sie, und schätze ihren moralischen Charackter – Sie haben viel Liebe, und Gutes mir und meine Kindern erwiesen, daß werde ich nie vergessen, ... so lange ich lebe." (Josephine to Beethoven, 1805, draft, in Schmidt-Görg 1957, p. 25.)

47   "**Ihr Herz muss die Kraft haben nein zu sagen**, eine traurige Pflicht." (Therese to Charlotte, 20 January 1805, in La Mara 1920, p. 54.)

48   "Sie wäre glücklicher gewesen als mit St[ackelberg]. Mutterliebe bestimmte sie – – auf eigenes Glück zu verzichten." (Therese's Diary, 4 February 1846, in Schmidt-Görg 1957, p. 23.) Note that Therese's comparison with Stackelberg, though with hindsight, clearly implies that the – supposed – alternative (to marry Beethoven instead) must be placed into the time of 1810 and following.

49   "... da du meine Treue gegen dich kennst, nie eine andre kann mein Herz besizen, nie – nie." (Beethoven to Josephine?, 6/7 July 1812, draft, in Pichler 1994, p. 371.)

50   "... Josephine bei ihren häufigen Besuchen nach Prag niemals im Gasthof logierte, sondern stets bei ihrer Schwägerin, der Gräfin Golz, wohnte. Das berechtigt zu der Vermutung, daß das Wiedersehen mit Beethoven sich in deren Hause in der Prager Neustadt zugetragen hat." (Goldschmidt 1977, p. 238 f.) According to Steblin (2007, p. 158, n. 50), Victoire Countess Golz was actually in Nemischl in early July 1812. It can be assumed that Josephine could have stayed in

Victoire's house in Prague despite her absence (Tellenbach 1983, p. 111) – and what better place to meet Beethoven secretly!

51   It should be emphasized that before Steblin (2002, 2007, 2009, 2009a), Goldschmidt (1977) and Tellenbach (1983) had also invested a lot of legwork to sift through many handwritten documents, often almost illegible and out of order, undated or damaged. One should also not forget that La Mara (1920) took advantage of access to part of the Brunsvik estate, with the result that from letters and diaries she was already able to surmise that Josephine (not Therese) was most likely the "Immortal Beloved". Likewise Kaznelson (1954), who used Therese's meanwhile (partly) published Diary. (Sadly, their research was completely ignored in America – perhaps because it was written in German?)

52   "Um die Antonia–Hypothese möglicherweise mit den ihr sachlich innewaltenden Widersprüchen endgültig zu verifizieren, bedarf es der Falsifizierung anderer sich anbietender Hypothesen." (Goldschmidt 1977, p. 166.)

53   A typical example how researchers continue to fall into Solomon's trap is how most recently, Walden (2011, p. 2) concedes that "of the three front-runners" (notice the matter being depicted like a sports event – which horse do you bet on?), Antonie – supposedly – "was the only [!] woman who **was** [!] in Karlsbad". As if absence of evidence were evidence of absence! And this from a lawyer: Walden claims to put his "case" for – Bettina Brentano forward with "evidence" like in a court case. But seriously, is lack of an alibi sufficient proof if the suspect had no reason to hide simply because she didn't do it (Antonie was in Prague and Karlsbad as previously agreed with Beethoven), and could it not be that the real "culprit" (Josephine) left no traces just because she had very valid reasons that nobody should know about it? Which fits well with all the previous years where the love between Ludwig & Josephine was kept **secret** – like the addressee of the letter of 1812.

54   "Ohne schlüssige Beweise des Gegenteils wird man sich nicht mehr voreilig von der zunehmend begründeten Annahme trennen wollen, daß die 'Unsterbliche Geliebte' schwerlich eine andere als die 'Einzig Geliebte' war." (Goldschmidt 1977, p. 296.)

55   "Es steht günstig um Solomons Antonia-Hypothese." (Goldschmidt 1977, p. 149.) This under the heading "Fragezeichen" [Questionmarks], however, he then concludes it with the verdict that "the Antonia hypothesis … is not so fully convincing that it excludes all others." […die Antonia-Hypothese … nicht so restlos überzeugend ist, daß sie jede andere ausschließt.] (Goldschmidt 1977, p. 165 f.)

56   Beahrs (1986, 1988, 1993) is an exception. See also Tellenbach (1987, 1993/1994) and Dahlhaus (1991).

*Submissiveness, deepest
devotion to your destiny ...
oh tough struggle!*[1]

Beethoven's Diary

In 1812, Beethoven began to write a fascinating and often moving "Diary" (as it was to be called). However, it was not really a diary in the usual sense of making daily (or regular) notes of the latest events and impressions, but just a notebook or scratchpad, into which he penned occasional remarks, observations, thoughts and reminders, and many copies and excerpts from various books he had read (mainly classics and about Eastern religion).

Maynard Solomon who edited this Diary, with comments, suspected that

> probably a personal crisis gave rise to the beginning of the diary.[2]

And he thought that such

> confession-diaries are often created just because of the absence of alternative outlets for the communication of personal feelings. ... In the autumn of 1812, Beethoven was in a state of increased isolation.[3]

Unfortunately, the original of this Diary is lost, and subsequent copies were not always reliable and truthful. This was not only because Beethoven's handwriting was notoriously illegible (thus always a challenge to any copyist), but also because much was cryptic, abbreviated, or simply in a kind of "code" that left the reader more bewildered than informed. It was just **not meant to be read** by anyone else.

The first two complete copies were made first by Anton Gräffer and then by Joseph Fischhof. As Solomon states:

> In Vienna, Fischhof and Gräffer were experts in music manuscripts, who knew each other well. ... There is no doubt that Fischhof's copy is in fact derived from the manuscript of Gräffer.[4]

We should bear these two important statements in mind, as Solomon decided (not unreasonably) to base his edition of Beethoven's Diary entirely on the very first copy, namely Gräffer's. After all, a copy of a copy can only get worse.

The very first note in Beethoven's Tagebuch was probably made around September 1812 (at least it is under the heading "1812", perhaps added by the copyist), and it is generally considered to reflect his state of mind in the aftermath of the encounter with his "Immortal Beloved":

> Submissiveness, deepest devotion to your destiny ... Oh tough struggle! – Do everything necessary to prepare for the long journey ... You are not allowed to be **human, not for you, only for others**, for you there is no happiness any more but in yourself, in your art – Oh God! give me the strength to defeat myself, nothing can bind me to life. –
>
> In this manner with A [?] everything goes to ruin – – –.[5]

The meaning of the letter "**A**" has puzzled researchers ever since. Could it have anything to do with the unknown "Immortal Beloved"? We already know that the whole love affair with Josephine was always kept – almost – perfectly secret.

But what could have been the meaning of such a sentence (referring to one "A"), anyway? Was it really a **name**, or maybe a place, or something else? If Josephine (or whoever else one would like to assume to have been the "Immortal Beloved") had left (or even betrayed) Beethoven, to stay with her husband – shouldn't we rather conclude that **he** was the one responsible for Beethoven's despair, that "with" **him**, "everything is destroyed"? (Steblin 2007, p. 153.)

And what about the three dashes "– – –": Is it possible that something was omitted or unreadable? And why? We should also not be surprised that Solomon, driven by his fixation on Antonie Brentano as the "one", concludes:

> "A" could be the first letter of the name of the addressee of Beethoven's letter to the "Immortal Beloved".[6]

This is unlikely, as Beethoven (affectionately, of course) referred to Antonie almost always as "Toni". We should also note here, that "in this manner, **with** A" translates the German "mit" simply by "with". However, in this context, where "A" is referred to as the **cause** of all the trouble, it makes more sense to render this instead as in this manner, **because of** A [?], everything goes to ruin.

Now the real puzzle is: Who was the mysterious person **behind** Beethoven's "Immortal Beloved" (whoever she was) that caused him such despair, and whose name he abbreviated to "A"? The solution was provided most convincingly by Steblin (2007, p. 153), who concluded that it must have been – Stackelberg! And the "A" was not an "A" really, but most likely "**St**".

This is not mere speculation, given the background of what we know already about Beethoven and Josephine. A closer look at both Gräffer's and Fischhof's copies of the Diary should give us some decisive clues: Even though Gräffer's was the first copy made (and indeed because of that), we cannot conclude that his rendering of what may have been an indecipherable letter in the original should be 100% correct. This is contradicted by the fact that the next copyist, Fischhof, who in turn copied Gräffer, was completely unable to copy this clearly identifiable "A" (see below) – but instead wrote something almost illegible that looks more like **two** letters scribbled on top of each other.

The only explanation for such a fumble on account of the experienced copyist Fischhof is that in this case he did **not** just copy Gräffer's version, but had a closer look at the original (and probably also talked to Gräffer himself). This cannot be ruled out; as Solomon himself states, both copyists knew and consulted with each other, and would have sought each other's opinion about doubtful passages, at least occasionally. Apparently, Gräffer did all the legwork first by creating his copy, in a legible handwriting; Fischhof then took the easier option to copy mainly – but perhaps **not exclusively** – from Gräffer's.

Thus, it appears that Fischhof probably learned from Gräffer about this passage and its – almost – unidentifiable "letter" (or letters?), and that Gräffer, for simplicity (or who knows, based on what assumption?) made up his mind and rendered it clearly as an "A". Fischhof then had a closer look again at the original, and copied it **more faithfully** – as an almost illegible scribble that could be anything from "A" (Antonie? Almerie? Amenda? Amalie? ...) or "D" (Dorothea?) or "J" (Josephine? Johanna?), to "K" (Karl?) or "R" (Rahel?) or "S" (Susanna?) or "T" (Toni? Therese? Teresa? ...) – or perhaps just a lowercase "t", with an uppercase "S" written over it (or slightly before): "**St**" (Stackelberg).

So when Solomon adds that
> Unlike in Fischhof's manuscript, the reading of the letter as "A" at this point in Gräffer's copy is unequivocal.[7]

then this is actually **not** a sufficiently valid reason to just follow Gräffer's **interpretation** (what else is it?), and to ignore Fischhof's only because it is less "unequivocal". The very reason **why** this strange difference came about needs explanation! – And, unfortunately for Solomon and all those who got fixated on the "A" – the only conclusion we can draw as a near certainty is: **This cipher was most likely anything but an "A"**.

It is important to realize that Gräffer when copying Beethoven's Diary was indeed **not always faithful** to the original, that he reinterpreted words or phrases and, most importantly, he **omitted** many passages (or replaced them by dashes "– – –"). Unfortunately, there is no way to even speculate what is missing (or what has been added or changed) – with the original being lost.

* * *

The job of being Beethoven's copyist was not an easy one (see the Chapter in the Appendix "Comparison of a Surviving Fragment of Beethoven's Diary with Gräffer's Copy"). The only thing we can say for sure is that despite Gräffer's confident rendering, the cryptic cipher Beethoven wrote in 1812 was almost certainly **not** an "A".

Below on the left, Gräffer's surprisingly clear and unmistakable "A" (from Steblin 2007, p. 152), and next to it, what Fischhof thought it looked like (from Tellenbach 1983, p. 122), both enlarged:

[1]   "Ergebenheit, innigste Ergebenheit in dein Schicksal ... o harter Kampf!" (Beethoven's Diary, in Solomon 2005, p. 29.)

[2]   "Wahrscheinlich bildete eine persönliche Krise den Anlaß für den Beginn des Tagebuches." (Solomon 2005, p. 1.) Note that this German edition was in fact edited, translated and annotated by the German Sieghard Brandenburg. Some background about this Diary can be found in Tellenbach (1983), pp. 283–285.

[3]   "Bekenntnis-Tagebücher entstehen oft gerade in Ermangelung alternativer Ventile für die Mitteilung persönlicher Gefühle. ... Im Herbst 1812 befand sich Beethoven in einem Zustand erhöhter Isolierung." (Solomon 2005, p. 2.)

[4]   "Als Wiener Spezialisten für Musikhandschriften waren Fischhof und Gräffer einander gut bekannt. ... Es gibt keinen Zweifel, daß sich das Fischhof-Manuskript tatsächlich von Gräffers Konvolut herleitet." (Solomon 2005, p. 12.) Tellenbach (1983, p. 284) discusses the possibility that there was an intermediate copy, which both Gräffer and Fischhof used as a starting point. This does however not affect the conclusions I am suggesting here.

[5]   "Ergebenheit, innigste Ergebenheit in dein Schicksal ... o harter Kampf! – Alles anwenden was noch zu thun ist um das Nöthige zu der weiten Reise zu entwerfen ... Du darfst nicht **Mensch** seyn, **für dich nicht, nur für andre**; für dich gibt's kein Glück mehr als in dir selbst in deiner Kunst – o Gott! gib mir Kraft, mich zu besiegen, mich darf ja nichts an das Leben fesseln. – Auf diese Art mit A [?] geht alles zu Grunde – – –." (Beethoven's Diary, in Solomon 2005, p. 29 f.) The three dashes "– – –" probably indicate that the copyist omitted something that he could not decipher. And in this context, it must have been something important.

[6]   "'A' könnte der Anfangsbuchstabe des Namens der Adressatin sein, an die Beethovens Brief an die 'Unsterbliche Geliebte' gerichtet war." (Solomon 2005, p. 30.) Against this, Harry Goldschmidt, in the last publication of his life, "'Auf diese Art mit A geht alles zu Grunde'. Eine umstrittene Tagebuchstelle in neuem Licht" ["In this manner with A everything goes to ruin." New Light on a Disputed Diary Note.], in: Harry Goldschmidt (ed.): *Zu Beethoven. Aufsätze und Dokumente.* [About Beethoven. Essays and Documents.] Vol. 3. Berlin: Neue Musik 1988, argues that "A" stands for Amalie Sebald, whom Beethoven may have intended to marry to compensate for the frustration he experienced after his encounter with the "Immortal Beloved" (whoever she was – but certainly not Amalie). Goldschmidt assumes this to have been a repeat of the episode with Teresa Malfatti two years before, to whom Beethoven proposed after Josephine got married again… Trouble is, Solomon and Goldschmidt are both wrong, simply because (as we shall see presently) this particular letter was **not** an "A"!

[7]   "Anders als im Fischhof-Manuskript ist die Lesart 'A' in der Gräffer-Kopie an dieser Stelle völlig eindeutig." (Solomon 2005, p. 30.)

*My view of your character ...
Once I am fully convinced of
this, I will calmly forget you,
and I will despise you.*[1]

Christoph von Stackelberg

An evaluation of Josephine von Brunsvik's tragic life would be incomplete without giving due consideration to Christoph Baron von Stackelberg, who was her companion, lover and husband for nearly 13 years – more than any other person of her acquaintance in her adult life (apart from Therese).

However, for most of this time he was conspicuous by his **absence**: After their wedding in 1810, he was frequently traveling to arrange financial matters (with ultimately disastrous effect); in 1811, Josephine did not want to sleep with him anymore and went on holiday without him; in June 1812, he left in a huff, only to return two months later to sign what was like a formal separation contract (the closest to a divorce, except that he but not Josephine was free to leave – which he did); in 1813 (at the time of Minona's birth), he disappeared for several months;[2] in 1814, he turned up only to "kidnap" his daughters and vanished again; in 1815, he returned with money but Josephine was not interested and went into hiding (being pregnant); in 1816, he moved back to Estonia (and had his brother Otto doing the dirty work of grabbing his children – just when Josephine had found them again); in 1817, Stackelberg's brief presence in Vienna is documented by a bond to Josephine that he signed.

And finally, in late 1819, he paid a visit to Vienna with the three girls, after which he left for good, while Josephine continued to waste away, and died, alone and lonely, a little more than one year later.

Was Stackelberg a "cruel" man?

* * *

After Josephine had to withdraw from her faithful friend Beethoven, mainly as a sacrifice to her children and because of the pressure by her family, it was Stackelberg whom she hired as a teacher and educator.

And after he had seduced her – most likely not with her full consent as she was weakened after yet another severe illness – the illegitimate child she bore him, combined with his threat to discontinue the education of her other children, left her with little choice but to marry him. At best, a marriage of convenience. And much inconvenience, because Stackelberg was disliked by everyone of the Brunsviks, and he remained a stranger to Viennese life.

We know from Therese's memoirs and diary notes as well as Josephine's diary, that already in 1809 Josephine began to withdraw from him. Even though she was pregnant with his child, she rejected any further advances by him. Instead, after her return to Hungary (in late 1809 or maybe 1810 – the date is uncertain), she renewed contact with Beethoven (by letter at least).

One could argue that especially Therese's view of Josephine's relationship to Stackelberg might be biased by jealousy – she complained about how he had outmanœvered her in Switzerland and Italy, regarding the education of the boys, and – to be alone with Josephine. But there is a significant difference to Therese's stance towards her sister's relationship with Beethoven: The composer was admired, adored and – we may say – also loved "as a like-minded spirit", by both sisters. In fact, this adoration and devotion by Therese was so strongly expressed (much more so than in any letter by, say, Antonie Brentano) that until the publication of the 13 Love Letters to Josephine in 1957, many thought that only Therese could have been the addressee of the mysterious "Letter to the Immortal Beloved".[3]

Of course, she was not. She kept her early vow to remain unmarried (as a "Priestess of Truth"), despite one or two romantic episodes. But she clearly expressed her view (in her private diary entries – not in her memoirs, which were obviously written for publication), that Josephine had loved Beethoven "passionately", and that she should have married him instead – not Stackelberg. And it was Therese, who stayed in contact with Beethoven, in

1811 (when he asked her for Josephine's drawing of an "Eagle looking towards the Sun"), and after 1812, on several occasions.

* * *

So who was this Stackelberg, who entered Josephine's life in 1808, married her in 1810, and then went on to ruin her financially (and physically and emotionally)? Astonishingly, very little is known about this man. He was born in 1777, as one of 16 children, and apparently – like his other 14 siblings – was always in the shadow of his younger brother Otto Magnus, who was to become a famous archaeologist.

There exists a biography of Otto (by his daughter Nathalie), with a few mentions of brother Christoph: Both studied at the University of Göttingen in Germany, Christoph went on to travel to Switzerland, and he became a follower of Pestalozzi. Winter 1803 until May 1804 saw Otto and Christoph in Geneva.

The biographer also reports the

> return of Otto to his home country, [and] a visit to brother Christoph in Vienna, who had meanwhile married a Hungarian Countess.[4]

In 1819, Christoph settled in Estonia, taking on a government position as a school principal – concerned mainly with religious education.

The pious man had found his calling.

> 1819. Christoph Baron von Stackelberg, born 1777 in Fähna in Estonia, pupil of Reval College, studied in Göttingen, concerned himself with education at Yverdon with Pestalozzi and corresponded with Franz von Baader, Jung-Stilling and others...[5]

A real gem is the following excerpt about

> the religious aspirations of Councilor and Knight Christoph Baron von Stackelberg, appointed in 1819 as Director of the High School at Reval as well as all other public schools under the Estonian Government, through the special trust of the then Curator, later Minister of Public Enlightenment, Prince Lieven. He [Stackelberg] tried, publicly and quietly here in Estonia, as well as in Switzerland and Germany in a slightly different way, like his contemporary and peer Frau von Krüdener née von Vietinghoff,[6] to encourage in all

> classes of society a more vibrant Christianity and a more stringent asceticism, whereby he set himself a lasting memory through the founding of his Sunday Schools and schools for the poor in Reval. This direction as initiated by him as well as the new teachers at the theological faculty in Dorpat was well received by the aristocracy of this country, especially by some highly educated and influential ladies...[7]

On an Estonian website, one can find a brief biographical note of *Adam Christoph von Stackelberg*, ending with his

> removal from office as the Director of the Estonian Province schools in 1834. It was clear that, despite a long period in office, his performance was not such a "rich blessing" as could have been expected.[8]

In the "Katalog der Deutschen Nationalbibliothek" [Catalogue of the German National Library], one finds under "Stackelberg, Christoph Adam/von" the following entry:

> Austria. Teacher and Nobleman, Husband of Josephine Brunsvik–Deym–Stackelberg, Beethoven's "Immortal Beloved".[9]

Stackelberg's career as a government official responsible for religious education (even though it ended in ignominy by dismissal) corresponds well with Therese's sarcastic description of his leaving in June 1812 to seek through prayer enlightenment from the Lord and the "Table of Rules" that he wrote up for the week of 5–11 July 1812, mixed up with Therese's – surviving – Diary (Steblin 2007, p. 163), which was suspiciously silent about the period from the end of June to the beginning of August 1812.

* * *

Most of what we know about Stackelberg is based on the memoirs, diaries and notes of Therese, as well as miscellaneous documents found in Josephine's estate. But among his surviving letters there is also a lengthy one to his wife that reveals much about how he perceived their relationship (in Skwara/Steblin 2007). It was written at the end of April 1815, after he had returned from Estonia with the news of having made an inheritance (after the death of one of his brothers), and apparently he made yet another unsuccessful attempt to get Josephine to follow him to his homeland.

Stackelberg begins with a reference to a dispute they had the day before:
> The openness with which you expressed yourself yesterday confirmed my view of your character. ... Once I am fully convinced of this, I will calmly forget you, and I will despise you. You show in your thoughts a vulgarity, with a shallow view of the human condition, and a shallow assessment of actions and characters. ... If however the vulgar is now what is vigorous and vivid in you, then I must lose that belief [that great things determine your actions] and I must despise you.[10]

Having set the scene, he follows up with a reminder of their happy past:
> ... you claim you never loved me, never wanted to marry me, that I have forced you to give yourself to me through all the tricks of seduction, ... that I was only interested in the sensual possession of you, even against your will, you say you understand that I did not mention anything about my financial circumstances in order to deceive you; you consider it a crime that I wanted to conclude our relationship only among us and without consulting your relatives, that I did not immediately after my arrival here participate in the life of the Big World ... and that inflamed your relatives against me more and more.[11]

He most accurately reiterates Josephine's point of view (as it matches the sisters' recollections) and contrasts it with his own:
> You have forgotten what made us both so happy and what the belief in a better life established within us. You forget that you often wavered in your opinion of me, soon you gave yourself to me in bliss, then you withdrew again; that I was prudish for a long time, did not touch you even slightly, that early on I expressed my belief that a closer union should be forever, when one could never again separate, that in Geneva already you gave yourself to me so nicely, without me having in the least compelled you, you say out of compassion, as a sacrifice, but I had to believe it was love. Only later on our journey did you no longer want to be united with me, and you said to me you could not love me; I considered this to be like a divorce and had to work against it as I have worked against it now.[12]

Understandably, he perceived Josephine's "sacrifice" to him as a precursor to an everlasting, happy marriage. Only he seems to forget that he was the one, who de facto divorced her when he left her (and seven children) two years before this letter was written, and he had three of their children forcibly removed by the police one year thereafter.

Stackelberg then appeals to their original romantic involvement:
> You forget completely that we were emotionally so excited that we forgot all worldly things, financial matters, the judgment of the relatives, reality, for we lived only in an idealistic world. ... Surely, it was not cunning that I did not mention my financial situation.[13]

Naturally, when blinded by love, who wants to talk about money? (Except that, according to Therese, the financial ruin caused by Stackelberg's ineptness had been the main reason for the breakdown of their marriage.)

Stackelberg (who was in Switzerland before 1809 and again after 1814) must have been infected by some fiercely puritan Calvinism:
> In silence I prayed to God to make me a good person, and useful to mankind.[14]

After this repeated self-aggrandizement as a pious and virtuous person, he finds it necessary to justify – again – the reason for abducting their children:
> I took our little children away, because I was convinced that it was the only way to pull them away from the sad conditions, the peril into which our circumstances had brought them. This was one of my noble actions, which you also interpret as a crime, explaining it to be out of my resentment and vindictiveness.[15]

One must wonder what purpose it serves to rub it in, once again, that – in Stackelberg's opinion (as he had denounced her with the police) – Josephine was a bad mother, who neglected her children...

He finally comes to the point:
> That the house and the boys are causing you to be in an improper situation, of this the latest proof is Andrehan's [Andrian's] admission by you. He is an out-and-out immoral vulgar person, given the indecent acts he committed with certain women. ... Circumstances cause you to take him into your house.[16]

This is not only just jealousy by a cuckolded husband – Stackelberg was in fact perfectly right to be incensed about

212

Andrian's character: This man was already known to the police having seduced (raped?) a young Countess in 1812 (Skwara/Steblin 2007, p. 187, n. 15).

This is indicative of Stackelberg's way of dissembling: After all, didn't he cause all the trouble in the first place by leaving his wife alone with four teenage children, a large house and a gallery, but no money? And shouldn't we expect a woman like Josephine – being frequently ill, having suffered many nervous breakdowns, and desperate for at least a little love and attention – to be susceptible to the charming advances of a young and handsome man?

No, Stackelberg keeps blaming his wife:

> He deceives you, you entrust him with your children and everything else, you have him with you from morning to evening, and you suspect nothing. You take on his principles, the worst one can think of, you consider him to be a great man, you call him our friend, you tell him many things about us, you admire the most ridiculous nonsense he says about education.
>
> What will people think, when the chambermaid says he is alone with you in your room in the morning, when you are still in bed? Are you not indifferent to the gossip to which this gives occasion? The opinions of Andrehan [Andrian], the misjudgment of his character reinforce my opinion that wickedness is more alive in you than high-mindedness.[17]

Remember how the Brunsviks were so incensed that the police believed the gossip about Josephine spread by servants? Who is (again) keen to hear what "the chambermaid says"?

Only a few weeks after this letter was written, someone (?) tipped off the police that Josephine's

> morality ... does not appear to enjoy a good reputation, and it is stated that she cannot be absolved from having given ground for conjugal quarrels.

Who is the hypocrite here?

* * *

At the end of the day, it does not matter whether Stackelberg was or was not intentionally cruel to Josephine. He certainly was a tormented soul, he had difficulties finding his way through life, especially in Austria and Hungary where he was rejected by high society, and from his point of view his relationship with the capricious Josephine was not always smooth sailing.

The catastrophic financial situation that he ended up with overwhelmed him probably more than the Brunsviks (and the Deyms), who at least had considerable assets. It is also possible (some say even likely) that he suspected that Minona was not his daughter – but he could not allow himself to risk a scandal, a divorce, and shame.

His best option was to disappear – again (after Minona's birth),[18] as he had disappeared the year before when the financial problems were too much for him. He did not have the guts to face his wife to discuss an amicable separation and the handing over of "his" three children; instead he called in the police to abduct them. A shocking, traumatizing experience for any loving mother, especially for the emotionally so unstable Josephine! It is hard to see any trace of paternal or conjugal love in this action by the enraged (vengeful?) husband.

And can we find an excuse for the subsequent smear campaign when Stackelberg acted as the obvious anonymous source reporting to the police about the "questionable" reputation of his wife? Didn't he deceive her by dumping the three daughters at a Bohemian deacon's place, claiming they would soon be returned to their mother (as Leyer wrote)?

And wasn't God on his (the religious fanatic's) side again when he was too busy traveling the world and sent his brother Otto to pick up the three girls for their final destination in far away Estonia, just in time as they were about to return into their heartbroken mother's arms?

Christoph Baron von Stackelberg (photo courtesy of the Estonian Historical Archives, Tallinn)

[1] "... die Ansicht ... von deinem Character. ... Wenn ich ganz davon ueberzeugt bin werde ich ruhig dich vergeßen, und werde dich verachten." (Stackelberg to Josephine, ca. 27 April 1815, in Skwara/Steblin 2007, p. 183.)

[2] It seems that Stackelberg was back home in December 1813.

[3] See Tenger (1890) for pure fiction and La Mara (1909) for a more scholarly work; also Rolland (1928).

[4] "Rückkehr Ottos in die Heimat, Besuch Bruder Christophs in Wien, der mittlerweile mit einer ungarischen Gräfin verheiratet war". (Nathalie Stackelberg 1882, p. 301.)

[5] "1819. Christoph Baron von Stackelberg, geb. 1777 zu Fähna in Estland, Zögling des revalschen Gymnasiums, studierte in Göttingen, beschäftigte sich mit der Pädagogik zu Yverdon bei Pestalozzi und stand im Verkehr mit Franz von Ba[a]der, Jung–Stilling und anderen..." (Geschichtsblätter des revalschen Gouvernements-Gymnasiums zu dessen 250jährigen Jubiläum am 6. Juni 1881, zusammengestellt und dargebracht von G. von Hansen. [Historical Notes of the Government College at Reval on its 250[th] Anniversary on 6 June 1881, collected and edited by G. von Hansen.]) Franz Benedict von Baader (1765–1841) was a German philosopher whose ambitious attempt to reconcile the Roman-Catholic with the Greek-Orthodox faith was rejected by the Russian Government. Johann Heinrich Jung-Stilling (1740–1817) must have been one of Stackelberg's favorite pals: He kickstarted his religious Œuvre in 1796 with a novel in four volumes called "Das Heimweh" [Homesickness], and he became the most popular religious writer of his time with edifying works like "Die Siegsgeschichte der christlichen Religion" [History of the Victorious Christian Religion] in 1799 and "Lehrsätze der Naturgeschichte für Frauenzimmer" [The Laws of Natural History for Womenfolk] in 1816.

[6] Barbara Juliane Baroness von Krüdener née von Vietinghoff (1764–1824), born in Riga (Latvia), was a religious mystic and author. She inspired Czar Alexander to enter the so-called "Holy Alliance".

[7] "... die religiösen Bestrebungen des im J. 1819 bei dem Gymnasium zu Reval als Director zugleich auch aller öffentlichen Lehranstalten des esthl. Gouvernements durch das besondere Vertrauen des damaligen Curators ..., nachmaligen Ministers der Volksaufklärung Fürsten Lieven berufenen Hofrath und Ritter Christoph Baron von Stackelberg. Dieser suchte öffentlich und im Stillen hier in Esthland, wiewohl in etwas anderer Weise, wie seine Zeit= und Standes=Genossin Frau von Krüdener, geb. v. Vietinghoff in der Schweitz und Deutschland in allen Classen der Gesellschaft lebendigeres Christenthum und strengere Ascetik anzuregen, wobei er durch die Gründung seiner Sonntags= und Armenschulen in Reval sich ein bleibendes Andenken stiftete. Auch bei der Aristokratie des Landes fand diese zugleich von den neuen Lehrern der theologischen Fakultät in Dorpat angebahnte Richtung hin und wieder, besonders bei einigen hochgebildeten einflußreichen Frauen vielen Anklang..." (Archiv für die Geschichte Liv–, Est– und Curlands, Volume 6. I. Entwurf zur Kirchen= und Religions=Geschichte Esthlands, von Gustav Carlblom, derzeitigem Prediger zu St.

Catharinae auf der Halb=Insel Ruckoe, nachmals Probst der Insural=Wieck und Assessor des kaiserl. esthl. Prov.=Consitorii zu Reval. § 11. Elfter Abschnitt. Von den religiösen und kirchlichen Verhältnissen in Esthland. Unter der Regierung des Kaisers Nicolai I. Von 1825 bis 1850 [Archive for the History of Livland, Estonia and Curland, Volume 6. I. Outline of the History of Church and Religion in Estonia, by Gustav Carlblom, current Preacher at St Catherine's of the Ruckoe Peninsula, later Probst of Wieck Island and Assessor of the Imperial Estonian Provisional Consitorii at Reval. § 11. Section Eleven. Of the Religious and Church Conditions in Estonia. Under the Government of Emperor Nicolai I. From 1825 to 1850], p. 33.)

[8] "A. C. von Stackelbergi Eestimaa kubermangu koolide direktori ametist tagandamise kohta 1834. aastal selgub, et vaatamata pikale ametiajale, polnud tema töötulemused nii 'õnnistusrikkad' kui võinuks oodata." (http://www.eha.ee/arhiivikool/index.php?tree_id=165, 8 Feb 2011) This website also contains the only picture of Christoph that I could find. – There is not a single word of Christoph to be found on the German website http://www.von-stackelberg.de/ (26 Dec 2010) – only Otto is mentioned, in much detail. An email request to service@von-stackelberg.de was not answered.

[9] "Österreich. Lehrer und Adliger, Ehemann von Josephine Brunsvik–Deym–Stackelberg, der 'unsterblichen Geliebten' Beethovens". (http://dnb.info/gnd/136160980, 2 Feb 2011) Still not quite correct as he was not an Austrian but an Estonian.

[10] "Die Offenheit mit der du dich Gestern äußertest, bestätigte mir die Ansicht ... von deinem Character. ... Wenn ich ganz davon ueberzeugt bin werde ich ruhig dich vergeßen, und werde dich verachten. Es zeigt sich in deinen Gedanken eine ... Gemeinheit, mit einer flachen Ansicht der menschlichen Verhältnisse, und einer flachen Beurtheilung der Handlungen und der Charactäre. ... Wenn aber das Gemeine jezt das Kräftige und Lebendige in dir ist ..., so verliere ich jenen Glauben [daß das Große deine Handlungen bestimme] und ich muß dich verachten." (Stackelberg to Josephine, ca. 27 April 1815, in Skwara/Steblin 2007, p. 183.)

[11] "... du vorgibst mich nie geliebt, mich nie heurathen wollen, ich habe durch alle Künste der Verführung dich gezwungen dich mir hinzugeben, ... es sey mir nur um den sinnlichen Besitz deiner, auch wider deinen Willen, zu thun gewesen, du gibst mir zu verstehen ich habe nichts von meinem Vermögen erwähnt um dich zu täuschen; du siehst es als ein Verbrechen an daß ich unsere Verbindung nur unter uns habe abschließen wollen und ohne deine Verwandte[n] darüber zu fragen, daß ich nicht gleich bei meiner Ankunft hier ... an dem Leben in der großen Welt Theil genommen habe ... und deine Verwandte[n] nicht noch immer mehr gegen mich aufzubringen." (Stackelberg to Josephine, ca. 27 April 1815, in Skwara/Steblin 2007, p. 183 f.)

[12] "Du hast vergeßen was uns beide so glücklich machte und was der Glaube an ein schöneres Leben in uns begründete. Du vergißt daß du in deinen Urtheilen ueber mich oft wanktest, bald mit Seeligkeit dich mir hingabst, bald dich zurückzogst; daß ich lange sehr sittsam war, nicht im mindesten dich berührte, daß ich dir frühe meine Ueberzeugung äußerte daß eine nähere Verbindung auf ewig

sey, man dann sich nie mehr trennen könne, daß du schon in Genf dich so schön mir hingabst, ... ohne daß ich im geringsten dich zwang, du sagst aus Mitleiden, aus Aufopferung, ich mußte aber glauben aus Liebe. Erst später auf der Reise hast du nicht mehr mit mir vereinigt seyn wollen und hast mir gesagt du könntest mich nicht lieben, daß ich dieses als eine Ehescheidung ansah u. dawider arbeiten mußte wie ich jezt dawider gearbeitet habe." (Stackelberg to Josephine, ca. 27 April 1815, in Skwara/Steblin 2007, p. 185.)

[13] "Du vergißt ganz[,] daß unsere Gefühle so hoch gespannt waren, daß wir alles Irdische, das Vermögen, die Urtheile der Verwandten, die Wirklichkeit vergaßen, denn wir lebten nur in einer ideali[sti]schen Welt. ... Sicher war es nicht aus List[,] daß ich von meinem Vermögen nicht sprach." (Stackelberg to Josephine, ca. 27 April 1815, in Skwara/Steblin 2007, p. 186.)

[14] "Ich betete in der Stille zu Gott mich gut zu machen, und nützlich den Menschen." (Stackelberg to Josephine, ca. 27 April 1815, in Skwara/Steblin 2007, p. 186.)

[15] "Ich nahm unsere kleinen Kinder weg, weil ich die Ueberzeugung hatte es sey das einzige Mittel sie aus den traurigen Verhältnißen zu reißen, in die zu ihrer größten Gefahr die Umstände uns versezt hatten. Das war eine meiner edlen Handlungen, die du auch als ein Verbrechen auslegst, sie aus meinem Groll, aus meiner Rachsucht erklärend." (Stackelberg to Josephine, ca. 27 April 1815, in Skwara/Steblin 2007, p. 186.)

[16] "Daß das Haus und die Knaben dich in Verhältniße bringen[,] die unschicklich sind, davon gibt den neuesten Beweis Andrehan's [Andrians] Aufnahme bei dir. Er ist jezt ausgemacht einer der unmoralischsten gemeinsten Menschen, giebt sich selbst mit seinen besonderen mit Weibern begangenen Unsittlichkeiten. ... Die Umstände machen daß du ihn ins Haus nimmst." (Stackelberg to Josephine, ca. 27 April 1815, in Skwara/Steblin 2007, p. 187.)

[17] "Er verstellt sich, du vertraust ihm deine Kinder an, alles an, du hast ihn vom Morgen bis an den Abend bei dir, u. ahndest nichts. Du nimmst seine Grundsätze an, die schlechtesten, die man sich denken kann, du häl[t]st ihn endlich gern für einen großen Mann, du nennst ihn unsern Freund, du theilst ihm mehreres über uns mit, den lächerlichsten Nonsens den er über Erziehung sagt, bewunderst du. Was sollen die Leute glauben, wenn das Stubenmädchen sagt, er sey des Morgens allein bei dir in deinem Zimmer, wenn du ... noch im Bette liegst? Können dir die Reden zu denen dies Gelegenheit gibt nicht gleichgültig seyn? Die Urtheile über Andrehan [Andrian], das Verkennen seines Wesens bestärkt mich in dem Urtheil es lebe jezt das Gemeine lebendiger in dir als das Höhere." (Stackelberg to Josephine, ca. 27 April 1815, in Skwara/Steblin 2007, p. 187.)

[18] According to Fritz Deym's memoirs (Steblin 2007, p. 173), Stackelberg was present at Minona's birth (contradicting Therese). It is possible that Fritz was dissembling here as he was very fond of his stepfather. There are also letters (still unpublished) indicating that Stackelberg was living again with Josephine in late 1813.

*When the wind blows over
it, she is gone,
And her place remembers
her no more.*[1]

Conclusion

6 July 2012 is the bicentenary of the day when Beethoven began to write a letter to his "Immortal Beloved", as it was to be called, misleadingly; really it was – yet another – letter addressed to the one and only woman he used to call his "**Angel**". This is the appropriate time to reflect on and (try to) once and for all clarify the relevance and the context of this event.

There is nothing to commemorate, let alone celebrate, though. 1812 was the year of crisis, of unexpected reunion, final consummation, and equally final – and irrevocable – separation. It had to be. Necessity spoke.

Hundreds of books and biographies have been written about Beethoven, dozens of movies and documentaries made his music and the main facts of his life known to everyone. And many, far too many myths and legends. But almost nothing (in English) has been published[2] about Josephine. For one and a half centuries, no one knew (or could even imagine) that there was a deep, intense, mutual love between Josephine and Ludwig – indeed from their very first meeting in 1799 until her death in 1821. And beyond. A love – as Ludwig lamented in his letters – that could not even be expressed in words.

* * *

It was Music. **Only** in Music. And Beethoven was the greatest master of this language, expressed in the most beautiful notes. There can be no doubt that **Josephine was the inspiration** behind his major works, his alter ego ("Mein Ich"). She spoke and continued to speak to him, especially in the years after 1812 when he was becoming increasingly deaf.

> I can only speak in a few words of that which the Spirit tells me in moments of calm. Our friendship can only be assumed to exist in such moments... Insofar as the soul speaks – it does not speak any more. – Spirits are silent.[3]

* * *

The point is not that there is no "proof" that Josephine was in Prague at the time (simply because this, like everything else about her relationship with Beethoven, was strictly kept secret – and we have to respect this). The point is that Josephine's and Ludwig's lives were so intricately intertwined during the time before as well as after 1812 that the Letter can, at best, be called a "missing link". Connecting two lives, one of which would eventually – after a less productive hiatus of almost six years – despite increasing deafness and ongoing troubles with a naughty nephew and his obstinate mother, culminate in the greatest musical achievements, unsurpassed ever since. The other life – Josephine's – turned out to be, sadly, the tragic completion of a fateful journey from a blissful youth in heaven-like surroundings and luxury towards the hellish experience of abandonment by her husband and her family, the loss of her children, misery and illness.

She was forever torn between her "enthusiasm" for music – Beethoven's music, and thus her feelings of affection for the one man, who understood her – and the strict rules of her class, her duties and responsibilities as a mother.

In a way she was a heroine, though a tragic one – struggling against a cruel fate which had cast the dice against her. As a woman she could not escape the chains of motherhood – and the restrictions imposed by her class. The latter condemned her to oblivion. Ultimately, successfully.

It is time to lift the veil. Josephine!

[1]   *Wenn der Wind darüber geht, so ist sie nimmer da, Und ihre Stätte kennt sie nicht mehr. (Psalm 103:16)*

This is quoted in http://www.lvbeethoven.com/Famille/FamilyTree–Minona.html (27 Apr 2011), under the heading "The enigma of Minona Stackelberg", supposedly the inscription on the headstone (no longer existing) on Minona's grave. Unfortunately, this story is full of errors.

[2]   The one notable exception is the excellent biography by Tellenbach (1983), extensively quoted in this book, but – being in German – almost completely ignored in the English speaking world. Some (like Solomon) could not avoid at least quoting the title of her book. But it seems hardly anyone cared to read (let alone translate) it. Recently, Steblin (2007, 2009) at last published articles in the English language – in a German journal.

[3]   "Ich kann nur mit wenig Worten von dem sprechen was der Geist zu mir spricht in den Augenblicken der Ruhe ... Unsere Freundschaft kann auch nur in solchen Augenblicken als existierend angenommen werden... Indem die Seele spricht – spricht sie nicht mehr. – Geister sind stumm." (Josephine to Beethoven?, 8 April 1818, draft, in Tellenbach 1983, p. 195.)

Appendix

Chronology

1770: 16 December (ca.), Ludwig van Beethoven born.

1775: 27 July, Therese Countess von Brunsvik born.

1777: 4 December, Christoph Baron von Stackelberg born.

1779: 28 March, Josephine Countess von Brunsvik born.

1799: Anna Countess von Brunsvik and her daughters Therese and Josephine meet Beethoven, who falls in love with the latter. But Josephine is then kindly asked to marry Joseph Count Deym…

1800: … to whom she sticks to weather the storm (whipped up by her mother). Ludwig and Franz Count von Brunsvik become friends.

1801: After two years of frustration, Ludwig briefly experiences again the feeling of love – induced by Josephine's flirtatious cousin Julie ("Giulietta") Countess Guicciardi (unrequited).

1802: Hearing problems result in Beethoven writing his "Heiligenstadt Testament". Josephine continues partying.

1803: A fateful move to the city of Prague…

1804: … where on 27 January, Count Deym dies of pneumonia, leaving Josephine with four children. Later that year, Ludwig composes the Song "An die Hoffnung" [To Hope] for Josephine, dedicated to her privately. December, Charlotte begins to notice Beethoven's frequent visits to Josephine.

1805: The year of the most passionate love letters. The year of (secret) Hope. The year of secrets.

1806: The year of Jealousy: Count Wolkenstein's courting of Josephine is clouding Beethoven's view.

1807: Josephine begins to yield to the increased pressure by her family. "The M" looks, sternly, at Ludwig (so he knows his place).

1808: Josephine travels with Therese to Pestalozzi in Switzerland to find a teacher for her children. They are impressed by a learned young man called Christoph Baron von Stackelberg. Meanwhile, Beethoven is yearning.

1809: Josephine comes home – with baggage. The teacher accompanying her – of lower rank, a stranger and not a Catholic – is not welcome as a new in-law by the other Brunsviks. To avoid a scandal, his illegitimate daughter is born in secret.

1810: February, Mother Anna reluctantly gives her consent to the marriage with Stackelberg. (It helps that he threatens to discontinue the education of the children.) It seems the wedding night is the second (and perhaps also the last) time Josephine sleeps with Stackelberg – the resulting second daughter is born nine months later (the first one is quietly accepted). This year is a "state of ferment" for Josephine. Beethoven is desperate and takes a foolish step (courting – unsuccessfully – Teresa von Malfatti).

1811: The year of (intensified) Family Life. Stackelberg is no party-goer, he sets up harsh rules of punishment for his (step)children in case they misbehave, and he prefers to read when his wife is weeping. Money that he does not have (Josephine's inheritance, loans from her relatives) is spent on purchasing an expensive estate in Moravia; Stackelberg signs all the documents. The deal falls through, and they end up financially broke.

1812: The year of Dissolution. A chance encounter and its aftermath. Stackelberg leaves his family to find enlightenment (which he does) and also more money (which he doesn't), and then comes back, to face the situation (Josephine is pregnant). Beethoven travels to Teplitz (via Prague) where he writes a letter, after missing an appointment. He later continues to write his thoughts into a Diary; in the first entry he is lamenting how someone (or something) identified by an unidentifiable letter (or two?) causes everything to "go to ruin". Josephine gives her unborn child to Therese.

- 1813: Minona = anonim? Or like the one in Goethe's *Werther*? In any case, Stackelberg is not interested in her, and is off again.
- 1814: The year of the Kidnapping. Stackelberg returns. He loves his family so much that he gets the police to forcibly remove "his" children. He dumps them at a Bohemian cleric's place, and vanishes again, to travel the world (in pious pursuit).
- 1815: The year of Tohuwabohu. Andrian the charlatan. Stackelberg turns up, has an argument with Josephine, and then writes her a letter expressing his contempt. He returns Police President Hager's favor by informing him about his wife's "morality". Meanwhile, Josephine as "Countess Mayersfeld" goes into hiding to give birth to Andrian's child.
- 1816: The year of the Last Yearning. Summer in Baden, the mute meets the deaf, for the last time. Josephine has to go through yet another traumatic experience when she has just found her little children again: Brother Otto von Stackelberg appears just in time to grab them.
- 1817: The year of Resignation. Except for Stackelberg, who turns up once more – to scrounge more money.
- 1818: The year of the the Last Letter. Josephine drafts a letter to (most likely) Ludwig about her (con)fusion – on Minona's fifth birthday.
- 1819: The year of the Final Visit – by Stackelberg. Therese is impressed how "her" little Minona has developed.
- 1820: The year of the final, terminal illness. Nervous consumption.
- 1821: 31 March, Josephine dies. Death and Oblivion.
- 1827: 26 March, Ludwig dies. He is buried next to Josephine.

Comparison of a Surviving Fragment of Beethoven's Diary with Gräffer's Copy

There happen to be two pages of Beethoven's Diary (part of entry #60d from 1815) that survived in his original handwriting – and comparing them with Gräffer's copy is quite revealing indeed. It is an excerpt that Beethoven copied from Zacharias <u>Werner</u>: *Die Templer auf Cypern* [The Templars on Cyprus], Berlin 1802. Beethoven himself did not copy quite correctly this part of a rather obscure drama, written in verse, but he underlined phrases that were close to his heart (for example, to "seek the higher good of **self-perfection in creating**").

* * *

Obviously Gräffer did not have access to the original text by Werner, and the many errors (and omissions) he made in copying Beethoven's Diary, even on these two pages, are quite significant – in fact, they make much of the text almost **meaningless**. It follows, side by side, first on the left, the first page of the original by Beethoven (in his original German; in Solomon 2005, p. 22), followed by my English translation, and then the second page (in Solomon 2005, p. 25), with Gräffer's copy in each case on the right (where insertions in square brackets were based on the original source; in Solomon 2005, p. 54 f.). Explanatory comments (to the notes in superscript) are following the text.

* * *

Beethoven:	Gräffer:
… ist der ächte Mensch Ein Sklave der Umgebung oder frey? <u>Reißt</u> er aus allen Stürmen, und, was mehr ist, aus allen <u>wonnen</u>[1] dieses lebens nicht sein bess'res ich? – die welt in seiner brust, ist sie ein Theil der Elementen-Masse; Und Kann, was oft in dieser wogt und gähret auf jene wirken? **Mensch!** Kannt du Erliegen? – N [Robert:] doch giebts Momente – ! Molaj[:] ja die giebt es freylich – Doch – Gott Sey dank – auch nur Momente – Wo der Mensch, von mächtiger Natur bezwungen, sein höh'res selbst ein spiel der Wogen in solchen augenblicken wähnt[,] zeigt die Gottheit unß jenen abstand zwischen ihr und unß; Sie **stra[h?]lt**[2] des Menschen frevelhafte[3] Kühnheit, ihr gleich zu seyn, und wirft[4] ihn in sein Nichts.	Ist der echte Mensch ein Sklave der Umgebung oder frey? Reißt er aus allen Stürmen, und, was mehr ist, aus allen – – –[1] dieses Lebens nicht sein besseres Ich? Die Welt in seiner Brust ist sie ein Theil der Elementen-Masse –Und kann was oft in dieser wogt und gährt auf jene wirken? <u>Mensch</u>! kannst du erliegen? – [Robert:] Doch gibt's Momente! <u>Molay</u>[:] ja die gibt es freylich – Doch Gott sey Dank auch nur Momente – wo der Mensch von mächtiger Natur bezwungen sein höheres Selbst ein Spiel der Wogen wähnt! in solchen Augenblicken zeigt die – – – Abstand zwischen ihr und der Gottheit einst; sie <u>strebt</u>? <u>strahlt</u>?[2] des Menschen räthselhafte[3] Kühnheit ihr gleich zu seyn, und wie oft[4] ihn in sein Nichts – – – –.

Beethoven:	Gräffer:
… is the real, true Man a slave of the Environment or free? Does he not <u>wrench</u> from all the storms, and what is more, from all the <u>pleasures</u>[1] of this life, his better self? – the World in his heart, is it part of the mass of Elements; and can what is often heaving and fermenting in this one affect the other one? **Man!** Canst thou succumb?	Is the real, true Man a slave of the Environment or free? Does he not wrench from all the storms, and what is more, from all – – –[1] of this life not his better self? – the World in his heart, is it part of the mass of Elements – and can what is often heaving and fermenting in this one affect the other one? <u>Man</u>! Canst thou succumb?
N [Robert:] yet there are moments –! <u>Molaj</u>[:] Sure there are – but – thank God – also only moments - Where Man, defeated by mighty Nature, imagines his higher self to be a play of the waves, in such moments the Deity shows us the distance between Him and us; He **shines**[2] [?] on Man's sacrilegious[3] audacity to be His equal, and throws[4] him into his void.	[Robert:] Yet there are moments! <u>Molay</u>[:] Sure there are – but – thank God – also only moments – where Man, defeated by mighty Nature, imagines his higher self to be a play of the waves! In such moments shows – – – – – distance between him and the Deity once; He <u>strives</u>? <u>shines</u>?[2] Man's puzzling[3] audacity to be like Him, and how often[4] him into his void.

Beethoven:	Gräffer:
[In s]olchem augenblicke sinkt selbst der weise [zu]m staub hinab – auch er ist sohn des Staubs, doch er erhebt[5] sich bald … Auch du wirst dich erheben, starker Robert, Robert[:][6] was kann ich thun? – Molay[:] Mehr als dein schicksaal seyn, den Hasser[7] lieben und das hohe Gut der Selbstvollendung im Erschaffen[8] suchen! … R[obert:] Erröthend beug ich mich vor deiner größe! – M.[olay:] das sollst du nicht – du sollst mich übertreffen – etc[.] sei ihnen Vater[9][,] den Menschen, die unter dir sind – der Mann der Einzelne kann öfters Mehr, als im Verein mit Tausend[,] denn schwer zu lenken sind der Menschen willen, und selten siegt der bessere Verstand.	… in solchen Augenblicken sinkt selbst der Weise zum Staub hinab – auch er ist Sohn des Staubs – doch er erholt[5] sich bald … Auch du wirst dich erheben starker [Robert!] [Robert:][6] was kann ihm [Molay:] mehr als dein Schicksal seyn, denn Hassen[7], Lieben und das hohe Gut der Selbstvollendung im Erschaffen[8] suchen … [Robert:] So erröthend beuge ich mich vor deiner Größe [Molay:] das solltest du nicht – du sollst mich übertreffen sey – – vorher[9] den Menschen[,] die unter dir sind[;] der Mann der Einzelne kann öfters mehr als im Verein mit Tausend[,] denn schwer zu lenken sind der Menschen Willen und selten siegt der bessere Verstand.

Beethoven:	Gräffer:
In such a moment even the wise man sinks down into the dust – he, too, is son of dust, but soon he gets up[5] ... You too will rise, strong Robert. Robert[:][6] What can I do? – Molay[:] Be more than your destiny, love the hater[7] and seek the higher good of self-perfection in creating!... R[obert]: Blushing I bow before your greatness! – M[olay]: That you shall not – you shall surpass me – etc. Be to them their Father[9], to the people who are beneath you – one man, as an individual, can often [achieve] more [alone] than together with thousands, for the intentions of men are difficult to control, and rarely wins the better reason.	... in such moments even the wise man sinks down into the dust – he, too, is son of dust – but soon he recovers[5] ... You too will rise, strong [Robert!] [Robert:][6] what can him [!] [Molay:] Be more than your destiny, than to hate[7], to love, and to seek the higher good of self-perfection in creating[8]... [Robert:] Thus, blushing, I bow before your greatness[.] [Molay:] you should not do that – you should surpass me, be – – before[9] the people who are beneath you[;] one man, as an individual, can often [achieve] more [alone] than together with thousands, for the intentions of men are difficult to control, and rarely wins the better reason.

* * *

Observations:

[1] "wonnen" [pleasures] replaced by "– – –". Being underlined, an important part of this sentence goes missing.

[2] "**stralt**" looks like a misspelled "**strahlt**" [**shines**], and Gräffer indicates his uncertainty by rendering it as "strebt? strahlt?" [strives? shines?]. However, both interpretations are meaningless in the context. Consulting the source reveals it to be "**straft**" [**punishes**] – and now it makes a lot of sense! (Note also how the immediately preceding sentence is jumbled up by Gräffer.)

³   "frevelhaft" [sacrilegious] was apparently so puzzling to Gräffer that he misread it as "räthselhaft" [puzzling].
⁴   "wirft" [throws] is misread as "wie oft" [how often], making the entire sentence meaningless.
⁵   "erhebt" [gets up] is misread as "erholt" [recovers] – at least, for once a roughly equivalent meaning.
⁶   "Robert" has been omitted by Gräffer twice here; the omission of the actors' names in several instances makes the text difficult to understand.
⁷   "den Hasser lieben" [love the hater] is rendered by Gräffer as "denn Hassen, Lieben" [than to hate, to love].
⁸   "das hohe Gut der Selbstvollendung im Erschaffen suchen" [seek the higher good of self-perfection in creating] – the central theme of Beethoven's life, here in a nutshell – but **not** underlined by Gräffer.
⁹   "Vater" [Father] is misread as "vorher" [before].

* * *

These are just the most obvious (and clearly misleading) copying errors in just two pages of Beethoven's Diary – but who cares what "Molay" exactly said to "Robert" in this drama! Note also how Gräffer usually indicated omissions by a number of dashes "– – –". Only he was not consistent as he more often than not wrote down interpretations of his own that simply did not make sense.

Bearing this in mind, Beethoven's first Diary entry concluding with "this way with **A** [?] everything goes to ruin – – –" should be taken with more than a grain of salt, given that "A" was an apparently clear and confident rendering by Gräffer of a most likely **illegible** cipher – at least Fischhof subsequently could not make sense of it. Note also that this sentence ended in several dashes "– – –" in Gräffer's copy, so there was something following (most likely important) that he either could not read – or found too embarrassing to write down...

Websites

http://www.beethovensite.eu/ or http://www.xs4all.nl/~ademu/Beethoven/: *De Beethovensite. Alles over Ludwig van Beethoven.* [The Beethoven Site. Everything about Ludwig van Beethoven.] All in Dutch, except for the first page which has a few FAQs answered in English. If you can read Dutch, this is by far the best and most comprehensive website about Beethoven's life, including a very detailed synoptic review of the lives of Josephine and Antonie.

http://www.lvbeethoven.com/: Very comprehensive "Euro" website in French/English/Spanish/Italian – the best one that is not in Dutch. As for the "Immortal Beloved", Cristina Barbieri's opinion is the most interesting:

> Josephine is the most likely candidate. Especially because the relation between the two of them had the required tone. Their love letters have a lot in common with the famous letter, and she was a very beautiful, cultured, musical young woman. ... The relation between them was ultimately impossible for the restrictions that the time put on such situations, and then the relation had receded to a spiritual level. This kind of spiritual link was mentioned in a mysterious letter written by Josephine in 1818 to an equally mysterious recipient. ... What is beyond any doubt is that the composer really loved a particular woman very much, and also that he loved her for a long time. The echoes of this love are in so much of his musical works. We can listen to this love in the vibrant bliss of so many passionate adagios, in the sorrow present in those painful tones, in so many melodies loaded with sadness and memories. ... **Our academics failed miserably** in revealing this particular mystery. There is more than a hint of voyeurism in the acute desire to "know". And our culture would only make some sordid media soap-opera out of a most sad and beautiful love story. [About Antonie Brentano:] To even consider that a man as open and frank as Beethoven evidently was, could maintain an affair with a friend's wife, and then share a roof with her and her husband (and child and maid) only a few days after such a passionate interlude ... Well, **it is a scenario simply unthinkable.** If someone had only read his diaries, his letters, his moral writings ... [Beethoven] would consider such an act, a terrible dishonourable behaviour. He would loathe such a treasonous act. That is why **the American hypothesis about the Immortal Beloved is completely unacceptable, absolutely psychologically unlikely.** (http://www.lvbeethoven.com/Amours/ImmortalAbout.html, 6 Feb 2011)

http://www.beethoven–haus–bonn.de/: The *Beethoven-Haus* in Bonn, Beethoven's museum on-line. German/English.

http://www.recmusic.org/lieder/b/beethoven.html: *The Lied, Art Song, and Choral Texts Page*. Info about each song's lyrics (often in multiple translations), origin, other versions, many interesting details.

http://www.unheardbeethoven.org/: Very good to find out about recordings of less well-known works – there are, after all, according to the latest Biamonti Catalogue, nearly 1000 of them. In order to gain a thorough understanding of Beethoven the composer and his development, you should invest a little more than just marvel at the *Choral* Symphony or being awe-struck by the thunder of the *Fifth*...

http://www.sjsu.edu/beethoven/: The **Ira F. Brilliant Center for Beethoven Studies** at *San José State University*. Under "Immortal Beloved", it is noncommittal: "The three leading candidates at the moment are Antonie Brentano, Josephine Brunswick, and Bettina Brentano." Take your pick!

http://raptusassociation.org/: "Ludwig van Beethoven – The Magnificent Master" by the **Raptus Association** *for Music Appreciation* (English/German), who also cannot make up their mind about the "Immortal Beloved":

> Solomon's research favors Antonie Brentano, Kaznelson's, Harry Goldschmidt's and Marie-Elisabeth Tellenbach's Josephine von Brunsvik, and Gail S. Altman's Countess Erdödy.

– though one somehow feels that there is a majority of reputable researchers "favoring" Josephine (and there are quite a few more – see under *Literature*). Isn't it time to take a vote?

* * *

I could find no Internet website exclusively or mainly dedicated to Josephine von Brunsvik. There is one in Hungarian about Therese (also Blanka Teleki, daughter of Charlotte), but with almost nothing about Josephine: http://brunszvikterez.hu/. It also contains two pictures allegedly showing Minona; however, they are considered doubtful (especially that of the younger woman).

The German site http://brunswicks.de/ hardly mentions Josephine (and also precious little besides); http://www.von–stackelberg.de/ is completely mum about Christoph. And most other (English) websites that I found (or stumbled across) that deal with "Beethoven" in one way or another, are pretty thin on biographical matters. Often they parrot bits and pieces that can clearly be traced to Solomon's various conjectures, and not surprisingly, this is often more **distorted** than even Solomon's views. A good (i.e., really bad) example is http://www.madaboutbeethoven.com/ which seems to be even more "mad" in the way how it glorifies and worships its star and author, one John Suchet...

Movies

There is not a single movie about Josephine von Brunsvik, and most of the few about Beethoven, where she has been given a supporting role, distort the facts beyond recognition.

* * *

The first ever film about the composer, called "Beethoven", was made in France in 1909 by Victorin-Hippolyte Jasset, with Harry Baur as Beethoven.

The next one was made in Austria in 1918, titled "Märtyrer seines Herzens" [Martyr of his Heart] a.k.a. "Beethoven und die Frauen" [Beethoven and Women] by Emil Justiz; Fritz Kortner played Beethoven. (Plot unknown.)

The plot of "Beethoven's Moonlight Sonata" (USA 1920, by James A FitzPatrick): Beethoven meets a pianist, discovers that she is blind, and then he is so moved that he has the candles put out and proceeds to improvise for her "in the moonlight"...

Two German movies followed: In 1927, "Das Leben des Beethoven" [Beethoven's Life] by Hans Otto, and "Luduvicus" by Manguri Ammilus in 1930. (Plots unknown.)

"**Un Grand Amour de Beethoven**" [Beethoven's Great Love] by Abel Gance (France 1936), again with Harry Baur as Beethoven, is **a great film** with a moving plot: Two young women, his pupils, are in love with him. Thérèse de Brunsvik's love remains unrequited, even though she and Beethoven are engaged for years; Juliette Guicciardi, whom Beethoven loves but who marries a Count, regrets her decision, but by then he and Thérèse are engaged...

Another French film was made in 1940 under the title "Sérénade" by Jean Boyer, followed by "New Wine" (USA 1941, by Reinhold Schünzel), and "Wen die Götter lieben" [Whom the Gods Love] (Germany 1942, by Karl Hartl). (Plots unknown.)

After the War, there was "Eroica" (Austria 1949, by Walter Kolm-Veltée) with Ewald Balser as Beethoven: He falls in love with Giulietta, who is even willing to leave her fiancé for him, whereas Therese thinks that, due to his talent, it is not Beethoven's destiny to lead a fulfilling relationship with a woman; nephew Karl also appears to add to Beethoven's worries...

In East Germany, a documentary "Ludwig van Beethoven" was made in 1954 by Max Jaap.

In 1961, Beethoven went to Disneyland (USA) to appear in a TV series as "The Magnificent Rebel" a.k.a. "Schicksals-Sinfonie" [Fateful Symphony] by Georg Tressler, with Karlheinz Böhm as Beethoven. (This film is a good little intro to the music of Beethoven for those who don't know anything about his life and work.)

Quite different (and highly disrespectful) was "**Ludwig van**" (West Germany 1969, by Mauricio Kagel), right on the eve of those many bicentenary birthday celebrations, reminding us that the composer had all but disappeared under a cobweb of myths and legends... This black and white film was intentionally dislodged, disturbed, aggressive.

Another documentary "Ludwig van Beethoven" appeared in West Germany in 1970, by Hans Conrad Fischer.

This was followed by "Beethoven – Tage aus einem Leben" [Beethoven – Days in a Life], a.k.a. "Der Compositeur" [The Composer] (East Germany 1976, by Horst Seemann), a biography showing episodes from Beethoven's life between 1813 and 1819. This seems to have been the first time that Josephine is at least mentioned. (Maybe, Harry Goldschmidt had a hand in it?)

"Fidelio" (France 1979, by Pierre Jourdan), with Gundula Janowitz, Jon Vickers, Theo Adam, and Zubin Mehta conducting the Israel Philharmonic Orchestra and the Chorus of the New Philharmonia, was one of more than a dozen recordings of Beethoven's only opera. It attempted to enliven the staged German-language performance at the *Roman Theater* at Orange by using odd camera angles and a constantly moving camera, though the result was panned by both opera lovers and film critics.

"Goshu the Cellist" (Japan 1982, by Isao Yakahata) is an animated film, full of poetry, a beautiful musical creation – a work of art for young and old, with Beethoven's *Pastoral* symphony at the centre of it.

"Le Neveu de Beethoven" a.k.a. "Beethovens Neffe" [Beethoven's Nephew], also "Beethoven – Die ganze Wahrheit" [Beethoven – The Whole Truth] (France 1985, by Paul Morrissey) with Wolfgang Reichmann as Beethoven, portrays the uncle as furious and tyrannical, obsessed and insanely jealous. Even though the film elicits a deep sympathy for his torment, it concentrates too much on only one aspect of his life – not surprisingly, given its plot being based on novels (like Magnani 1972).

A TV documentary "The Immortal Beethoven" was made in Canada (1987, by Israela Margalit).

And in Germany, a film "Freunde, diese Töne" [Friends, those Sounds] (1990, by Klaus Lindemann), with Mathias Herrmann as Beethoven. (Plot unknown.)

A comedy or children's story "Beethoven Lives Upstairs" (USA 1992, by David Devine) was made for TV.

In Germany appeared "Le mécano de l'oreille" [The Mechanic of the Ear] (1994, by Gert Jonke). (Plot unknown.)

The long overdue soap opera picture, Hollywood-style, and appropriately (mis)named "Immortal Beloved" (USA 1994, by Bernard Rose), with Gary Oldman as Beethoven, received nevertheless only "mixed" reviews. The (disintegrated) plot is simply beyond belief: It turns out that she is none other than his hated sister-in-law Johanna! To say that this way of depicting Beethoven (he also appears to be more of a womanizer) is "distorted", is putting it mildly. Even the music (beautiful though it is – but that can't be helped, no?) is rather misrepresented and misrepresenting. In short: If the aim was to create a fantasy, a myth that is most unlike what is known about Beethoven's so-called "Immortal Beloved", and confuse people's minds for good measure, then this film was a resounding success! – Proof:

> I watched the movie *Immortal Beloved* and was surprized how close the movie was to this book [Solomon's *Beethoven*], although the book wasn't [!] mentioned in the credits. Of course, the movie made up the bit about the I[mmortal] B[eloved] being B[eethoven]'s sister-in-law but Solomon suggested [!] the love/hate relationship between the two. (http://www.amazon.com/Beethoven–Revised–Maynard–Solomon/product–reviews/, 6 Feb 2011)

See also Lewis <u>Lockwood</u>: "Film Biography as Travesty: *Immortal Beloved* and Beethoven." The Musical Quarterly 81/2, 1997, pp. 190–198.

As if this was not enough, "La Musique de l'amour: Un amour inachevé" [The Music of Love: An Unfinished Love] (France 1996, by Fabrice Cazeneuve), a TV soap that appeared also in German under the more revealing title "Minona – Zaubermacht der Musik" [Minona – The Magic Power of Music], tells the entirely fictitious story of Minona looking for her famous father.

Outstanding and beautiful, but little known, is the Canadian film on DVD "**Immortal Spirit**" (2000, by Bernar Hébert) in the series "The Great Composers" (with 2 Bonus CDs), with Pascal Contamine as Beethoven, showing a truly astonishing biographical and choreographic staging of the String Quartet #10 in *E flat major* "The Harp" Op. 74 (see http://www.lvbeethoven.com/Fictions/FictionFilmsImmortalSpirit.html, 6 Jan 2011).

"Fidelio" (USA 2002, by Brian Large) with Karita Mattila, Ben Heppner, and James Levine conducting The Metropolitan Opera Orchestra & Chorus, is another TV recording of the opera, this time staged like a modern-day gangster movie...

An excellent and beautiful TV film dedicated to a single work is "**Eroica**" (UK 2003, by Simon Cellan-Jones) with Ian Hart as Beethoven and Claire

Skinner as Josephine. The plot happens to be fairly accurate as far as historical truth goes: 9 June 1804 is the date of the first (private) performance of Beethoven's third symphony in the palace of Prince Lobkowitz. Midway during the performance, Beethoven tries to get his lover, a widow named Josephine von Deym, to marry him, but she refuses because of the unfair laws regarding child custody – she is a member of the nobility, and cannot marry a commoner without losing guardianship of her children.

If "Immortal Beloved" by Rose was not fantastic and fictitious enough, "Nesmrtelná milenka" [Lover Beyond Death] (Czech Rep. 2005, by Josef Císaovsky) is yet another TV Film, based on a totally fictitious plot: The long dismissed speculation that one Almerie Esterházy (a woman Beethoven never even met) was his secret love (see Rita Steblin: "Beethoven's Immortal Beloved: Evidence against Almerie Esterházy". Abstracts of Papers Read at the Meeting of the American Musicological Society, Sixty-Seventh Annual Meeting, November 15–18, 2001, p. 45; http://www.ams–net.org/abstracts/2001–Atlanta.pdf, 11 May 2011).

"Beethoven's Hair" a.k.a. "Beethovens Haar" (USA/Germany 2005, by Larry Weinstein), based on the book of the same title by Martin (2000), examines the exciting discovery that the lead content in a surviving lock of the composer might point to a possible cause of his death by lead poisoning. Given the many still unresolved mysteries about his health, deafness and other illnesses, this does not fully solve the riddle – though it is highly interesting as the story involves the horrors of the Holocaust.

"Copying Beethoven" a.k.a. "Klang der Stille" [Sound of Silence] (USA 2006, by Agnieszka Holland) with Ed Harris as Beethoven is a fantasy, a made-up story to give us some insight into what might have been; the screenplay is very "inventive".

"Beethoven – Genie am Abgrund" [Beethoven – Genius on the Brink] (Germany 2009, by Gero von Boehm) in the TV series "Giganten" [Giants], with Uwe Ochsenknecht as Beethoven, was called "bombastisc", though it does have a short scene with Josephine as the "Immortal Beloved". Plus interviews with Beethoven scholars, including Rita Steblin.

"In Search of Beethoven" (UK 2009, by Phil Grabsky) is a documentary, dominated by Anglo-American "experts" (so you can guess who they think the "Immortal Beloved" was). Maudlin, sentimental. Despite the acclaim it received (after the much better "In Search of Mozart"), one is left with the feeling that he did not really find him! A (still questionable) selection of lots of excellent music is just not enough.

List of Songs

"**Als die Geliebte sich trennen wollte**" [When the Beloved Wanted to Separate] WoO 132, originally "Empfindungen bei Lydiens Untreue" [Feelings about Lydia's Infidelity]. Text: Stephan von Breuning (1774–1827).

"**Andenken**" [Memory] WoO 136. Text: Friedrich von Matthisson (1761–1831). Also set to music by Carl Maria von Weber (1786–1826) in 1806, Ferdinand Ries (1784–1838) in 1810, Franz Schubert (1797–1828) in 1814 and Antonio Salieri (1750–1825) in 1825.

"**An die Geliebte**" [To the Beloved] WoO 140. Text: Josef Ludwig Stoll (1778–1815). Also set to music by Franz Schubert (1797–1828) in 1815.

"**An die Hoffnung**" [To Hope], 1st setting, Op. 32; 2nd setting, Op. 94. Text: Christoph August Tiedge (1752–1841), from *Urania*, Erster Gesang [First Song]: "Klagen des Zweiflers" [The Doubter's Lamentations].

"**An die ferne Geliebte**" [To the Distant Beloved] Op. 98. Text: Alois Jeitteles (1794–1858).

"**Empfindungen bei Lydiens Untreue**" [Feelings about Lydia's Infidelity] WoO 132, later renamed "Als die Geliebte sich trennen wollte" [When the Beloved Wanted to Separate]. Text: Stephan von Breuning (1774–1827).

"**God Save the King**" WoO 157#1. Text: Henry Carey (1687?–1743).

"**Ich denke dein**" [I Am With You] WoO 74#1. Text: Johann Wolfgang von Goethe (1749–1832), as "Nähe des Geliebten" [Closeness of the Beloved]. Also set to music by Franz Schubert (1797–1828) in 1821.

"**Ich liebe dich so wie du mich**" [I love you as much as you love me] WoO 123, a.k.a. "Zärtliche Liebe" [Tender Love]. Text: Karl Friedrich Wilhelm Herrosee (1764–1821).

Italian Love Songs Op. 82.

"**Resignation**" WoO 149. Text: Paul von Haugwitz (1791–1856).

"**Sehnsucht**" [Yearning] Op. 83#2. Text: Johann Wolfgang von Goethe (1749–1832), 1802. Also set to music by Franz Schubert (1797–1828) in 1814.

"**Sehnsucht**" [Yearning] WoO 134. Text: Johann Wolfgang von Goethe (1749–1832), from *Wilhelm Meisters Lehrjahre*: "Nur wer die Sehnsucht kennt" [Only He Who Knows Yearning]. Also set to music by Franz Schubert (1797–1828), 1815 to 1826 (6 versions).

"**Sehnsucht**" [Yearning] WoO 146. Text: Christian Ludwig Reissig (1783–1822+).

Six Songs Op. 75.

"**Wonne der Wehmut**" [The Bliss of Melancholy] Op. 83#1. Text: Johann Wolfgang von Goethe (1749–1832), 1775. Also set to music by Franz Schubert (1797–1828) in 1815.

"**Zärtliche Liebe**" [Tender Love] WoO 123, a.k.a. "Ich liebe dich so wie du mich" [I love you as much as you love me]. Text: Karl Friedrich Wilhelm Herrosee (1764–1821).

* * *

See http://www.recmusic.org/lieder/b/beethoven.html for more details.

List of Works

Op. = Opus, a work with an assigned Number (by Beethoven or a publisher; there are 138). **WoO** = "Werk ohne Opus-Nummer" (Work without Opus Number, as catalogued by Kinsky & Halm; there are 205 plus an Appendix of 18). **Hess** = Catalogue of other Works with neither Opus nor WoO Number (there are 335 plus an Appendix of 66). There is now also a nearly complete Catalogue of all known compositions by (or attributed to) Beethoven, by **Biamonti** (849 entries plus an Appendix of ca. 100), including many sketches, fragments and spurious works – see http://www.lvbeethoven.com/Oeuvres/ListBiamonti01.html.

Ideally, each of these compositions, when mentioned in the text, you should be playing in the background!

* * *

Op. 1: 3 Piano Trios, 1792–1794, ded. Prince Lichnowsky.

Op. 2: 3 Piano Sonatas, 1793–1795, ded. Joseph Haydn.

Op. 3: String Trio in *E flat major*, 1794.

Op. 11: Trio for Piano, Clarinet/Violin & Cello in *B flat major*, 1797-1798, ded. Countess von Thun.

Op. 12: 3 Sonatas for Piano & Violin, 1797–1798, ded. Antonio Salieri.

Op. 17: Sonata for Piano & Horn in *F major*, 1800, ded. Baroness Braun.

Op. 21: Symphony #1 in *C major*, 1799–1800, ded. Baron van Swieten.

Op. 27#2: Piano Sonata #14 "quasi una Fantasia" in *C sharp minor* ("Moonlight"), 1800–1801, ded. Giulietta Countess Guicciardi.

Op. 31: 3 Piano Sonatas, 1802.

Op. 32: Song "An die Hoffnung" [To Hope], 1st setting, 1804–1805, ded. Josephine Countess Deym (secretly).

Op. 35: 15 Variations with Fugue for Piano in *E flat major*, on a theme from the ballet *Die Geschöpfe des Prometheus* Op. 43 ("Eroica Variations"), 1802, ded. Prince Lichnowsky.

Op. 36: Symphony #2 in *D major*, 1801–1802, ded. Prince Lichnowsky.

Op. 37: Piano Concerto #3 in *C minor*, 1800–1803, ded. Prince Louis Ferdinand of Prussia.

Op. 43: Ballet Music "Die Geschöpfe des Prometheus" [The Creatures of Prometheus], 1800–1801, ded. Princess Lichnowsky.

Op. 47: Violin Sonata #9 in *A major* ("Kreutzer"), 1802–1803, ded. Rodolphe Kreutzer.

Op. 53: Piano Sonata #21 in C *major* ("Waldstein"), 1803–1804, ded. Ferdinand Count von Waldstein.

Op. 54: Piano Sonata #22 in F *major*, 1804.

Op. 55: Symphony #3 in E flat *major* "Eroica", 1803, ded. Prince Lobkowitz.

Op. 57: Sonata in F *minor* "Appassionata", 1804–1805, ded. Franz Count von Brunsvik.

Op. 68: Symphony #6 in F *major* "Pastoral", 1807-1808, ded. Prince Lobkowitz & Count Razumovsky.

Op. 69: Cello Sonata #3 in A *major* ("Inter Lacrimas et Luctum"), 1807–1808, ded. Baron von Gleichenstein.

Op. 72: Opera *Fidelio*, 1814.

Op. 74: String Quartet #10 in E flat *major* "The Harp", 1809, ded. Prince Lobkowitz.

Op. 75: 6 Songs, 1809, ded. Princess Kinsky.

Op. 78: Piano Sonata in F sharp *major* ("À Thérèse"), 1809, ded. Therese Countess von Brunsvik.

Op. 81a: Piano Sonata #26 in E flat *major* "Das Lebewohl" a.k.a. "Les Adieux" [The Farewell], 1809–1810, ded. Archduke Rudolph.

Op. 82: 5 Italian Love Songs, 1809–1810.

Op. 83#1: Song "Wonne der Wehmut" [The Bliss of Melancholy], 1810, ded. Princess Kinsky.

Op. 83#2: Song "Sehnsucht" [Yearning], 1810, ded. Princess Kinsky.

Op. 85: Oratorio *Christus am Ölberge* [Christ on the Mount of Olives], 1803–1804.

Op. 86: Mass in C *major*, 1807, ded. Prince Kinsky.

Op. 91: Battle Symphony "Wellingtons Sieg, oder die Schlacht bei Vittoria" [Wellington's Victory, or the Battle of Vittoria], 1813, ded. King George of England.

Op. 92: Symphony #7 in A *major*, 1811–1812, ded. Moritz Count von Fries.

Op. 93: Symphony #8 in F *major*, 1812.

Op. 94: Song "An die Hoffnung" [To Hope], 2nd setting, 1813–1815.

Op. 95: String Quartet #11 in F *minor* "Quartetto serioso", 1811–1812, publ. 1816, ded. Nikolaus Zmeskall.

Op. 96: Violin Sonata #10 in G *major*, 1812, ded. Archduke Rudolph.

Op. 98: Song Cycle "An die ferne Geliebte" [To the Distant Beloved], 1816, ded. Prince Lobkowitz.

Op. 106: Piano Sonata #29 in B flat *major* ("Hammerklavier"), 1816–1818, ded. Archduke Rudolph.

Op. 109: Piano Sonata #30 in *E major*, 1820, ded. Maximiliane Brentano.

Op. 110: Piano Sonata #31 in *A flat major*, 1821–1822.

Op. 111: Piano Sonata #32 in *C minor*, 1821–1822, ded. Archduke Rudolph.

Op. 120: 33 Variations for Piano in *C major* on a Waltz by Diabelli, 1819–1823, ded. Antonie Brentano.

Op. 123: Mass in *D major* "Missa Solemnis", 1819–1823, ded. Archduke Rudolph.

Op. 125: Symphony #9 in *D minor*, 1817–1824, ded. King Friedrich Wilhelm III of Prussia.

Op. 135: String Quartet #16 in *F major*, 1826, ded. Johann Nepomuk Wolfmayer.

Op. 136: Cantata "Der glorreiche Augenblick" [The Glorious Moment], 1814.

WoO 1: Ballet Music "Ritterballett", 1790–1791.

WoO 14#7: Contredance for Orchestra in *E flat major*, 1800–1802.

WoO 33: 5 Pieces for Musical Clock, 1799.

WoO 39: Allegretto for Piano Trio in *B flat major*, 1812, ded. Maximiliane Brentano.

WoO 57: Andante grazioso con moto for Piano in *F major* ("Andante favori"), 1803–1804 ("Josephine's Theme"). Written for Josephine.

WoO 59: Bagatelle for Piano in *A minor* ("Für Elise"), 1810, ded. Teresa von Malfatti?.

WoO 63: 9 Variations for Piano in *C minor* on a March by Ernst Christoph Dreßler, 1782, ded. Countess Wolf-Metternich.

WoO 74: Song "Ich denke dein" [I am with you] plus 6 Variations for Piano Duet in *D major*, 1799–1803, ded. Therese Countess von Brunsvik & Josephine Countess Deym.

WoO 78: 7 Variations for Piano in *C major* on "God Save the King", 1802–1803.

WoO 79: 5 Variations for Piano in *D major* on "Rule Britannia", 1803.

WoO 123: Song in *G major* "Ich liebe dich so wie du mich" [I love you as much as you love me], a.k.a. "Zärtliche Liebe" [Tender Love], 1795, publ. 1803.

WoO 132: Song in *E flat major* "Als die Geliebte sich trennen wollte" [When the Beloved Wanted to Separate], originally "Empfindungen bei Lydiens Untreue" [Feelings about Lydia's Infidelity], 1806.

WoO 134: Song "Sehnsucht" [Yearning], 4 settings, 1807–1808.

WoO 136: Song in *D major* "Andenken" [Memory], 1808.

WoO 140: Song "An die Geliebte" [To the Beloved], 1st setting, 1811 (2nd setting, 1814). Written for Regina Lang.
WoO 146: Song in *E major* "Sehnsucht" [Yearning], 1816.
WoO 149: Song in *D major* "Resignation", 1817.
WoO 157#1: English Folksong Setting "God Save the King", 1817.
WoO 168#1: Canon "Das Schweigen" [Silence], 1816.
WoO 200: Piece for Piano in *G major* "O Hoffnung!" [Oh Hope!], 1818.

Hess 90: Ballet Music "Die Geschöpfe des Prometheus" [The Creatures of Prometheus] for Piano (arr. Op. 43), 1801, ded. Princess Lichnowsky.
Hess 107: Grenadier March for Mechanical Clock in *F major*, 1798.
Hess 109: Opera *Leonore, oder Der Triumph der ehelichen Liebe* [Leonore, or The Triumph of Conjugal Love], 1st version, with Overture *Leonore II*, 1804–1805.
Hess 110: Opera *Leonore, oder Der Triumph der ehelichen Liebe* [Leonore, or The Triumph of Conjugal Love], 2nd version, with Overture *Leonore III*, 1805–1806.

* * *

Dedications: There seems to be considerable confusion about the term "Dedication", the major synonyms of which are "Devotion", "Allegiance", "Loyalty", even "Devotedness". The German word "**Widmung**" can be translated as "dedication" or simply "**inscription**". It did not necessarily mean that a composer was in some sense "dedicated" emotionally to the person(s) whose name(s) appeared on the title of a composition, unless there was some qualification like "in loving memory" or such like. In Beethoven's case (see Thayer, in Forbes 1967, p. 107), the dedicatee was usually just a person who had paid (or was expected to do so) for this privilege, and/or more often than not one of his patrons (or their wives). This applies also to Josephine and Therese to whom "Ich denke dein" WoO 74 was dedicated – not at all as a declaration of love really (maybe secretly), but simply as a symbolic thank-you for their hospitality. Likewise the famous "Moonlight" Sonata, dedicated to Julie Guicciardi, again **not** as a sign of love but as "retaliation" for a gift Beethoven received from her mother. Certainly Franz von Brunsvik (dedicatee of the "Appassionata") deserved this for his life long friendship and financial support of Beethoven (as stated by Therese). And of course Therese (Op. 78), who gave him a painting and much help besides. Sure enough, Beethoven did not dedicate compositions to anyone whom he did not like – witness his scratching out the name of Napoleon on the title page of the *Eroica*!

But to conclude that he **must** have been in love with Antonie Brentano more than 10 years before when he dedicated the Piano Sonata Op. 111 to her in 1823 (and then only the English edition!) – this is stretching credibility. In fact, Beethoven thus expressed indeed his gratitude (or indebtedness one should say, quite literally), but to her husband Franz Brentano, who had given him significant amounts of money (usually as non-repayable "loans"). Which Beethoven in turn may have used to support the ailing Josephine (although there is of course no hard evidence for this). And many of the compositions that can be shown to have a meaningful connotation with Josephine are conspicuously left undedicated, the last of them being the Piano Sonata Op. 110 – her Requiem. It was originally dedicated to Antonie Brentano (Goldschmidt 1977, p. 118).

Literature

Anton Schindler (**1840**): *Biographie von Ludwig van Beethoven.* [Biography of Ludwig van Beethoven.] Münster.
>First ever biography, full of errors, omissions, myths and various attempts at self-aggrandizement. Even so, it has dominated the common picture of Beethoven for more than a century (even today – it is listed among the "Standard Literature" of the Beethoven-Haus!). It does not contain a single word about Josephine or Therese.

Nathalie von Stackelberg (**1882**, ed.): *Otto Magnus von Stackelberg. Schilderung seines Lebens und seiner Reisen in Italien und Griechenland (nach Tagebüchern und Briefen).* [Otto Magnus von Stackelberg. Description of his Life and his Travels in Italy and Greece (according to Diaries and Letters).] Heidelberg: Winter.
>Contains a few references to his brother Christoph.

Mariam Tenger (**1890**): *Beethoven's Unsterbliche Geliebte.* [Beethoven's Immortal Beloved.] Bonn: Nusser.
>Probably the first, but rather fictional, account, pointing to Therese. Dismissed by La Mara (1909, p. 17) as a "chimera". Tenger's fiction fooled several serious Beethoven scholars for years, just as Solomon's fabrications would do so decades later.

La Mara (**1909**) [Ida Maria Lipsius]: *Beethovens Unsterbliche Geliebte. Das Geheimnis der Gräfin Brunsvik und ihre Memoiren.* [Beethoven's Immortal Beloved. Countess Brunsvik's Secret and her Memoirs.] Leipzig: Breitkopf & Härtel.
>("1909" is shown on the title page, whereas on the following inside page it says "Published November 15th 1908" and "Copyright 1908 by Breitkopf & Härtel". 1909 is probably the year when it actually appeared in print.) La Mara assumed that Therese von Brunsvik was (secretly) Beethoven's beloved, based mainly on second-guessing by some of the later descendants of the Brunsvik family whom she had interviewed. The major value of La Mara's book is in publishing the Memoirs of Therese – a very lively and readable account, not only of her own (long and reasonably happy) life, but also of her sister Josephine's (short and unhappy) life. And, of course, her never-ending adoration of Beethoven. However, all this was filtered with the aid of hindsight, some details are incorrect, and the crucial events of 1812 in particular are entirely missing (or are wrapped up with those of 1813).
>Ida Maria Lipsius (1837–1927) was born into a musical family and became a music historian, publishing under the pseudonym "La Mara". She was a close friend of Franz Liszt and wrote biographies

about many composers, from Haydn to Berlioz, from Gluck to Chopin. And of course Beethoven.

Wolfgang A Thomas-San-Galli (**1910**): *Beethoven und die unsterbliche Geliebte: Amalie Sebald. Goethe, Therese Brunswik und anderes; mit Benutzung unbekannten Materials.* [Beethoven and the Immortal Beloved: Amalie Sebald. Goethe, Therese Brunsvik and Others; Using Unknown Documents.] Munich: Wunderhorn.

> Checked out the "List of cure and bath guests" of 1811 and 1812 in Teplitz and Karlsbad, concluding: "Amalie Sebald seemed to me to have been the one." (One wonders why he overlooked Antonie Brentano...)

La Mara (**1920**) [Ida Maria Lipsius]: *Beethoven und die Brunsviks. Nach Familienpapieren aus Therese Brunsviks Nachlaß.* [Beethoven and the Brunsviks. According to Family Documents from Therese Brunsvik's Estate.] Leipzig: Siegel.

> After discovering various letters and other documents (at least what was accessible in the aftermath of the First World War), she corrected her previous view and was now convinced that Josephine was the one. La Mara was the first to get it right.

Romain Rolland (**1928**): *Beethoven the Creator. The Great Creative Epochs: I. From the Eroica to the Appassionata.* [Beethoven. Les grandes époques créatrices. I. De l'Héroïque à l'Appassionata.] Transl. Ernest Newman. New York: Garden City.

> Had been in contact with Marianne Czeke, who provided him with parts of Therese's Diary and other information.

Marianne Czeke (**1938**): *Brunszvik Teréz grófno naplói és feljegyzései.* [Countess Therese Brunsvik's Diaries and Notes.] Vol. 1. Budapest.

> Contains Therese's Diary and notes up to 1813 (in German and French), with an introduction in Hungarian.

Siegmund Kaznelson (**1954**): *Beethovens Ferne und Unsterbliche Geliebte.* [Beethoven's Distant and Immortal Beloved.] Zürich: Standard.

> First thorough analysis that clearly identifies Josephine, based on Therese's Diaries and Minona's date of birth – just before the "13 Letters" became known.
>
> Siegmund Kaznelson (1893–1959) was a Polish Zionist, who moved to Israel in 1937. First obsessed with the idea that Rahel Varnhagen was the "Immortal Beloved" (and then, instead, the "Distant" one). After evaluating the Brunsvik sisters' diaries, he came up with the correct solution. Only, he was (like La Mara) virtually ignored by the musicological establishment.

Stephan Ley (**1957**): *Aus Beethovens Erdentagen* [Of Beethoven's Days in this World], chapter "Eine unsterbliche Geliebte Beethovens" [An Immortal Beloved of Beethoven], pp. 78-85. Siegburg: Schmitt.

> "Only on the negative side has one been able to arrive at certain conclusions: neither Giulietta Guicciardi, nor Amalie Sebald, nor

> Bettina Brentano can be considered any longer, and not even Therese Brunsvick, who for a long time was seriously regarded as the recipient of the famous love letter. But curiously enough, it is precisely the same documents which shed a definitive light, in the negative sense, on Therese which bear witness to Beethoven's passionate love for her sister Josephine." (p. 78)

Joseph Schmidt-Görg (**1957**, ed.): *Beethoven: Dreizehn unbekannte Briefe an Josephine Gräfin Deym geb. v. Brunsvik.* [Beethoven: Thirteen Unknown Letters to Josephine Countess Deym née von Brunsvik.] Bonn: Beethoven-Haus.

> With comments by the editor, and also some of Josephine's draft letters. A first attempt to interpret (and date) these letters. Unfortunately, he did not see the effects of the pressure by the Brunsvik family to terminate the relationship, and therefore misinterpreted the last letters as reflecting a "cooling down" – as an irreversible termination in fact. He wrongly concluded that therefore the later Letter to the "Immortal Beloved" must have been to someone else. Matters were not helped by the fact that this edition of the "13 Letters" (in German) did not become widely known, even less read and understood. The "mystery" (and thus the lack of profound knowledge and understanding) continued – until Solomon filled the void with a mischievous claim...
>
> It could be argued that this book by Schmidt-Görg is a **disgrace**, not only because it is so widely quoted these days, but filled with errors. It is also noteworthy that this former head of the Beethoven-Archiv in Bonn already knew these 13 letters in 1949, but would not allow Kaznelson access to them (Goldschmidt 1977, p. 464, n. 19). It was Schmidt-Görg's disqualification of Josephine as the Immortal Beloved (together with the German Beethoven establishment's ignoring of Kaznelson) that paved the way for Solomon.
>
> (This book is usually sold with a certain picture on the title page, supposedly depicting Josephine. This amateur portrait of a fat, blond woman is one of Therese's mythical heads and has nothing to do with Josephine. Lampi is probably rolling in his grave for having this painting assigned to him in such official places as the Beethoven-Haus!)

Dana Steichen (**1959**): *Beethoven's Beloved.* New York: Doubleday.

> Steichen discerned two distinct musical ideas in works Beethoven dedicated to Countess Erdödy (the "Beloved theme" and the "Goddess theme"), which she then traced in over 40 works as evidence "of the composer's lifelong love for Countess Erdödy." (p. 20)

Emily Anderson (**1961**, ed.): *The Letters of Beethoven.* 3 vols. London: Macmillan.

> Even though the "13 Letters" were included, many of her translations were critisized as not always accurate (examples in

Tellenbach 1983, pp. 37, 249). Only mentioned here because it is so often referenced. (I have provided my own translations.)

Walter Riezler (**1962**): *Beethoven*. 8th ed. (1st ed. 1936) Zürich: Atlantis.

> Still very much the "standard" German biography. Follows Kaznelson regarding Josephine being his "only love".

Editha & Richard Sterba (**1964**): *Ludwig van Beethoven und sein Neffe. Tragödie eines Genies. Eine psychoanalytische Studie.* [Ludwig van Beethoven and his Nephew. The Tragedy of a Genius. A Psychoanalytic Study.] Munich.

> German authors who argued for nephew Karl as the "Immortal Beloved". First (to some extent, successful) attempt to muddy the waters with lurid psychoanalytical speculations (soon to be surpassed by Solomon).

Joseph Schmidt-Görg (**1966**): "Wer war 'die M.' in einer wichtigen Aufzeichnung Beethovens?" [Who was "the M." in an Important Note by Beethoven?] *Beethoven-Jahrbuch* 1961/64, pp. 75–79. Bonn.

> Shows that according to watermarks this document must be dated to 1807.

Elliot Forbes (**1967**, ed.): *Thayer's Life of Beethoven*. 2 vols. 2nd ed. Princeton: University Press.

> Still the classic among Beethoven biographies, begun by Thayer, who published the 1st edition of the 1st volume in German in 1866. After his death in 1897, Hermann Deiters and later Hugo Riemann worked hard to complete what amounted to thousands of pages (in 5 volumes) of detail about almost everything that was known about Beethoven during the nineteenth century (i.e., almost nothing about the "Immortal Beloved"). The edited and revised German version appeared from 1907 to 1917. An English version was published by Henry Krehbiel in 1921, and Forbes edited this to a shortened English version in 1964 (1st ed.).
>
> The major advantage of this tome is also its main shortcoming: It has a lot of data, but its interpretation and presentation (e.g., dating) are still based on what was the established knowledge of essentially one (though tireless) man more than 100 years ago.

Joseph Schmidt-Görg (**1969**): "Neue Schriftstücke zu Beethoven und Josephine Gräfin Deym." [New Documents about Beethoven and Josephine Countess Deym.] *Beethoven-Jahrbuch* 1965/68, pp. 205–208. Bonn.

> Contains another letter by Beethoven to Josephine (April/May 1807), and more letters by Josephine to Beethoven from 1805.

Jean & Brigitte Massin (**1970**): *Recherche de Beethoven*. Paris: Fayard.

> French authors who identified Josephine as the "Immortal Beloved".

Luigi Magnani (**1972**): *Il nipote di Beethoven*. [Beethoven's Nephew.] Torino: Einaudi.
> Being a (well-written) novel, expect more myth and fiction than reality.

Maynard Solomon (**1972**): "New Light on Beethoven's Letter to an Unknown Woman." *The Musical Quarterly*, Vol. 58/4, pp. 572–587.
> First time the audacious suggestion was made public that Antonie Brentano could have been the "Immortal Beloved" (mainly because she was there).

Virginia Oakley Beahrs (**1972**): "New Light on Beethoven's Immortal Beloved?" *Michigan Quarterly Review*, Volume XI/3, pp. 177-185.
> Identified the letter "A" in Beethoven's Diary with his friend Amenda, suggesting (like the Sterbas) a homoerotic tendency!

Harry Goldschmidt (**1977**): *Um die Unsterbliche Geliebte. Ein Beethoven-Buch*. [About the Immortal Beloved. A Beethoven Book.] Leipzig: Deutscher Verlag für Musik.
> Begins with a thoughtful and comprehensive weighing up of all the arguments presented by his friend Solomon in favor of Antonie, followed by a detailed presentation of and then a synoptic comparison with the evidence supporting Josephine. The latter the clear winner.

Marie-Elisabeth Tellenbach (**1983**): *Beethoven und seine "Unsterbliche Geliebte" Josephine Brunswick. Ihr Schicksal und der Einfluß auf Beethovens Werk*. [Beethoven and his "Immortal Beloved" Josephine Brunsvik. Her Fate and the Impact on Beethoven's Œuvre.] Zürich: Atlantis.
> First (and so far only) **comprehensive biography** of the woman who was Beethoven's "one and only". Even though still limited by what was accessible at the time, draws all the right conclusions. Like Goldschmidt, only available in German (i.e., effectively ignored in America).

Virginia Beahrs (**1986**): "The Immortal Beloved Revisited." *Beethoven Newsletter* 1/2, pp. 22–24.
> This time she correctly identifies Josephine.

Marie-Elisabeth Tellenbach (**1987**): "Beethoven and the Countess Josephine Brunswick." *The Beethoven Newsletter* 2/3, pp. 41-51.

Virginia Oakley Beahrs (**1988**): "The Immortal Beloved Riddle Reconsidered." *Musical Times*, Vol. 129/1740, pp. 64–70.
> Extended version of her previous article, refuting Solomon.

Susan Lund (**1988**): "Beethoven: a true 'fleshly father'?" *Beethoven Newsletter* 3/1, pp. 6-11; 3/2, pp. 36-40.
> Argues that Beethoven was the father of Antonie Brentano's son Karl Josef, born 8 March 1813! Wasn't this to be expected after Solomon suggested Antonie, and many felt more and more

uncomfortable with the fact that Minona was born exactly 9 months later, and Stackelberg was away? The claim that Karl Brentano was Beethoven's son either assumes that he fathered him actually four weeks before that encounter in Prague (somehow), or that Karl was born prematurely - extremely unlikely, as in those days this usually resulted in miscarriage (Antonie was already a mother of five).

Maynard Solomon (**1988**): *Beethoven Essays*, chapter "Recherche de Josephine Deym". Cambridge, Mass.: Harvard University Press, pp. 157–165.

> Written in a polemic style, a futile attempt to discredit the evidence in favor of Josephine as the most likely "candidate" by pouring scornful ridicule on her "advocates". By (mis)interpreting letters around the time in question, speculates that Josephine and Stackelberg "must" have been (1) both in Vienna, (2) together and (3) happily so! Overall, sadly, disgraced by a prevailing misogynistic attitude.

Marie-Elisabeth Tellenbach (**1988**): "Künstler und Ständegesellschaft um 1800: die Rolle der Vormundschaftsgesetze in Beethovens Beziehung zu Josephine Gräfin Deym." [Artists and the Class Society in 1800: the Role of Guardianship Laws in Beethoven's Relationship to Josephine Countess Deym.] *Vierteljahrschrift für Sozial- und Wirtschaftsgeschichte* 2/2, pp. 253-263.

> Shows that "it was a case of guardianship which was the main reason why Countess Josephine Deym, the **only** woman to whom he wrote passionate love letters ... distanced herself from him in 1807, although she specifically responded to his love." (p. 253)

Carl Dahlhaus (**1991**): *Ludwig van Beethoven: Approaches to his Music*. Oxford: University Press.

> Concludes that "internal evidence" (p. 247) points to Josephine.

Barry Cooper (**1991**, ed.): *The Beethoven Compendium. A Guide to Beethoven's Life and Music*. London: Thames & Hudson.

> You should have this on your book shelf.

Virginia Beahrs (**1993**): "Beethoven's Only Beloved? New Perspectives on the Love Story of the Great Composer." *Music Review* 54, no. 3/4, pp. 183-197.

> "Solomon goes to considerable lengths to establish what he considers the composer's 'deeply rooted inability to marry'. Suggesting that 'Oedipal connotations may have intensified Beethoven's anxieties', he considers 'pursuit of the unattainable woman a necessary (though painful) condition of the creative achievement'. ... Was there for him in fact ... one deep and lasting passion for a certain dear one, marriage to whom was precluded, not by psychological inhibitions of the inner man, but by prohibitive heart-breaking externals?" (p. 183) "Where is any evidence whatsoever of true romantic love for even such dear ones

as Marie Erdödy or Dorothea von Ertmann, Therese Malfatti or Antonie Brentano? Although all have been advanced as Beethoven's unknown Immortal Beloved, the assessment is unsupported by the record or by any known correspondence. Intimate friends of Beethoven, true, one and all; but loves? There is one, however, and **only one**, to whom Beethoven did pour his heart out in impassioned declarations of undying love remarkably similar to the phraseology of the anguished letter to his Immortal Beloved ... That one is his 'BELOVED AND ONLY J' – Josephine." (p. 184)

Marie-Elisabeth Tellenbach (**1993/1994**): "Psychoanalysis and the Historiocritical Method: On Maynard Solomon's Image of Beethoven." *Beethoven Newsletter* 8/3, pp. 84–92; 9/3, pp. 119–127.

> This publication resulted in Solomon's resignation from the advisory board of the *Newsletter*'s publisher – which was a major blow to them, given Solomon's reputation in the USA and the fact that they were still a fledgling society.

Ernst Pichler (**1994**): *Beethoven. Mythos und Wirklichkeit.* [Beethoven. Myth and Reality.] Vienna: Amalthea.

> A biography written like a mixture of a novel and a long essay. He (re)tells many of the "myths" without actually destroying them (like Bettina Brentano's fantasies). Nevertheless, as far as most relevant events in Beethoven's life go, a truthful record of what must have been "reality". He dismisses convincingly Solomon's "lonely" speculations and gives sufficient consideration to the relevance of Josephine in Beethoven's life.

Ulrich Noering (**1995**): *Beethoven und Ungarn.* [Beethoven and Hungary.] Budapest: TóKa-PR-System; publ. in French as: *Ludwig van Beethoven et l'immortelle bien-aimée.* [Ludwig van Beethoven and the Immortal Beloved.] Marseille: Via Valeriano.

> Also published in Hungarian.
>
> In 1984, Ulrich Noering founded the "Gesellschaft der Ungarnvereine" [Association of Hungary Clubs] in Stuttgart, later to become the "Deutsch-Ungarische Freundschaftsgesellschaft" [German-Hungarian Friendship Association] (http://www.neuezeitung.hu/dokumentumok/NZg_05-2002.pdf, 24 Jan 2011).

Theodore Albrecht (**1996**, ed.): *Letters to Beethoven & other Correspondence.* 3 vols. University of Nebraska Press.

> Complements the translations into English of Beethoven's letters by Anderson (1961); however, many wordings are questionable, especially in the translations of the letters by Josephine to Beethoven (they are also often dated incorrectly).
>
> It is a shame that this edition was not co-ordinated with the German edition of Beethoven's correspondence (see following); the many discrepancies are annoying.

Sieghard Brandenburg (**1996**, ed.): *Ludwig van Beethoven: Briefwechsel. Gesamtausgabe.* [Ludwig van Beethoven: Letters. Complete Edition.] 8 vols. Munich: Henle.

> The long awaited "definitive" edition, with many corrections of spelling and dating. However, this German edition of all the German correspondence by the most German of all composers has this to say about the so-called "Letter to the Immortal Beloved": "On the problem of identifying the 'Immortal Beloved' see the summary by Maynard Solomon, *Antonie Brentano and Beethoven*, also *Recherche de Josephine Deym*, in: Beethoven Essays ...; there also the recent literature on the subject." [Zum Problem der Identifizierung der "Unsterblichen Geliebten" zusammenfassend Maynard Solomon, *Antonie Brentano and Beethoven* sowie *Recherche de Josephine Deym* in: Beethoven Essays...; dort auch die neuere Literatur zu dem Thema.] (Vol. 2., p. 272)
>
> This is (once again, in the tradition of Schmidt-Görg 40 years earlier) a **disgrace**, for various reasons: (1) The quoted article about Antonie does not deal at all with the problem of "identification". (2) The other article (about Josephine) does not aid much in this regard as it is just a polemic, trying, vainly, to refute the (meanwhile many) "Deym advocates". (3) These two specialized articles do **not** "summarize" anything. (4) The "recent literature" is of course nowhere "summarized" by Solomon, or even properly quoted. If anything, he represents that branch of esoteric American scholarship that consistently **refuses** to accept the latest [!] German research (as opposed to scholars like Beahrs). The upshot is that the (mostly) **German** readers of these "Letters" are told to obtain any additional knowledge from an **English** source – as if there were no useful ones in German! (Or was this the price to pay to get the likes of Solomon and Lockwood to lend their names as co-editors?)

Gail S Altman (**1996**): *Beethoven: A Man of His Word – Undisclosed Evidence for his Immortal Beloved.* Anubian Press.

> Won some undeserved fame for making the untenable suggestion that Marie Countess Erdödy was the "Immortal Beloved". More valuable for shredding Solomon's conjecture.

Marie-Elisabeth Tellenbach (**1996**): "Noch eine Geliebte Beethovens gefunden – oder erfunden? Zu Klaus Martin Kopitz: 'Sieben volle Monate': Beethoven und Theresa von Zandt." [Yet Another Beloved of Beethoven Found – or Invented? About Klaus Martin Kopitz: "Seven Whole Months": Beethoven and Theresa von Zandt.] *Musica Germany* 50/2, pp. 78-83.

> Never heard of Zandt? Never mind, as long as it's not Josephine, you can get published with any old phantasy...

Maynard Solomon (**1998**): *Beethoven.* 2nd ed. New York: Schirmer.

> As in the 1st edition in 1977, repeats the rather vague speculations regarding Antonie, adding some of the polemics from his previous "Recherche" essay. On http://www.amazon.com/, it is "hailed as a masterpiece for its original interpretations of Beethoven's life and

music" (by the salesmen) because "Maynard Solomon is a leading authority on Beethoven". But among several "Customer Reviews", one can find profound observations like this:

> "Solomon's psychoanalysis irritated me. ... The book is written from a psychoanalytic point of view that all may not find convincing. ... I found his attempts to psychoanalyze Beethoven annoying, and seemingly **rooted more in conjecture rather than solid facts**. Even the chapter on the Immortal Beloved, which I found so impressive the first time I read the book, seems now to me based more upon a process of elimination **rather than solid scholarship**. ... I've encountered much greater depth in far more accessible styles of writing. ... I found this book **unreadable and extremely boring**. It was so dense with **meaningless detail** that the narrative flow virtually ceased – the endless inclusion of irrelevant detail sucked the life right out of the book for me. ... A whole chapter about Solomon's guess (all 'Beethoven Scholars' have one) as to the identity of the Immortal Beloved, to whom Beethoven wrote (but may not have mailed) an ardent love letter – then **no real attempt to make this supposed relationship relevant to the man's life and work**. ... Most of the mistranslations, misinformation, and inaccuracies of the original book have been carried over into this version. Although **soundly criticized** by mainly European scholars, this book **continues to dazzle American** academicians who have never bothered to double-check the primary source material from which quotes have been taken. **Truncated quotes, misquotes, and half-truths** support theories which the information in original form would have easily shown as **false**. The psychoanalyses included are **ludicrous** and often based on misrepresentations of facts. A strong caveat to all readers." (http://www.amazon.com/Beethoven-Revised–Maynard–Solomon/product–reviews/, 6 Feb 2011)

Marie-Elisabeth Tellenbach (**1998**): "Psychoanalyse und historisch-philologische Methode. Zu Maynard Solomons Beethoven- und Schubert-Deutungen." [Psychoanalysis and Historiocritical Method. On Maynard Solomon's Interpretations of Beethoven and Schubert.] *Analecta Musicologica* 30/II, pp. 661–719.

> A reply to Solomon, who inflicted his questionable "psychoanalytic" speculations not only on Beethoven but also on Schubert (and elsewhere, Mozart).

Marie-Elisabeth Tellenbach (**1999**): "Die Bedeutung des Adler-Gleichnisses in Beethovens Brief an Therese Gräfin Brunswick. Ein Beitrag zu seiner Biographie." [The Meaning of the Eagle Allegory in Beethoven's Letter to Therese Countess Brunsvik. A Contribution to his Biography.] *Die Musikforschung* 4.

Oldrich Pulkert (**2000**): "Beethoven's Unsterbliche Geliebte." [Beethoven's Immortal Beloved.] *Beethoven Journal* 15/1, pp. 2-18.

> Suggests one Almerie Esterházy, whom Beethoven did not even know. Now that surely tops it. (And if you wonder why the

respected *Beethoven Journal* publishes such utter nonsense ... read on:)

William Meredith (**2000**): "Mortal Musings: Testing the Candidacy of Almerie Esterházy against the Antonie Brentano Theory." *Beethoven Journal* 15/1, pp. 42-47.

> "... **we lack evidence of a connection between Almerie and Beethoven**... I must reiterate that **we have no such evidence [!] of a passionate love relationship between Antonie and Beethoven either**, just of a close friendship; for Josephine, ... we know he was indeed passionately in love with her in 1805-1807 at least." (p. 47) Still bewildered? So am I.

Russell Martin (**2000**): *Beethoven's Hair. An Extraordinary Historical Odyssey and a Musical Mystery Solved*. London: Bloomsbury.

> Although its conclusion – that the high amount of lead in a surviving lock of Beethoven's hair could provide an explanation for his many mysterious illnesses and the cause of his death – remains controversial, this book is also a moving account of the people of **Denmark**, the only country whose people saved all their Jews during the Holocaust.

Wolfhart von Stackelberg (**2001**): "Ohne Beethoven klänge Estnisch anders." [Without Beethoven, Estonian would Sound Differently.] *Nachrichtenblatt der Baltischen Ritterschaften* [Newsletter of the Baltic Knighthoods] 169/1, pp. 4–7. Lüdenscheid.

> A direct descendent of one of Christoph's brothers provides a short overview of what now seems to be the adopted "family myth", claiming that Christoph knew all along that Minone was Beethoven's child...

Klaus Martin Kopitz (**2001**): "Antonie Brentano in Wien (1809–1812). Neue Quellen zur Problematik 'Unsterbliche Geliebte'." [Antonie Brentano in Vienna (1809–1812). New Sources to the Difficulties with the "Immortal Beloved".] *Bonner Beethoven-Studien*, vol. 2, pp. 115–146.

> Rather valiant (but in the end, futile) attempt to salvage Solomon's "Antonie hypothesis" by (mis)interpreting a letter by Franz Brentano (who was seeking a teacher for his son, without apparently bothering to tell his wife – yet) as a supposedly clear indication that their marriage was on the rocks; thus no wonder that Antonie spontaneously (for one night at least) flew into Beethoven's arms!

Rita Steblin (**2002**): "Josephine Gräfin Brunswick-Deyms Geheimnis enthüllt: Neue Ergebnisse zu ihrer Beziehung zu Beethoven." [Josephine Countess Brunsvik-Deym's Secret Revealed: New Results about her Relationship to Beethoven.] *Österreichische Musikzeitschrift* 57/6, pp. 23–31.

Lewis Lockwood (2003): *Beethoven. The Music and the Life.* New York: Norton.

> Thoughtful and readable account of biographical events and their historical context. As for the "Immortal Beloved", he offers nothing more than parroting his friend Solomon.

Maynard Solomon (2005, ed.): *Beethovens Tagebuch 1812–1818.* [Beethoven's Diary 1812–1818.] 2nd ed. (1st ed. 1990.) Bonn: Beethoven-Haus.

> With an introduction and some useful comments by the editor, who – not surprisingly – seizes upon the first entry where a doubtful letter is copied incorrectly as an "A". (Of course, it is not "Antonie", as he likes us to believe.)
>
> Note: This book is the German version of the same one edited by Solomon in English (published in 1982) - the translation of his comments and the whole editing were actually done by Sieghard Brandenburg of the *Beethoven-Haus* in Bonn.

Rita Steblin (2005): *A History of Key Characteristics in the 18th and Early 19th Centuries.* 2nd ed. (1st ed. 1983). University of Rochester Press.

> Presents historical documentation for the symbolic meaning of C minor as the Requiem key, with the implication that Beethoven's Piano Sonata Op. 111, rather than Op. 110, might have been Josephine's true Requiem. This was the last piano sonata Beethoven ever wrote, the high trills symbolize the unity of their souls in heaven. Fittingly, Op. 111 was also Beethoven's farewell from the Piano Sonata, from the Piano in fact – and his farewell from Josephine, who had become his favorite piano pupil 22 years before, and was his one and only beloved. Forever.

Rita Steblin (2005a): "Reminiscences of Beethoven in Anton Gräffer's unpublished Memoirs: A Legacy of the Viennese Biography Project of 1827." *Bonner Beethoven-Studien* 4, pp. 149–189.

Dietrich Haberl (2006): "Beethovens erste Reise nach Wien – Die Datierung seiner Schülerreise zu W. A. Mozart." [Beethoven's First Journey to Vienna – Dating his Study Trip to W A Mozart.] *Neues Musikwissenschaftliches Jahrbuch* 14, pp. 215–255.

Rita Steblin (2007): "'Auf diese Art mit A geht alles zugrunde'. A New Look at Beethoven's Diary Entry and the 'Immortal Beloved'." *Bonner Beethoven-Studien* 6, pp. 147–180.

> At last an article in English that summarily and with much (often new) documentary evidence argues most convincingly that the "Immortal Beloved" was Josephine and no one else. Concentrates on the mysterious "A" in Beethoven's first Diary entry that caused so much confusion. The surprising result is that whatever Beethoven might have scribbled in an almost illegible way, it was most likely not an "A". Instead, if anything, "St" (= Stackelberg) is the most meaningful interpretation!

Dagmar Skwara/Rita Steblin (**2007**): "Ein Brief Christoph Freiherr von Stackelbergs an Josephine Brunsvik-Deym-Stackelberg." [A Letter by Christoph Baron von Stackelberg to Josephine Brunsvik-Deym-Stackelberg.] *Bonner Beethoven-Studien* 6, pp. 181–187.

> Offers great psychological insights into why their relationship was (from the beginning) so "troubled". Stackelberg revealing his true character.

Gabriele Hatwagner (**2008**): *Die Lust an der Illusion – über den Reiz der "Scheinkunstsammlung" des Grafen Deym, der sich Müller nannte.* [The Pleasure of Illusion – about the Appeal of the "Fake Art Collection" of Count Deym, who Called himself Müller.] Diplomarbeit [Thesis Paper], Vienna University. (http://othes.univie.ac.at/850/1/2008–08–04_8302575.pdf, 6 Feb 2011)

Yayoi Aoki (**2008**): *Beethoven – Die Entschlüsselung des Rätsels um die "Unsterbliche Geliebte".* [Beethoven – The Decryption of the Riddle about the "Immortal Beloved".] Munich: Iudicium.

> Aoki claims to be a "leading feminist", and she came up with her sensational new discovery (namely Antonie Brentano) after "long years of research" and supposedly based on "thus far unknown sources". Maybe unknown in Japan, as she refers to the – flawed – article by Kopitz (2001). This book is full of the most ridiculous nonsense, like Beethoven was the true father of Minona Stackelberg, and Antonie forgave him for sleeping with Josephine – as he did this by mistake! And the translation from the Japanese is by one "Annette Boronnia" – an all too obvious anagram of "Antonie Brentano"…
>
> The "Antonie Hypothesis" has by now truly evolved – from the audacious and unlikely through the speculative and incredible, to the ridiculous and farcical.

Rita Steblin (**2009**): "'A dear, enchanting girl who loves me and whom I love': New Facts about Beethoven's Beloved Piano Pupil Julie Guicciardi." *Bonner Beethoven-Studien* 8, pp. 89–152.

> Very interesting study with much detail about the only other woman with whom Beethoven (according to his own letters) ever was in love – though only very briefly. Steblin also corrects many genealogical inaccuracies.

Rita Steblin (**2009a**): "Beethovens 'Unsterbliche Geliebte': des Rätsels Lösung." [Beethoven's "Immortal Beloved": the Riddle Solved.] *Österreichische Musikzeitschrift* 64/2, pp. 4–17.

> German version of her article in Bonner Beethoven-Studien, vol. 6.

Rita Steblin (**2009b**): "Beethoven's Name in Viennese Conscription Records." *Beethoven Journal* 24/1, pp. 4–13.

Edward Walden (**2011**): *Beethoven's Immortal Beloved. Solving the Mystery*. Lanham, Maryland: Scarecrow.

By adding even more to the (supposed) "Mystery", he thinks the bubbly Bettina Brentano must have been the one, because Beethoven wrote her a (one) friendly letter in 1811 (the year she married and went away) which he ended by using, jocularly, the intimate "Du" form of addressing. More importantly, Walden does not seem to believe that Bettina actually **forged** love letters by Beethoven (and a few more things besides) – he takes them as "evidence" instead. If anything, this latest book demonstrates at least (and again) that Solomon's conjecture is (even in America) still not unequivocally accepted. However, it also shows once more that to this day the mountain of research by European scholars has not yet percolated through the musicological culture in America – Walden does not quote any of it.

Index

1

1812 · 33, 88, 90, 93, 94, 95, 141, 151, 156, 157, 159, 160, 161, 164, 165, 174, 176, 178, 179, 180, 181, 182, 187, 189, 192, 202, 203, 205, 210, 219, 225, 247, 248, 256

185, 187, 188, 189, 191, 192, 200, 203, 204, 208, 233, 234, 243, 245, 251, 254, 256, 257, 258
Aoki · 258
Appassionata · 160, 193, 242, 244, 248
Artaria · 148
Auckland · 7
Austria · 62, 107, 111, 124, 210, 214, 235

A

Adam, Theo · 236
Albrecht, Theodore · 253
Albrechtsberger · 11
Almerie Esterházy · 204, 238, 255
Altman · 234, 254
Amalie Sebald · 204, 206, 248
Amenda · 30, 204, 251
An die ferne Geliebte · 126, 239, 242
An die Geliebte · 175, 239, 244
An die Hoffnung · 42, 51, 58, 128, 157, 180, 186, 199, 224, 239, 241, 242
Andante favori · 39, 43, 160, 185, 243
Anderson, Emily · 249
Andrian · 112, 118, 119, 126, 152, 187, 212, 213, 226
Angel · 5, 7, 23, 38, 39, 93, 102, 156, 161, 163, 164, 167, 168, 180, 181, 189, 219
Anna von Brunsvik · 12, 18, 23, 24, 33, 56, 110, 129, 143, 177, 224, 225
Antonie Brentano · 21, 41, 77, 105, 127, 151, 160, 165, 166, 168, 169, 170, 172, 173, 174, 175, 176, 177, 178, 179, 180, 182,

B

Baader · 209
Baden · 56, 125, 126, 128, 177, 226
Barbieri · 233
Baur, Harry · 235
Beahrs · 251, 252, 254
Beethoven, Carl van see Carl van Beethoven · 11
Beethoven, Johann van see Johann van Beethoven · 11
Beethoven, Johanna van see Johanna van Beethoven · 49
Beethoven, Karl van see Karl van Beethoven · 49
Beethoven-Haus · 7, 233, 247, 249, 257
Berg · 186
Berlioz · 248
Bettina Brentano · 77, 173, 174, 201, 234, 249, 253, 259
Bhagavad-Gita · 121
Biamonti · 234, 241
Bigot · 174
Blanka Teleki · 234
Boehm, Gero von · 238
Bohemia · 33, 81, 108, 123, 124, 182
Böhm, Karlheinz · 236

Bonn · 7, 10, 11, 27, 39, 76, 169, 233
Brandenburg · 206, 254, 257
Braunschweig · 12
Breitkopf & Härtel · 90
Brentano, Antonie see Antonie Brentano · 77
Brentano, Bettina see Bettina Brentano · 77
Brentano, Clemens see Clemens Brentano · 174
Brentano, Franz see Franz Brentano · 77
Brentano, Maximiliane see Maximiliane Brentano · 177
Brentano, Toni (Antonie) see Toni (Antonie) Brentano · 175
Breuning · 150, 239
Bridgetower · 34
Brilliant · 193, 234
Brunsvik, Anna see Anna von Brunsvik · 12
Brunsvik, Charlotte see Charlotte von Brunsvik · 7
Brunsvik, Franz see Franz von Brunsvik · 9
Brunsvik, Joseph see Joseph von Brunsvik · 109
Brunsvik, Therese see Therese von Brunsvik · 7
Budapest · 12, 33, 36, 52, 98, 169
Burgmüller · 80
Burstein · 79
Burton · 7

C

Canada · 7, 236
Carl van Beethoven · 11, 49, 103, 120
Carlsbad · 62, 98
Cassandra · 19, 36, 63, 74
Cellan-Jones · 237
Charlotte von Brunsvik · 7, 12, 24, 27, 37, 44, 51, 53, 73, 74, 112, 157, 189, 224, 234
Chopin · 186, 248
Christ on the Mount of Olives · 175, 242

Christoph von Stackelberg see Stackelberg, Christoph von · 9
Clemens Brentano · 174, 175
Cooper, Barry · 14, 252
Czech Republic · 181, 190
Czechoslovakia · 180
Czeke · 13, 169, 248

D

Dahlhaus · 79, 252
Deiters · 197, 250
Denmark · 256
Deym, Fritz see Fritz Deym · 25
Deym, Joseph · 18, 19, 23, 24, 30, 33, 36, 37, 152, 173, 174, 181, 182, 198, 224, 258
Deym, Josepha see Josepha Deym · 37
Deym, Viky see Viky Deym · 23
Dezasse · 118
Diabelli · 199, 243
Diana, Princess · 182
Disneyland · 236
Don Giovanni · 186
Dornbach · 97, 98
Dorothea Ertmann · 204

E

East Germany · 236
Eger · 86
Eleonore · 111
Emilie · 113, 119, 126
Empfindungen bei Lydiens Untreue · 47, 239, 243
England · 106, 199
Erdödy · 234, 249, 254
Eroica · 28, 33, 45, 235, 237, 241, 242, 244, 248
Ertmann, Dorothea see Dorothea Ertmann · 204
Esterházy · 165
Esterházy, Almerie see Almerie Esterházy · 204
Estonia · 9, 89, 90, 183, 207, 209, 210, 214
Esztergom · 72

eternally devoted · 69
Eternity · 140, 141

F

Fähna · 209
faithful · 54, 55, 67, 68, 93, 163, 165, 166, 167, 208
faithfulness · 54, 93, 147, 158, 163, 165, 166, 167, 179, 189, 192
Fanny Giannatasio del Rio · 125
Fidelio · 51, 107, 174, 236, 237, 242
Fischhof · 202, 204, 205, 232
Florence · 67
Forbes · 197, 250
France · 235, 236, 237
Frankfurt · 62, 127, 166, 173, 177
Franz Brentano · 26, 41, 77, 148, 151, 173, 175, 178, 185, 200, 256
Franz von Brunsvik · 9, 12, 23, 24, 53, 82, 98, 112, 119, 143, 152, 157, 158, 160, 173, 183, 193, 224, 242, 244
Franzensbrunn · 94, 98, 165, 166
Franziska von Hohenheim · 25
Fritz Deym · 25, 105, 108, 109, 110, 112, 143, 147, 169, 192, 218
Für Elise · 76, 243

G

Gallenberg · 27, 28, 158
Gance, Abel · 29, 235
Geneva · 67, 73, 209, 211
Genoa · 67
George of England · 242
Germany · 209, 235, 236, 237, 238
Giannatasio, Fanny see Fanny Giannatasio del Rio · 125
Giovane, Julia von · 26
Giulietta · 157, 235, 241, 248
Gleichenstein · 66, 76, 242
Gluck · 248
God Save the King · 33, 104, 239, 243, 244

Goethe · 12, 17, 63, 74, 94, 111, 173, 176, 239, 240, 248
Goldschmidt · 24, 25, 33, 41, 49, 111, 151, 161, 169, 175, 180, 190, 191, 192, 195, 206, 234, 236, 249, 251
Golz · 23, 25, 93, 190, 200
Gotha · 62
Göttingen · 209
Gottschall [Gottschalk] von Stackelberg · 107
Grabsky · 238
Gräffer · 202, 203, 204, 205, 227, 228, 229, 230, 231, 232, 257
Gran · 72
Greece · 247
Greytown · 7
Guicciardi, Julie see Julie Guicciardi · 27
Gumpendorf · 172

H

Haberl · 13, 257
Hacking · 103
Hager · 97, 109, 110, 226
Hammerklavier · 140, 160, 242
Handel · 106
Harris, Ed · 238
Hatwagner · 18, 258
Haydn · 11, 18, 241, 248
Heaven · 5, 93, 111, 112, 152, 158, 162, 166, 189, 220
Hébert · 237
Heiligenstadt · 31
Heiligenstadt Testament · 31, 56, 94, 156, 224
Helena · 126
Henry the Lion · 12
Heppner · 237
Herder · 103, 106, 120
Hernals · 98
Hesiod · 121
Hess 107 · 26, 244
Hess 109 · 244
Hess 110 · 244
Hess 90 · 29, 244
Holland, Agnieszka · 238
Hollywood · 237

Holocaust · 238, 256
Homer · 115
Hope · 42, 47, 51, 52, 79, 128, 157, 180, 186, 224, 239, 241, 242, 244
Hungary · 12, 16, 45, 141, 143, 180, 181, 190, 208, 214, 253

I

Ich denke dein · 17, 43, 52, 66, 198, 239, 243, 244
Ich liebe dich so wie du mich · 159, 239, 240, 243
Ilias · 115
Immortal Beloved · 29, 33, 41, 56, 88, 94, 105, 156, 157, 165, 167, 168, 169, 170, 171, 176, 179, 180, 181, 183, 187, 188, 190, 193, 200, 201, 203, 204, 208, 210, 219, 233, 234, 237, 238, 247, 248, 249, 250, 251, 253, 255, 256, 257, 258, 259
Israel Philharmonic Orchestra · 236
Italy · 29, 62, 67, 98, 208, 247

J

Janitschek · 194
Janowitz · 236
Japan · 236
Jaretzki · 8
Johann van Beethoven · 11, 99
Johanna van Beethoven · 49, 120, 204, 237
Joseph Deym see Deym, Joseph · 18
Joseph von Brunsvik · 109
Josepha Deym · 37
Josephine's Theme · 39, 160, 243
Julie Guicciardi · 27, 30, 157, 158, 192, 224, 235, 244, 258
Jung-Stilling · 209

K

Kagel · 236

Karl van Beethoven · 49, 103, 120, 126, 148, 204, 250
Karlsbad · 74, 81, 86, 94, 98, 165, 166, 170, 178, 179, 187, 188, 201, 248
Kaznelson · 41, 157, 169, 201, 234, 248, 249, 250
Kinsky · 93, 99, 242
Koblenz · 76
Kopitz · 80, 254, 256, 258
Krehbiel · 197, 250
Kreutzer · 34, 241
Krüdener · 209

L

La Mara · 13, 26, 41, 157, 169, 186, 197, 201, 216, 247, 248
Lang, Regina · 175, 244
Leitzmann · 125
Leonore · 45, 51, 107, 160, 174, 244
Levine, James · 237
Ley, Stephan · 248
Leyer · 108, 123, 124, 214
Lichnowsky · 42, 48, 157, 180, 185, 241
Linz · 99
Lipsius · 157, 247, 248
Liszt · 247
Lobkowitz · 104, 172, 238, 242
Lockwood · 14, 79, 237, 254, 257
Lorenz · 80
Lund, Susan · 251

M

Magnani · 120, 236, 251
Mahler · 186
Malfatti, Teresa · 76, 77, 158, 178, 204, 206, 225, 243
Maria Laura von Stackelberg · 72
Martin, Russell · 238, 256
Martonvásár · 7, 12, 19, 24, 44
Marxism · 194
Massin · 198, 250
Mattila · 237

Maximiliane Brentano · 177, 199, 243
Mayersfeld · 119, 125, 226
Mehta · 236
Meredith · 193, 200, 256
Metropolitan Opera · 237
Metternich · 6, 109
Minona · 9, 94, 102, 103, 107, 140, 144, 157, 184, 198, 207, 214, 221, 226, 248, 258
Missa Solemnis · 140, 151, 160, 243
Mont Blanc · 63
Mont Cenis · 63
Moonlight · 29, 158, 193, 235, 241, 244
Moravia · 33, 73, 225
Mozart · 10, 11, 18, 170, 181, 186, 198, 238, 255, 257
Müller · 18, 258
my everything · 38, 43, 93, 156, 161, 164, 166, 167, 168

N

Napoleon · 79, 91, 95
Narayena · 121
Nathalie von Stackelberg · 198, 209, 247
Nature · 165, 229
Nemischl · 93, 169, 200
New Philharmonia · 236
Noering · 253

O

Obermayer, Therese · 99
Oldenburg · 7
Oldman · 237
Oliva · 144
only beloved · 43, 55, 75, 189
Op. 1 · 14, 241
Op. 106 · 140, 160, 242
Op. 109 · 199, 243
Op. 11 · 19, 241
Op. 110 · 151, 160, 185, 199, 243, 245, 257
Op. 111 · 169, 199, 243, 245, 257
Op. 12 · 26, 241

Op. 120 · 199, 243
Op. 123 · 160, 243
Op. 125 · 160, 243
Op. 135 · 165, 243
Op. 136 · 111, 243
Op. 17 · 31, 241
Op. 2 · 14, 241
Op. 21 · 34, 241
Op. 27#2 · 27, 241
Op. 3 · 14, 241
Op. 31 · 159, 185, 199, 241
Op. 32 · 45, 185, 199, 239, 241
Op. 35 · 29, 241
Op. 36 · 34, 241
Op. 37 · 34, 241
Op. 43 · 29, 241, 244
Op. 47 · 34, 241
Op. 53 · 39, 242
Op. 54 · 160, 199, 242
Op. 55 · 29, 33, 242
Op. 57 · 160, 242
Op. 68 · 242
Op. 69 · 64, 160, 242
Op. 72 · 242
Op. 74 · 237, 242
Op. 75 · 199, 240, 242
Op. 78 · 160, 242, 244
Op. 81a · 75, 79, 160, 242
Op. 82 · 45, 239, 242
Op. 83#1 · 75, 160, 240, 242
Op. 83#2 · 75, 239, 242
Op. 85 · 175, 242
Op. 86 · 165, 242
Op. 91 · 106, 107, 111, 242
Op. 92 · 107, 111, 242
Op. 93 · 107, 160, 199, 242
Op. 94 · 45, 128, 239, 242
Op. 95 · 160, 242
Op. 96 · 160, 169, 242
Op. 98 · 126, 239, 242
Otto von Stackelberg · 124, 136, 207, 209, 214, 226, 247

P

Pantheism · 117
Pastoral · 165, 236, 242
Pestalozzi · 62, 63, 68, 82, 110, 209, 225

Peters, Karl · 171, 172
Pichler · 8, 253
Pisa · 67
Plutarch · 135, 136
Prague · 33, 36, 81, 86, 87, 88, 90, 93, 94, 97, 170, 178, 179, 181, 182, 188, 190, 191, 201, 220, 224, 225
Prater · 102
Prometheus · 28, 241, 244
Prussia · 111
Pulkert · 255
Pyrmont · 125, 126
Pythagoras · 106

Q

Quartetto serioso · 160, 242

R

Rahel Varnhagen · 204, 248
Raptus Association · 234
Razumovsky · 242
Requiem · 151, 160, 185, 199, 245, 257
Resignation · 135, 136, 160, 226, 239, 244
Reval · 89, 209
Rickets · 12
Riemann · 197, 250
Ries, Ferdinand · 31, 125, 127, 199, 239
Riezler · 250
Ritterballett · 11, 243
Röckel · 80
Rolland · 28, 41, 169, 216, 248
Rose, Bernard · 237
Rudolph · 78
Rule Britannia · 33, 243
Russia · 89, 107, 111, 123

S

Salieri · 11, 239, 241
Savoy · 63
Schindler · 150, 156, 157, 247

Schmidt-Görg · 157, 169, 177, 249, 250, 254
Schnepfenthal · 62
Schönberg, Baron · 62
Schönbrunn · 44
Schubert · 109, 170, 186, 239, 240, 255
Schumann · 186
Sebald, Amalie see Amalie Sebald · 204
Sehnsucht · 63, 75, 128, 160, 163, 239, 240, 242, 243, 244
Skinner, Claire · 238
Skwara · 118, 210, 213, 258
Slovakia · 181
Solomon · 21, 105, 125, 169, 170, 171, 172, 174, 176, 177, 178, 179, 180, 182, 183, 184, 185, 186, 187, 188, 190, 191, 192, 193, 202, 203, 204, 205, 221, 234, 237, 249, 251, 252, 253, 254, 255, 256, 257, 259
Solothurn · 63
Stackelberg, Christoph von · 9, 10, 61, 62, 63, 66, 67, 68, 72, 73, 74, 81, 82, 86, 87, 88, 89, 95, 97, 98, 102, 103, 107, 108, 109, 110, 112, 118, 119, 123, 124, 125, 126, 136, 143, 144, 152, 157, 160, 181, 182, 183, 184, 187, 198, 204, 207, 208, 209, 210, 211, 212, 213, 214, 215, 224, 225, 226, 252, 257, 258
Stackelberg, Gottschall [Gottschalk] see Gottschall [Gottschalk] von Stackelberg · 107
Stackelberg, Maria Laura see Maria Laura von Stackelberg · 72
Stackelberg, Nathalie see Nathalie von Stackelberg · 209
Stackelberg, Otto see Otto von Stackelberg · 124
Stackelberg, Theophile see Theophile von Stackelberg · 72
Stackelberg, Wolfhart see Wolfhart von Stackelberg · 7
Staudenheim · 90
Steblin · 7, 18, 25, 28, 29, 40, 58, 72, 81, 86, 88, 94, 95, 98, 105, 108, 113, 118, 125, 144, 164, 166, 169, 181, 190, 192, 193,

198, 200, 203, 204, 205, 210, 213, 218, 221, 238, 256, 257, 258
Steichen · 249
Sterba · 250
Stolberg, Countess · 62
Suchet · 234
Swafford · 7
Swieten · 241
Switzerland · 62, 123, 208, 209, 212, 225

T

Tallinn · 7
Tasso · 111
Tchaikovsky · 186
Teleki · 24, 44
Teleki, Blanka see Blanka Teleki · 234
Tellenbach · 54, 82, 105, 115, 123, 125, 126, 159, 169, 171, 172, 180, 190, 192, 193, 201, 205, 206, 221, 234, 250, 251, 252, 253, 254, 255
Tenger · 216, 247
Teplitz · 90, 94, 98, 173, 178, 225, 248
Teresa Malfatti see Malfatti, Teresa · 76
Thayer · 177, 178, 197, 250
Theophile von Stackelberg · 72, 81
Therese von Brunsvik · 7, 10, 12, 13, 16, 17, 18, 19, 24, 33, 36, 37, 43, 51, 52, 53, 62, 63, 67, 68, 72, 73, 74, 81, 82, 83, 86, 88, 89, 90, 94, 95, 97, 98, 102, 103, 107, 108, 109, 110, 111, 112, 119, 124, 125, 126, 128, 129, 130, 136, 141, 143, 144, 145, 147, 148, 150, 151, 152, 157, 160, 177, 184, 189, 204, 207, 208, 210, 212, 224, 225, 226, 234, 235, 242, 243, 244, 247, 248, 249, 255
Thomas-San-Galli · 248
Tiedge · 239
Toni (Antonie) Brentano · 175, 178, 203, 204

Traun · 97
Trautenau · 108, 123, 124
Trautmannsdorf · 81
Troppau · 48

U

USA · 192, 235, 236, 237, 238, 253

V

Varnhagen · 93
Varnhagen, Rahel see Rahel Varnhagen · 204
Vickers · 236
Vienna · 7, 10, 11, 12, 13, 16, 19, 27, 33, 44, 48, 55, 62, 73, 86, 89, 97, 104, 107, 111, 118, 124, 136, 141, 144, 150, 165, 166, 172, 173, 175, 183, 202, 207, 209, 252, 256
Viky Deym · 23, 81, 87, 110, 150

W

Währing · 6, 150
Walden · 7, 195, 200, 201, 259
Waldstein · 11, 39, 242
Wegeler · 27, 30, 76, 168
Wellington · 107, 111, 242
Werner, Zacharias · 227
Werther · 226
West Germany · 236
Westphalia · 125
Wiener Neustadt · 151
Witschapp · 73, 74, 81, 86
Wolfhart von Stackelberg · 7, 83, 256
Wolkenstein · 47, 152, 186, 224
Wonne der Wehmut · 75, 160, 240, 242
WoO 1 · 11, 243
WoO 123 · 159, 239, 240, 243
WoO 132 · 47, 239, 243
WoO 134 · 63, 160, 239, 243
WoO 136 · 66, 239, 243
WoO 14 · 29, 243

WoO 140 · 175, 239, 244
WoO 146 · 128, 240, 244
WoO 149 · 135, 136, 160, 239, 244
WoO 157#1 · 106, 239, 244
WoO 168#1 · 106, 244
WoO 200 · 45, 244
WoO 33 · 26, 243
WoO 39 · 199, 243
WoO 57 · 39, 160, 185, 199, 243
WoO 59 · 76, 243
WoO 63 · 13, 243
WoO 74 · 20, 43, 185, 198, 239, 244
WoO 78 · 33, 243
WoO 79 · 33, 243

Y

Yearning · 66, 128, 156, 163, 167, 225
Yverdon · 62, 209

Z

Zandt · 254
Zärtliche Liebe · 159, 239, 240, 243
Zmeskall · 30, 157, 160, 171, 242
Zum schwarzen Roß · 33, 93

Early Reader Comments

"… very interesting take on Beethoven's life and times!" - R.R. in C.

* * *

"I wish to extend my hearty congatulations on a job well done. Your book is so interesting to read (you write so well!) and it also meets all of the academic requirements that are expected of a scholarly work. So, I hope it willl satisfy both worlds: the general reader and the Beethoven scholar alike." - R.C.S. in W.

* * *

"I am very excited with your Josephine book! I thought it seemed quite plausible but it's only when all the facts are brought together that it becomes absolutely convincing. It's a wonderful book. Maybe someone will do a film on the truth one day. After having been interested in this for a long time, what I am reading is really astounding. I can't speak highly enough of what you've done. Well done. You've really done something fantastic. It will gradually make its way in the world, I'm sure. This one may grow slowly but there are a lot of people who will need to hear the story of these two poor, star-crossed lovers and will be moved by it, and awareness of what happened will gradually spread." - M.H.B. in S.

* * *

CPSIA information can be obtained at www.ICGtesting.com
Printed in the USA
269575BV00010B/42/P